The Story of the American Flag

By Bud Hannings

Copyright © 2001 A.D.
Seniram Publishing Incorporated
P.O. Box 432, Glenside, Pennsylvania 19038
Phone - 215-887-3524   Fax - 215-887-8762
Website - http://www.usmilitaryhistory.com
E-Mail: Seniram@usmilitaryhistory.com

Third Printing
Library of Congress Control Number - 2001126026
ISBN Number - 0-922564-02-7
Printer Fernhill Press, Hatfield, Pennsylvania

This book is presented to:

From:

Table of Contents

Quote of the Day: "Smile, You're An American."

The Story of the American Flag.

Throughout the ages, nations from all parts of the world have carried standards as symbols of their respective states, and in many instances as a sign to others of their approaching armies or naval armadas. This practice as in ancient times continues; however, many of these ensigns, some of which had actually been signs, rather than flags, have been obscure for thousands of years. As the world progressed, standards changed as one nation would vanquish another, while others would be the victors only to later be themselves dominated by a new and stronger adversary. Many of the names relating to these sects and states are relegated to obscurity, except for notations in history books and occasional films that depict the specific periods that predated the modern era. Among these would be the Achaeans, Ionians Arcadians, Teutons, Scythians and Sarmatians that existed between 4000 B.C. and 300 B.C. in places such as Greece, Germany, and Russia.

The Hsia and Shang (Yin) Dynasties dominated China between 1994 B.C. and 1523 B.C. and the Hittitie Empire ruled in Asia Minor (Turkey) about 1200 B.C., during what was known as the first "Dark Age of Cappadocia. Afterwards, this area, ruled by the Hittitie Empire was taken over by Assyrian and Phrygian influences, which then brought about what was known as the Neo-Hittitie period. Subsequently, during the 6th Century (B.C.), the Persians arrived in Cappadocia.

Meanwhile, in Greece, about 1100 B.C., the Phocians, a group of the Dorians forcefully moved to the Euripus River, while other groups of the Dorians headed south toward the Gulf of Corinth, the latter driving further toward the Peloponnese where they evicted the inhabitants and suppressed those who remained. Some of those who fled the region migrated to Lacedaemon where they became known as helots, while others were pushed to Thessaly; the latter were known as penestae. The Dorians eventually conquered Argolid, Laconia and Magara. The Dorians, of Greek ancestry, assumed their name from Dorus, the son of the mythological goddess, Hellen. They originated somewhere southwest of Macedonia in the mountainous area in Epirus. As they expanded their territory, they advanced into Peloponnesus to evict the Achaeans, and from there they moved through Crete, Italy, Asia Minor and Sicily; however, Crete and Sparta are usually thought of as having had standard Dorian rule. These invaders marked the rapid decline of the in-place Greek culture and are considered to be at blame for a period of decline.

During the period about 332 B.C., the forces of Alexander the Great occupied the area, previously ruled by the Hittitie Dynasty, terminating the "Dark Age. With the arrival of the Greeks, came Hellenism, which then influenced the region. However, during the Second Century (B.C.), Roman influence began to dominate the region and in fact, the Kings of Cappadocia are elevated to power and removed from the throne by choice of the Romans, the latter having come into power about 753 B.C. when Romulus became king and founded Rome.

The world continued to swirl in turbulence as conflicts became ever-present and more states evolved. Nonetheless, it would take volumes to detail all of these. As new states began to develop, the challenge for domination was rarely suspended and the thirst for land and power remained un-quenched. Several of these rivalries

3

would last for centuries and of these, a few still remain uneasy with each other.

More familiar names were also added to the rolls of prominent leaders of the past such as, Julius Caesar of Rome, Hannibal of Carthage, Constantine the Great (Roman Empire), Attila the Hun, Charlemagne of France, Canute, the Viking, Saladin of the Fatimid Dynasty, the latter seizing Jerusalem during 1187, reigniting the Crusades. Ghengis Khan later appeared, leading the Mongols. All the while, Europe was involved in various power struggles, as nations such as Austria, England, France, Germany, Hungary, Italy, Poland, Spain, Russia and the Scandinavian countries dealt with power struggles within the respective countries and often these nations also were simultaneously at war with an adversary. At times, the various allies changed allegiance during the conflicts. England and France during 1387 had engaged in an on-again off-again conflict known as the "Hundred Years War, yet they had earlier participated as allies in the Crusades against the Moslems.

Conflict continued between the Christian countries and the Moslems with wars being fought in Italy, Spain, Africa and the Middle East and different Christian sects battled each other. Power struggles and open warfare persisted in Asia as competing dynasties emerged in China and Japan. The Balkans, often became the ignition point of warfare, and in India and Afghanistan, there was frequent combat. The world was during these times frequently at war, and seldom at peace. Often, separate flags were being carried by different factions of the identical family, as each attempted to dominate the particular nation. Sovereigns sometimes killed their spouses to gain power and at times, a threat could come from a child. Civil war was an ordinary occurrence. The transfer of power was rarely a peaceful transition.

One of the most prominent of the ancient flags was that of the Roman Empire, but many others in Asia and Europe disappeared forever. And there were some future states that had not come to be part of the world of nations. One of these would emerge from a distant land that up until the latter part of the 15th Century was not even known to exist. However, due to the persistence of one man, Christopher Columbus, with the support of King Ferdinand and Queen Isabella of Spain, a new continent in what was known as the New World was discovered during 1492. From that discovery, a new flag was eventually hoisted to join the nations of the world, but not before an excruciating test of endurance that lasted nearly 300 years.

Columbus had petitioned the court in Spain about ten years prior to finally receiving an affirmative answer and it came just at the time that the King and Queen, both Catholic Monarchs, had subsequent to a prolonged conflict, ejected the Moors from Spain. King Ferdinand and Queen Isabella focused on spreading Christianity throughout the world. Columbus had convinced the sovereigns that he could find a sea route to the East Indies and that he would help spread Christianity.

On Friday, 3 August 1492, with the ensign of Spain atop the mast, Columbus began his quest to find a westward sea route to the East Indies, thought by many at the time to be non-existent. He embarked from Palos, Spain with a three-ship flotilla, the *Nina*, *Pinta* and *Santa Maria*. It was a harrowing voyage and many of the crew had been apprehensive since the first day at sea, but despite their great fears and a temporary mutiny that occurred on 10 October, land was spotted during the early morning hours of 12 October, 1492. Columbus, however, had not succeeded in finding a sea route to the East Indies, rather he had discovered a new land, unknown to the world on the opposite side of the Atlantic Ocean.

Columbus upon reaching land, knelt to the ground in thanksgiving to God. He named the island San Salvadore (San Salvador) and soon after, he discovered another island which he called Conception. Columbus' discovery opened the gateway to the New World and the first banner to claim it was the Spanish flag. Others would follow and this new land would become a separate challenge for the powers in Europe to test each other's mettle and determine who would dominate this area, soon to be described as a land of riches and paradise.

Following the Spanish, the British ensign arrived during June of 1497 when an expedition led by Sebastian Cabot and his father John, discovered an island off Labrador which they named Prima Vista. Shortly thereafter, they spotted another island which they named St. John's Island. At the time, the Cabots had relocated from England to Venice and they had become citizens of Venice, but their expedition was under the auspices of the English through a patent issued by King Henry VII. The king's mandate directed them to explore the territory north of those lands discovered by the Spanish and they too were to spread Christianity to the new lands. The Cabots, while at Labrador, continued to explore the region. They sailed an additional nine hundred miles along the coast of North America, but like Columbus, the Cabots were unaware of the depth and extent of the discovery and somewhat dismayed that they too had failed to find the sea route to the East Indies.

The French arrived in the New World during 1504 and established fisheries off Newfoundland, bringing yet a third flag to the New World. By 1512, the Spanish flag began to fly over another part of the New World. On 27 March, Easter Sunday, the day the Spanish refer to as Pascua de Flores, an expeditionary force from Porto Rico (Puerto Rico) under Ponce de Leon discovered the peninsula that separates the Gulf of Mexico from the Atlantic Ocean. On 2 April, Ponce de Leon, while searching for the "fountain of youth," discovered the east coast of Florida. During 1513, the Pacific Ocean was discovered by Balboa and during 1534, Cortez explored lower California.

The English during 1587 under Sir Walter Raleigh, established a colony at Roanoke Island (NC), but the settlers mysteriously vanished while Raleigh was in England. During 1607, England established its first permanent settlement in America at Jamestown, Virginia, while the Spanish expanded their territory in Florida and points west. They founded Santa Fe, New Mexico during 1609. By 1610, another banner arrived to wave over America as the Dutch established a settlement on Long Island, New York and they constructed some primitive shelters on Manhattan Island, basing their claim on Henry Hudson's voyage of the previous year to Lower New York, bringing the total number of European flags in America to four, followed by a fifth during 1624, when colonists from Denmark arrived in New Jersey.

During 1620, the Pilgrims (Puritans) aboard the *Mayflower* arrived off

Massachusetts on 9 November. The Ship anchored in Cape Cod Harbor and the Pilgrims established a constitution (Mayflower Compact) on 11 November, 1620. Some of the passengers (total 100-102 people) landed on 21 December at Plymouth, Massachusetts, but most stayed aboard ship until the following spring. At that time they began to establish friendly relations with the Indians including the Pokanokets and the Narragansetts, but later, hostilities broke out. These clashes with the Indians spread to other parts of New England as the colonies expanded.

Meanwhile, the colonists and the Indians in Virginia continued to quarrel. During March 1622, the Indians under Opechancanoough, sought retaliation for the murder of an Indian brave, igniting hostilities with the colonists. Intermittent warfare continued for twenty-four years.

Another flag, that of Sweden arrived on the shores of America during 1638 when Peter Minuit established Fort Christina on the west bank of the Delaware River in close proximity to present day Wilmington, Delaware. The Swedes purchased more land from the Indians that stretched between Trenton Falls to Paradise Point (Cape Henlopen). They established a settlement at Wicaco (Philadelphia, Pennsylvania). The Swedes named their territory "New Sweden,." but the Dutch challenged the action and claimed the identical land for the Netherlands. William Kieft, the Governor of New Netherlands, vehemently protested, claiming the country for the Dutch. Nevertheless, by 1641, the Dutch, aligned with the Swedes, attacked the British colonists at New Amsterdam, which resulted in rising tensions. The British were overwhelmed, forced to pay ransom and compelled to take an oath of allegiance to Sweden. War also erupted between the Dutch (New Netherlands) and the Algonquins; the conflict lasted until 1645.

During February 1643, in New Netherlands, the Tappan Indians, having been attacked by the Mohawk Indians, fled towards the Dutch territory for safety, but the Dutch instead offered a ruse and later killed the Indians, prompting retaliation by other Indian nations in the region. The Dutch, insufficiently armed and lacking sufficient numbers were unable to withstand the attacks. The Indians, retired, but Dutch survivors were taken as captives. Other Dutch colonists, terrified by the raids, took flight and headed for New Amsterdam. During April, the Indians sought and gained peace; however, later, during autumn, hostilities again broke out and continued until 1645. At that time, only five or six of about thirty settlements survived. Nonetheless, the Dutch rebuilt and maintained their attempts to reach a dominating position in the New World.

By 1654, the Dutch lost Fort Casimir to the Swedes and during the following year, the Dutch embarked from New Amsterdam to recapture it. They arrived in Delaware Bay during September 1655 and with little effort, they compelled the Swedes to surrender. The victory over the small garrison nevertheless brought New Sweden back into the possession of New Netherlands. The territory stretching from the Brandywine to Bombay Hook (part of Delaware) was purchased by the city of Amsterdam in Holland, and renamed, changing New Sweden to New Amstel. The Dutch vanquished the Swedes, but they continued to clash with the English and both claimed the west bank of the Delaware Bay.

The English held Maryland, but the Dutch insisted that it was under the Dutch flag due to their earlier claim. Later, during the summer of 1673, a Dutch fleet arrived at New York and captured the British fort and garrison without a fight to again bring New York under the Dutch colors. Later, during 1674, the fort and New York reverted back to the English in accordance with the Treaty of Westminster, which stipulated by mutual consent that all conquered territory was to be restored.

During June 1675, ongoing trouble between the colonists and the Indians escalated in Massachusetts. At Plymouth, some Indians accused of killing a man the previous year were tried by a jury, half Indian and half white, and the verdict was guilty. Each of the accused were sentenced to death by hanging. Following the executions, some other men of the tribe sought retaliation by killing about eight more colonists at Swansea, Rhode Island, igniting "King Philip's War." The violence spread to other tribes and hostilities continued into the following year. The fighting nearly annihilated the Narragansetts.

South of Massachusetts, during 1676, the colonists in Connecticut manning Fort Saybrook were confronted by troops out of New York, led by the mayor, Edmund Andros who informed them that the territory between the Hudson and the Connecticut Rivers was being claimed by the Duke of York (later King James II) in accordance with his patent. The colonists rejected the action and refused even to listen to Andros and his ultimatum. Andros, however, sensed the confidence of the colonists and chose to return to Long Island, rather than fight for the fort. Sparks of independence for the colonies began to emerge. In the meantime, colonists in New York protested the policies of Andros and the Duke of York.

In Virginia, the colonists and the Indians continued to engage in warfare, causing many plantations to be burned. Also, a conflict developed between Governor Sir William Berkeley and the colonists in Kent County, Virginia led by Nathaniel Bacon. The colonists had requested additional protection against the Indians to no avail and they protested against what they considered to be extremely high taxes. The insurrection was known as "the Grand Rebellion." The Virginia assembly passed encouraging legislation on the 4th of July, 1676, 100 years prior to the Declaration of Independence, but soon after, on the 1st of October of the same year, Bacon succumbed and with his death, the rebellion ended.

While the colonists in America continued to acquire additional stability, the tensions in Europe between France and England again exploded into hostilities. During June of 1689, France declared war against England. The conflict was known as "King William's War" in the colonies and as the "War of the League of Augsburg," (also known as the War of the Grand Alliance) in Europe. The hostilities continued until 1697 when England, France, Holland and Spain signed the Peace of Ryswick. However, soon after, hostilities again erupted.

During May of 1702, England declared war against France and Spain ("War of the Spanish Succession"). The conflagration continued until 1713 and it was not limited to Europe, as the French Catholics in Canada and the Protestants in New England engaged in hostilities. In the American Colonies, the war was known as Queen Anne's War. A treaty (Peace of Utrecht) signed between England, France, and Spain terminated the war, but Holy Roman Emperor Charles VI, allied with the English since 1704, continued the hostilities with the French. Following the conclusion of the war, France conceded Great Britain's supremacy in the American fisheries. And she also ceded Acadia, the Hudson Bay, Newfoundland and St. Kits. Subsequent to the capitulation of Acadia, the French moved to occupy Cape Brereton, Nova Scotia, a French possession. Although the English held the upper hand in the quest for domination in America, the struggle continued and the European powers were unable to keep peace for a sustained period of time.

By 1718, some players again changed sides. France and Spain which had only recently been allied against England and the Grand Alliance, commenced hostilities against each other. This conflict lasted until 1721. To further complicate the issue, the French, aligned themselves with England and the other members of the Triple Alliance, the Netherlands and the Holy Roman Empire. The conflict extended to America during May, 1719 when a French fleet arrived at Pensacola, Florida. The Spanish fort there was taken by the French, lost again to the Spanish and later during September of the same year, it was again captured by the French. At the termination of hostilities (1721), the fort reverted back to Spain. Also, the French moved their headquarters (New Orleans) back to Biloxi, Mississippi. Meanwhile, the Spanish occupied Texas (1720), to prevent the French from gaining it.

The French, at Fort Rosalie in Natchez (Mississippi), during November 1729, issued an ultimatum to the Natchez Indians, demanding that they vacate their village to make room for a French plantation. The Natchez, however, ignored the demand and instead, launched an attack that killed nearly all the French there. Only a few of the French were spared and they were held as prisoners. After news of the massacre spread, the French bolstered their defenses at New Orleans.

By 1732, America had many flags, but none had gained total dominance. And still, there was no serious consideration that the colonists were in a position to obstruct any of the major powers. Nevertheless, the English colonies were tiring of the conditions imposed upon them, and they grew weary of the policies of the crown. Many of the colonists had arrived in America to seek a new life and religious freedom, but here too, the word freedom was not necessarily for everyone and not only the Negroes sustained humiliation. During June of 1732, King George II, of England granted a Charter (duration twenty-one years) to General James Edward Oglethorpe and others. It stipulated that the territory should be carved out between the Savannah River and the Alatamaha and from the Atlantic to the Pacific Ocean into the province of Georgia. The king also stipulated that it was "in trust for the poor," with the caveat that the land was to be open to Jews, but no Papists (Catholics) would be permitted to settle in the Colony (Georgia). During the following year, the English Parliament passed the Molasses Act, to the dismay of the colonists. The discontent among the Americans began to intensify.

In Louisiana, the French again encountered difficulty with Indians, the Chickasaws. French forces advanced from Illinois and from New Orleans in a coordinated move to trap the Chickasaws at their territory (present day Lee County, Mississippi.). The contingent from New Orleans failed to arrive as scheduled, but those from Illinois led by Major Pierre D'Artaguette reached the rendezvous point on 9 May. After waiting for some time for the force under Bienville to arrive, the French, still lacking full strength, chose to attack. The Chickasaws repelled the assault and the Indians that had accompanied the French, hurriedly abandoned the area. The French were mauled and those who were able, attempted escape, but many, including D'Artaguette were captured and subjected to death by torture. One prisoner was spared to permit him to return to New Orleans with the news of the incident. Meanwhile, Bienville's force arrived. Despite the loss of the other force, he launched an attack, but it also failed. The French survivors retired to Mobile (Alabama). Jean Baptiste Bienville concluded a peace with the Chickasaws during March 1740. The Chickasaws continued to dominate the territory between Baton Rouge and Illinois. During July 1740, the Chickasaws sent a party of about eighty braves to Georgia, but they arrived in search of a treaty with the English colonists. Oglethorpe and the Chickasaws came to terms and agreed to a pact.

Although the colonists still sought more independence, their ties with England remained strong and loyal. During 1739, when the Anglo-Spanish War (War of Jenkin's Ear) erupted, colonists were among the British forces. England declared war against Spain on 23 October, but the conflict did not spread to the colonies. It was primarily confined to naval warfare in the West Indies. But afterwards, during 1740, the conflict expanded when the War of Austrian Succession (King George's War) ignited. The conflagration spread to Canada and the American colonies once again bringing to the forefront, the question of which country and flag would survive to dominate America?

A British naval force of about 35,000 soldiers and sailors, which included American colonists arrived off Jamaica to attack the Spanish at Cartagena during January of 1741. The British debarked about 6,000 troops and they were able to successfully destroy the Spanish fortifications, but the torrid tropical weather nearly destroyed the British while they prepared to attack Cuba. By July, thousands of troops succumbed. Subsequently, during 1742, the Spanish embarked from Cuba and unsuccessfully attacked the English at Fort William on Cumberland Island at the mouth of the St. Mary's River, Georgia. Undaunted, the Spanish then assaulted Fort Frederica on 7 July, but here too, the British prevailed. Despite two major setbacks, the Spanish again attacked Fort William, and yet again, the English prevailed. Following the third defeat, the Spanish survivors returned to Cuba.

During 1744, a French force embarked from Cape Brereton and launched an attack against the English at Fort Canseau, Nova Scotia. The stunned Englishmen, unaware of ongoing war between England and France, were quickly overwhelmed. The French destroyed the fort and transported about eighty captives to Louisburg, which became known as the "Gibraltar of America." In the meantime, Indians allied with the French unsuccessfully stormed British-held Annapolis, Nova Scotia. Meanwhile, the American colonists became incensed by the actions of the French, but retaliation was delayed until April 1745. At that time, about one hundred vessels transporting nearly 9,000 troops from the combined colonies of Connecticut, Massachusetts and New Hampshire, led by William Pepperell (Maine), embarked from Massachusetts to attack the French at Louisburg. The colonists' flotilla, bolstered by a British fleet, arrived at the objective on 30 April and supported by the British armada, the Americans executed a seven-week siege that compelled the French to capitulate on 17 June, 1745. The French later attempted to retake the fortress at Louisburg, but en route, the armada was devastated by the combination of inclement weather and the simultaneous arrival of a plague which devastated the crews. The French suffered more misfortune during 1746. A 38-vessel fleet, en route to Canada and Nova Scotia to reinforce the garrisons was intercepted and captured by the British on 3 May.

In New York, during 1747 a combined force of Frenchmen and Indians seized and destroyed Fort Massachusetts (Williamstown), which stood opposite Crown Point, Lake Champlain. Meanwhile, in Massachusetts, the Colonists repulsed the French and their Indian allies at Charlestown and at Concord. Other English colonies, primarily Virginia, had begun gathering forces to aid the effort against the French. About 8,000 troops formed to embark; no British fleet arrived to transport them.

The War of Austrian Succession, fought between England, Austria, Holland and Sardinia against France and Spain, concluded with the signing of a peace (peace of Aix-la-Chapelle, 1748). Russia, under Elizabeth, entered the hostilities late on the side of Austria. As a term of the treaty, Silesia went to Prussia. Another condition of the peace reached across the Atlantic Ocean. France regained Cape Brereton and Louisburg, to the dismay of the American colonists who had earlier captured it. In an effort to appease the colonists, England compensated them. The termination of the latest war did little to stabilize Europe or the colonies in America, and within a short while, due to a lingering dispute between the French and the Americans, another conflict erupted.

Following five years of fruitless negotiations with the French, it became apparent that only sheer force would prompt the French to depart the contested area where the Alleghany and Monongahela Rivers converge (present day Pittsburgh, Pennsylvania) and return to Canada. During April 1754, the French captured a group of English colonists who were constructing a fort. After seizing the captives, the French established Fort DuQuesne. Meanwhile, Governor Robert Dinwiddie of Virginia initiated action to extricate the French. Shortly thereafter, a colonist, Captain Trent, while involved in an effort to enlist traders and backwoodsmen in the Ohio Valley for the upcoming campaign, was captured by the French, an action that tripped the wire to ignite the French and Indian War, the conflict which will determine whether the French or the English would dominate America.

The initial hostilities, without a declaration of war, broke out during the latter part of May 1754, when a force from Virginia under George Washington skirmished with and defeated a French contingent in the vicinity of Fort DuQuesne in the Ohio Valley. The skirmish led to a full-scale war that continued until September 1760, with the fighting occurring on both sides of the Atlantic. In Europe, the conflict was known as the "Seven Years War."

While the French bolstered Fort DuQuesne, Pennsylvania, the colonial militia also in Pennsylvania and under George Washington, augmented the recently constructed Fort Necessity while awaiting British reinforcements. During early

10

July, 1754, the French with their Indian allies forced Washington to surrender Fort Necessity. On 4 July, 1754, Washington, leading his command, departed the fort which was soon after burned by the French. Washington returned with his command to Virginia, following the first and only time that he capitulated.

During July, 1755, the French inflicted another stinging defeat upon the British-Colonial force near Fort Duquesne, and while in retreat, the French pursued them back to the vicinity of the former site of Fort Necessity at Great Meadows (Uniontown, Pennsylvania) on 13 July During the fighting at Great Meadows, George Washington had been repeatedly struck, but not wounded. He later stated in a letter to his brother: "By the all-powerful dispensation of Providence, I have been protected beyond all human probability or expectation; for I had 4 bullets through my coat, and two horses shot under me, and escaped unhurt, although death was leveling my companions on every side of me." Daniel Boone also participated at this battle. Later, Boone will explore Kentucky (1767-1769).

About fifteen years after the rout, an Indian Chief who had been engaged against the colonists, traveled to the forks of the Kenhawa and Ohio Rivers in search of Washington. The Chief was convinced that Washington had been blessed with some special protection. The chief also claimed that during the fighting, he had personally selected Washington as a target and with his rifle, fired at him no less than fifteen rounds. Continuing, the chief maintained that he also ordered his braves to target Washington, but none could slay him. Years later in New Jersey near Princeton during the fight for independence, Washington would ride to the front of his faltering troops to halt a retreat and rally them for the fight. As he reached the front, and rallied his troops, Washington was also in the immediate front of the Redcoats. Both sides opened fire with Washington standing dead-center; however, without explanation, he stood amidst the enfilade of fire and emerged unscathed.

During September 1755, an English-colonial force at Fort William Henry defeated the French at the battle of Lake George, New York. Later, during July, 1757, the French and their Indian allies continued their attempts to seize Fort William Henry. On 23 July, a contingent of colonial troops, aboard twenty barges, attempted to intercept an advancing French force, but misfortune struck and only two barges escaped a pernicious trap. The troops who were unable to escape, but were able to avoid death by drowning were either killed or captured by the Indians allied with the French. Those captured were cooked and eaten as a meal. Soon after, during August, Fort William Henry fell to the French. Subsequent to the surrender, French General Louis Joseph Montcalm de Saint Veran guaranteed the safety of the English, but once the French departed, the Indians took matters into their own hands.

One survivor of the horror scene, Israel Putnam (later General during the War for Independence) described what he observed: " ...The fires were still burning. The smoke and stench offensive and suffocating. Innumerable fragments, human skulls, and bones, and carcasses, half consumed, were still frying and broiling in the decaying fires..." Continuing, Putnam described the scene of the women: "...More than 100 women, butchered and shockingly mangled, lay upon the ground still weltering in their gore..." Despite the fall of the fort, the French were unable to penetrate further, to the jubilation of the colonists who were acutely aware of the actions and intent of France's Indian allies. General Montcalm returned to Canada. Nonetheless, Massachusetts continued to enlarge its colonial forces. Soon after, about 20,000 troops were available to meet any new threat from the French.

During May 1758, a British-Colonial force marched to seize French-held Louisburg (Louisbourg), Nova Scotia and during early July, they launched an unsuccessful attack against Fort Carillon (Fort Ticonderoga), New York. Shortly thereafter on 27 July, the British seized Louisburg and with its capture, the English also gained Cape Brereton in its entirety as well as St. John's Island (later Prince Edward Island). Afterwards during August, the colonists and the English seized and destroyed French-held Fort Frontenac (Kingston, Ontario Canada). Subsequently, the English and the colonists were told that Ft. Duquesne was lightly defended. On 21 September, a vanguard force of about 800 troops, launched an unsuccessful assault against the fort and lost about 300 killed.

During October, 1758, the French attempted to destroy the English-colonial forces at Loyal Hanna, Pennsylvania, but here the English held firmly and thrashed the French and their Indian allies. The English followed up that success with another move against Fort Duquesne during November, but the French, rather than face the superior force chose to burn the fort and evacuate the area. The French departed on 14 November under cover of darkness. On the following day, the British flag was hoisted and the fort became Fort Pitt. By the end of 1758, the fortunes of war seemed to tilt the momentum to the British, prompting them to plan an assault against Quebec, Canada. A British fleet embarked during June 1759 and following a siege and a fierce battle, the fortress-city fell to the British during September 1759. The loss of Quebec was a severe, but non-fatal blow to the French, who still had large numbers of troops at Montreal. The commander there believed he could hold for the winter and by the following spring, defeat the English.

During April, 1760, the French (about 10,000) advanced against British-held Quebec, but the British, rather than remain on the defensive, also advance and intercepted the French before their assault was launched. The two sides clashed on 26 April, and on the field, the French prevailed, but the British strategy actually saved Quebec and bought more time. Meanwhile, the Americans continued to mass their forces. On 5 September, 1760, about 18,000 troops (English, colonists and allied Indians) moved against Montreal, Canada and within three days, the French surrendered Montreal, terminating the war. One French diplomat subsequently stated: "They (Americans) will no longer need her protection. She (England) will call on them to contribute toward supporting the burdens they have helped to bring on her, and they will answer by striking for independence."

The long enduring story of America from her discovery during 1492 until the end of the French and Indian War seemed finally to bring about a conclusion and resolve the unanswered question as to whom would dominate America? At that point in time, following the capitulation of France, it was apparent that England's colors would soon be flying all across the land.

Once the French and Indian war concluded, the colonies were still confronted by many problems, including more taxes imposed by the crown to pay for the costly wars, and continuing difficulties with some Indian tribes. In South Carolina, the colonists, supported by British troops, engaged the Cherokees to avenge the deaths of colonists that had occurred during the previous year at Fort Loudon. And in Massachusetts, dissent was rapidly growing as the colonists were subjected to unlawful British searches to inspect for infractions of the law. Meanwhile, customs officials in Massachusetts applied for the "issue of writs," an action which further ignited the passions of the colonists, whose minds and souls were leaning towards self-government, with freedom and liberty, as well as being accorded all the rights and privileges of all Englishmen. The colonists continued to seek support from the crown and relief from what was thought to be taxation without representation, but hearty seeds of liberty had already taken root across the land. Consequently, while the colonists continued to plead for some relief from the king, patriots were simultaneously preparing for independence if no other options became available.

On 25 October 1760, King George II, succumbed. The policies of his grandson, King George III, would become the primary factor which determined whether or not the colonists would clash with England. Meanwhile, relations between the Americans and the Indians continued to be strained. In Pennsylvania, the Indians under Pontiac rebelled (Pontiac's War) during 1763, but they sustained a setback at the Battle of Bushy Run (August 5-6) that preserved Fort Pitt. The Indians allied against the British and colonists included the Chippewas, Delawares, Hurons, Miamis, Ottawas, Senecas and Shawnees; the hostilities continued until 1766, when a treaty was signed between Pontiac and the British. Meanwhile, King George III, issued the proclamation of 1763 which concerned the land west of the Appalachians. This action by the King which granted land to the Indians was considered by the colonists to be interference with American affairs. The proclamation was followed during 1764 by the Sugar Act and to the consternation of the colonists, England burdened America with the Stamp Act of 1765. The road towards liberty nudged closer during 1765. Talk of independence flourished throughout the colonies and even more frequently in Virginia. The rugged path became more clear and inviting when English troops, with fixed bayonets, debarked at Boston during September of 1768.

Tensions between the crown and the colonies continued to build and confrontations between the British troops and colonists became a common occurrence. During March, 1770, English troops fired upon civilians in Boston, causing some fatalities, and by the latter part of 1773, the patriots, opposed to the king's policies, dumped a cargo of tea into Boston harbor. King George responded the following year by having Parliament pass the Intolerable Acts of 1774, which were totally opposed by the colonists. By that time, it appeared as if the breaking point had been reached. The voices of the patriots were subsequently raised higher and more often. Thomas Jefferson, would state, "The God who gave us life; gave us liberty at the same time." Meanwhile, Daniel Boone, a Pennsylvanian, was cutting the Wilderness Road in Kentucky (1775), while under attack by Shawnees.

Patrick Henry, a Virginian, bellowed during March of 1775: "There is no retreat but in submission in slavery. Our chains are formed, their clanking may be heard in the streets of Boston. The war is inevitable, and let it come. I know not what course others may take, but for me, give me liberty or give me death." In the meantime, the British took steps to suppress what appeared to be the initial signs of an insurrection. English troops attacked the colonial arsenal in Salem, Massachusetts, but discovered that the Americans had anticipated the action and removed the stores. The patriots also took other measures to counteract the British threat. George Washington, on the suggestion of fishermen, ordered the fishing ships in and around Boston harbor to be armed. The diminutive fleet, dubbed the "Web Foot Regiment," later seized some British vessels including an arms-laden ship.

By April 1775, a patriot, Paul Revere, in a letter to Doctor Jeremy Belknap: "If the British went out by water, we would show two lanterns in the North Church steeple and if by land, one as a signal." In Massachusetts, on 18 April, about 700 British troops were spotted crossing the Charles River en route to Concord to seize the arsenal, prompting the famous ride of Paul Revere, William Dawes and Doctor Samuel Prescott to alert the colonists of the approaching British troops.

On 19 April, 1775, at Lexington, Massachusetts upon the approach of the British, the American commander, John Parker issued the order: "Don't fire unless fired upon, but if they mean to have a war, then let it begin here." The first shot was fired, although it was never determined whether it was by the British or the colonists. The initial shot became known as "the shot heard round the world." The English destroyed the ammunition at Barrett's farm and came under attack by militia. The British under pressure from patriots withdrew towards Concord, and from there they marched to Boston to await reinforcements.

At Breed's Hill, just under Bunker Hill, on 17 June, 1775, Colonel William Prescott issued his general order: "Don't fire till you see the whites of their eyes." The British attacked and eventually won the day, but the patriots prior to extinguishing their ammunition late in the day, made their presence known. The British force of 2,000 troops sustained 1,050 casualties, including 476 killed. Ninety British officers were slain, about 12 percent of the British officer casualties of the entire war. The Americans lost 140 killed, 271 wounded and 30 captured. The Redcoats anticipated an easy victory, but they hadn't factored in the fierce spirit of liberty and freedom that had galvanized these unorthodox rag-tag troops. The colonists, most of whom were farmers and craftsmen, would have much to learn to grasp victory from England, which at that time held the world's most formidable army and navy. The green and undisciplined Minutemen and the American Militia rallied under their commander-in-chief, George Washington.

On 2 July 1776, twelve of the thirteen colonies accepted a resolution by Virginia's Richard Henry Lee to adopt a declaration of independence. New York abstained, but later affirmed. On 4 July, 1776, the Continental Congress declared its independence from England: "A Declaration by the Representatives of the United States in General Congress Assembled." The document was signed by John Hancock, with the other signatures coming later. After the affirmation of New York, on 19 July, by order of Congress, the Declaration was properly inscribed on parchment as, "The Unanimous Declaration of the United States of America; 56 patriots sign the declaration, which ended with the words: "And for the support of this declaration with a firm reliance on the protection of Divine Providence, we mutually pledge our lives, our fortunes and our sacred honor."

Later, also in Philadelphia, during 1787, the Constitution of the republic of the United States was born. It was followed during 1791 by the Bill of Rights, the first ten amendments to the Constitution. It is this document, the Constitution, referred to by George Washington, James Madison and others as "the Miracle in Philadelphia," that each successive President of the United States swore to protect and defend. And it is the identical Constitution that members of the United States Armed Forces have sworn to protect and defend.

The Constitution, flanked by the Stars and Stripes is the great work of the ages and the foundation of law in the United States. It guarantees certain inalienable rights including, free speech, the right to assemble, religious freedom, the right to vote and the right to bear arms. It also provides an opportunity (not a guarantee) to pursue happiness. It is conceivable, possible and probable that the Constitution has been referred to as a miracle due to its ingenious method of setting up a republic with three branches of government to counter balance each other and ensure that government does not overwhelm its citizens, and for its ability to organize smooth transitions from one administration to another, a stark contrast from the various governments in the Old World. The peaceful transition of power for more than 200 years, from president-to-president, underscores the genius of the Constitution.

Neither freedom nor liberty are free, nor is the right to vote to select government officials; however, under the Constitution it is your right as an American to vote for government officials who will honor their oath to the Constitution. During June, 1776, Thomas Paine wrote: "Society in every state is a blessing, but government even in its best state, is but a necessary evil; in its worst state, an intolerable one." Nevertheless, for the Constitution to remain strong, it is imperative that every eligible American shows loyalty to the Constitution by voting to prevent a tyrant or tyrannical government from gaining power and abolishing individual rights.

When you see the flag pass by, remember that every patriot that has rallied to her side in the service of the United States Army, Navy, Coast Guard, Air Force and Marine Corps for more than 200 years, has served to protect you and your family. The Stars and Stripes is the symbol of freedom, the vanguard of Liberty, and the invincible spine of the indefatigable American spirit. She is the soul of liberty, the velvet threads of golden glory, the symbol of our pride and our heritage and the blood of our ancestors as well as the oxygen for our posterity. The Stars and Stripes in her majestic beauty shall always sail the seas, blanket the stars and trumpet the advance of her endless line of heroes, the vanguard of Liberty. They will continue to march in noble cadence to safeguard the dignity, character, and honor of the flag.

Yes, the Stars and Stripes, the symbol of the land we love, is your flag. You are part of the "Grand Ole Flag." Never be embarrassed to pledge allegiance to your flag and your country, one nation under God, the United States of America.

General (President) Ulysses S. Grant:

"No name is so great that it should be placed upon the flag of our country."

The Following is a snapshot (time line) view of the history of the Stars and Stripes and the Patriots who rallied round the "Grand Ole Flag."

Through these pages, pass the finest fighting men in the world as they press forward to defend Liberty and preserve the American legacy. The Grand Ole Flag not only flies atop our magnificent mountains, amidst our precious valleys and from sea to sea, she has also journeyed to the moon.

This is her story!

The Stars and Stripes Through the Years
The War For Independence (American Revolution)

March 1760 - Cherokee Indians unsuccessfully attack Fort Loudoun, S.C. During August, it surrenders; colonists are afterwards killed or captured by Cherokee. Subsequently, reinforcements arrive and after hard fighting, the Cherokee are compelled to sue for peace.
September 8 1760 - The French surrender to the English at Montreal, making England the dominant country in America.
October 25, 1760 - England - King George II, succumbs. He is succeeded by his grandson, George III, who reigns until 1820.
Spring 1763 - Pontiac gathers tribes to fight the settlers in the Ohio Valley.
May - June 1673 - Fort Sandusky, Fort St. Joseph (Niles, Michigan), Fort Miamis (Ft. Wayne, Ind.) fall to Pontiac's warriors during May. During June, Fort Quiatenon (Lafayette, Ind.), Fort Michilmilimac (Michigan), Fort Presque Isle (Erie, Pa.), Fort Venango (Pa.) and Fort Le Boeuf (Pa.) fall. The settlers along the frontier are in great jeopardy as most of the garrisons had been massacred. However, primary forts, Detroit, Pitt and Niagra are not seized. Troops under Colonel Bouquet rush from Carlisle Barracks, Pa. to bolster Fort Pitt, but before the columns reach it a major battle occurs at Busy Run.
August 5-6, 1763 - Battle of Bushy Run, Pennsylvania - (Pontiac's War). Fort Pitt is saved. The Indians had anticipated help from the French, but none arrives. Bouquet's victory saves the frontier from crumbling under Pontiac's sweeping attacks. A treaty is later signed with the Chippewa and Ottawa tribes and Pontiac an Ottowa chief, signs a treaty with the British during 1766.
January 19, 1770 - British troops clash with Sons of Liberty (Golden Hill, NY).
March 5, 1770, - The Boston Massacre - British troops fire upon civilians.
May 10, 1773 - British Parliament passes the Tea Act.
December 16, 1773 - The Boston Tea Party- Patriots dressed as Mohawk Indians dump a cargo of tea into Boston harbor.
March 1774 - **England** - British Parliament passes the Intolerable Acts - They are: The Boston Port Act, The Massachusetts Government Act, The Quartering Act, The Impartial Administration of Justice Act, and the Quebec Act.
April 22, 1774 - In New York, patriots dump a cargo of tea into the harbor.
September 5, 1774 - The First Continental Congress meets at Carpenter's Hall, in Philadelphia, Pa. Peyton Randolph is elected president of the Congress.
October 10 1774 - Battle of Point Pleasant (Western Virginia) - Virginia militia against Cayuga, Delaware, Shawnee and Wyandots (former Hurons and Tiontati).
April 19, 1775- The Skirmish at Lexington and Concord (Massachusetts).
May 10, 1775- Colonists seize British-held Fort Ticonderoga, New York.
May 20, 1775 - The 13 colonies agree on articles of union and confederation. Also, while Congress is in session, Peyton Randolph resigns as president of

Congress. He is replaced by John Hancock.
June 14, 1775 - The Continental Congress adopts the New England (Continental) Army. This day is recognized as the birthday of the U.S. Army.
June 17, 1775- Battle of Bunker Hill (fought on Breeds Hill), Massachusetts.
July 3, 1775- George Washington, appointed Commander on 15 June, takes command of the Continental Army at Cambridge, Massachusetts.
October 13, 1775- Congress authorizes establishment of a Naval Committee, which essentially is the beginning of the U.S. Navy.
November 10, 1775-The Marine Corps is founded (Philadelphia).
November 13, 1775 - A U.S. force under General Montgomery seizes Montreal.
November 1775 - The Second Continental Congress creates the U.S. Navy. On 2 December, Esek Hopkins becomes the first Commander-in-Chief of the Navy.
December 11 1775 - Battle of Great Bridge - Virginia militia against Loyalists.
December 30, 1775- Battle of Quebec (Canada). U.S. Gen. Montgomery dies.
1776 - Betsy Ross of Philadelphia makes the first American flag. Some historians question this, but others are convinced it is fact. The Betsy Ross flag contains the 13 stars in a circle. At this time U.S. vessels heading to sea required a flag, and often used that of their respective colonies to avoid problems. An armed vessel at sea intercepted by English warships would be considered a pirate vessel if not flying national colors and the captured crew would be hanged.
February 27, 1776 - The Battle of Moore's Creek Bridge (North Carolina).
March 3, 1776 - Marines (first expedition) capture Forts Montagu & Nassau, Bahamas and raise the U.S. Flag for the first time over a foreign country.
March 17, 1776 - The British evacuate Boston, Massachusetts.
June 7, 1776 - Americans under General Sullivan unsuccessfully attack British at Three Rivers (Penna.), then withdraw to Ft. Ticonderoga, NY.
June 28, 1776 - A British land and sea attack is repelled at Fort Moultrie, Charlestown (later Charleston), South Carolina. The British commander, Sir Peter Parker, finds his pants afire from an American shell as the fleet is retiring.
July 4, 1776 - Congress adopts Declaration of Independence; it is signed by John Hancock and Secretary Charles Thomson. The other 55 signatures come later.
July 8, 1776 - The Declaration of Independence is publicly read for the first time by John Nixon at the Pennsylvania State House (later Independence Hall).
July 20, 1776 - Cherokees attack Eaton Station, NC; Militia retaliates (21st).
August 2, 1776 - The engrossed Declaration of Independence is signed by some members of Congress. Other signatures come later.
August 3, 1776- U.S. fleet battles British ships on the Hudson at Tarrytown, NY.
August 14, 1776 - The British gather the largest fleet ever to appear in U.S.
August 27-29, 1776 - Battle of Long Island (New York).
September 16, 1776 - Battle of Long Island, NY.
September 22, 1776 - Captain Nathan Hale is executed as a spy by the British.
October 11, 1776 - The Naval Battle of Lake Champlain (New York).
October 13, 1776 - Naval Battle of Split Rock (near Lake Champlain). The surviving U.S. ships from Lake Champlain. The British occupy Crown Point.
October 28, 1776 - The Battle of White Plains (New York).
November 1, 1776 - Henry Laurens is elected President Continental Congress.
November 16, 1776 - The British capture Fort Washington, New York.
December 12, 1776- Congress abandons Philadelphia; it moves to Baltimore.
December 25-26, 1776 -Battle of Trenton (New Jersey). Marines participate.
1776 - In Connecticut, David Bushnell creates a submarine. During 1777, it fails in attacks against the British; he is humiliated and he changes his identity.
January 3, 1777 - The Battle of Princeton (New Jersey). Marines participate.
January 7, 1777 - General George Washington moves to the Watchtung Mountains in New Jersey (30 miles from British) to establish winter quarters.
May 1777 - The British at Ft. Dearborn instigate Indian attacks against frontier.
May 23-25, 1777 -The Battle of Sag Harbor (New York).
June 14, 1777- The American Flag is officially mandated by Congress.
June 26, 1777 - Battle of Scotch Plains, New Jersey.
July 6, 1777 - The Americans evacuate Fort Ticonderoga, New York.

17

August 3-6, 1777 - Battle of Ft. Stanwix (renamed Ft. Schuyler) Rome, New York. It is legend only (not based on fact) that the Stars and Stripes is hoisted.
August 6, 1777- The Battle of Oriskany (New York)- Militia ambushed by British and Indians. General Nicholas Herkimer is killed.
August 16, 1777- The Battle of Bennington (fought in New York, not Vermont).
August 22, 1777 - The British lift the siege of Ft. Stanwix and retire to Canada.
August 29, 1777 - Battle of Newton (Elmira, NY) - Kentucky Riflemen and artillery units battle Indians and Tories.
September 3, 1777 - Battle of Cooch's Bridge & Welsch Baptist Church, Del.
September 9-11, 1777- The Battle of Brandywine (Pennsylvania).
September 18, 1777 - The Continental Congress again abandons Philadelphia.
September 19, 1777- The First Battle of Saratoga (New York).
September 21, 1777 -The British ambush the Americans (Paoli, Penna.).
September 26, 1777 - Massacre at Grave Creek (W. Va.)- Indians ambush militia.
October 4, 1777- The Battle of Germantown (Philadelphia, Pennsylvania).
October 7, 1777- The Second Battle of Saratoga (Bemis Heights-New York). British General John Burgoyne surrenders.
October 21, 1777- Colonists at Fort Mercer, N. J. attacked by Hessians.
November 8, 1777 - British abandon Ft. Ticonderoga & Mt. Independence, VT.
November 15, 1777 - Continental Congress adopts Articles of Confederation.
November 16-20, 1777- The British attack Fort Mifflin, (Pennsylvania).
December 7, 1777- The Battle of Edge Hill (Abington, Pennsylvania).
December 19, 1777- The Continental Army arrives at Valley Forge, Pa.
December 23, 1777- A Plot to replace George Washington with Gen. Gates fails.
January 5, 1778 -Battle of the Kegs (Pa.)British fire at floating kegs.
January 10, 1778 - Marines on vessel *Rattletrap* depart Fort Pitt for Louisiana.
Jan. 27, 1778- Naval-Marine force captures Fort Nassau, Bahamas (2nd time).
February 6, 1778 - France agrees to aid U. S (treaty of aid).
February 9, 1778 - Daniel Boone captured by Shawnees; he escapes during June.
February 14, 1778- The USS *Ranger* arrives in France and is greeted by a French fleet which fires a salute, accepting the U.S. flag as a national ensign.
February 23, 1778 - Baron von Steuben arrives at Valley Forge. He uses a French training manual and transforms the U.S. Army into a disciplined force.
March 3, 1778 - The Articles of Confederation take effect.
March 13, 1778 - England, informed of France's alliance with the American colonies, declares war upon France.
April 23, 1778 - John Paul Jones attacks England and seizes a fort at Whitehaven (where Scotland meets England).
April 24, 1778- The USS *Ranger* captures the HMS *Drake* (off Ireland).
May 1, 1778 - An American force under General John Lacey, encamped at Hatboro, Pennsylvania (Crooked Billet) comes under attack by British troops. The Americans en route to Valley Forge escape, but 26 men are killed.
May 15, 1778 - Americans capture Cahokia, Illinois on Mississippi River.
June 6, 1778 - The U.S. rejects a British peace proposal.
June 18, 1778 -The American Army reenters Philadelphia, Pennsylvania.
June 27, 1778- The Battle of Monmouth (New Jersey). Mary Hays becomes a hero at this battle and becomes known as "Molly Pitcher."
July 2, 1778 - Continental Congress returns to Philadelphia.
July 3, 1778 - Loyalists and Indians massacre settlers in Wyoming Valley, Pa.
July 4, 1778- George Rodgers Clark captures British-held Kaskaskia (Indiana).
July 8, 1778 - West Point becomes General George Washington's headquarters.
July 10, 1778 - France declares war against England.
July 20, 1778 - George Rodgers Clark seizes Vincennes (Ft. Sackville), Indiana. The British retake it on 17 December.
September 28, 1778 - The British attack a U.S. Cavalry unit at Tappan, N.Y.
August 23, 1778 - Indians attack troops from Ft. Muncy, Pa.
November 11, 1778 - Indians & Loyalists massacre settlers (Cherry Hill, NY).
Dec. 9, 1778 - Virginia annexes land captured by G. R. Clark (County of Ill.).
December 29, 1778 - Savannah, Georgia falls to the British.

January 6 - 9, 1779 - The British attack Fort Sunbury, Georgia.
January 10, 1779 - The French transfer a rundown vessel, the *Duc de Durad*, to John Paul Jones. It is renamed the *Bonhomme Richard.*
January 29, 1779 - The British seize Augusta, Georgia.
February 3 1779 - Battle of Port Royal Island, South Carolina.
February 14 - 1779 - Battle of Kettle Creek, Georgia.
March 3, 1779 - Battle at Briar Creek, near Augusta (North Carolina).
April 1779 - Colonial troops from North Carolina and Virginia launch retaliatory raids against the Chickamauga Indians in Tennessee.
May 10, 1779 - British troops torch Portsmouth and Norfolk, Virginia.
June 1, 1779 - The British seize Stony Point and Verplanck Point, New York, but they fail to seize their primary objective, West Point..
June 19, 1779 - The British begin to abandon Charleston, South Carolina. As they move towards Savannah, Georgia a battle erupts at the Stono River.
June 23, 1779 - British and American troops skirmish at Springfield, NJ.
July 1779 - Loyalists burn several Connecticut towns including Norwalk and Fairfield and the British destroy ships in the harbor at New Haven.
July 5, 1779 - The British seize Black Rock Fort, Connecticut.
July 15, 1779 - American troops recapture Stony Point, New York.
July 28 1779 - Loyalists (Butler's Rangers) attack Fort Freeland (Pennsylvania).
July-August - 1779 - The fleet of Dudley Saltonstall is lost to the British because he fails to attack on the Penobscot estuary (Maine).
August 19, 1779 - General Henry Lee (father of Robert E. Lee) attacks the last British garrison in New Jersey at Paulus Hook (Jersey City).
August 29, 1779-Battle of Newton (Elmira), N.Y. (Indians and Loyalists).
September 23, 1779- Naval Battle between the USS *Bonhomme Richard* and the HMS *Serapis* off France. The British demand surrender and John Paul Jones responds: "I have not yet begun to fight."
September 1779 - A force under General John Sullivan destroys 40 Cayuga and Seneca villages (Western Frontier) in retaliation for massacre of settlers.
September 3-October 9, 1779- Battle of Savannah (Georgia).
September 26, 1779 - A British fleet transporting about 8,000 troops embarks from New York for Charleston, South Carolina.
January 1780 - A U.S. force (using sleighs to cross the frozen sound) attacks Staten Island, NY. The British retaliate & attack Newark & Elizabethtown, NJ.
May 12, 1780- Charleston, S.C., under siege since the previous February, falls to the British (worst defeat of the war). Ft. Moultrie had fallen on 6 May.
May 25, 1780 - The 13th Connecticut Regiment attempts mutiny at Morristown.
May 26, 1780 - An English-Canadian and Indian force attacks St. Louis (Spanish-control) and Cahokia under George Rogers Clark.
May 29, 1780 - A skirmish occurs between Americans and British cavalry at Waxhaw, South Carolina. The Americans hoist a white flag to no avail.
June - September 1780 - Clarksville (Ft. Jefferson), Ky., attacked by Indians.
July 11, 1780 - About 8,000 French troops arrive at Newport, Rhode Island.
July 12-25, 1780 - U.S. forces clash with the British at Williamstown Plantation, Cedar Springs, Gowen's Old Fort Prince, and Hunt's Bluff, S.C.
July 1780 - American force under Colonel Archibald Lochry surprise-attacked in Ohio(Cincinnati) while en route to meet George Rogers Clark.
August 3, 1780 - George Washington, unaware that Benedict Arnold is a British spy, appoints him commander of West Point (New York).
August 6, 1780 - Battle of Hanging Rock Creek (near Heath Springs, S.C.).
August 16, 1780- The Battle of Camden, South Carolina. Baron De Kalb, wounded eleven times, is killed. His loss is a severe blow to the Americans.
August 18, 1780 - U.S. forces again clash with Banastre Tarleton's cavalry at Fishing Creek. Also, another battle rages at Musgrove's Mill, South Carolina.
September-28-29, 1780 - Francis Marion's (Swamp Fox) troops defeat a force of Loyalists at Black Mingo, South Carolina.
October 2, 1780 - British Major John Andre (Benedict Arnold's accomplice) is

captured in civilian clothes and hanged as a spy.

October 7, 1780- Battle of King's Mountain, North Carolina. British Major Patrick "Bulldog" Ferguson is mortally wounded at this battle. He succumbs while leaning against a tree with his infamous whistle still dangling from his teeth. This defeat prevents British General Cornwallis from invading N.C.

October 16, 1780 - Indians led by a British officer attack Royalton, Vermont.

November 9, 1780 - The British attack Americans at Fishdam Ford, S.C.

November 20, 1780 - British cavalry under Banastre Tarleton attack troops under General Thomas Sumter at Blackstock's (Cross Keys, South Carolina).

December 11, 1780 - The Battle of Long Cane (South Carolina).

December 13, 1780 - Marion defeats the Br. 64th Regiment at Halfway Swamp.

January 3, 1781 - The British capture Jamestown, Virginia, but they fail to seize their primary target, Thomas Jefferson.

January 5-7, 1781 - The British led by the traitor Benedict Arnold seize Richmond, Virginia, held by only a small force.

January 17, 1781 -Battle of Cowpens, South Carolina.

January 23, 1781 - Tories engage a Colonial force at Wiggin's Hill, S.C.

January 25, 1781 - American forces under Henry Lee and Marion, the Swamp Fox attack a British-held Fort at Georgetown, South Carolina.

February 7, 1781 - The Board of War and Ordnance, originally the War Office is succeeded by a Secretary at War; the position is filled on October 30, 1781.

February 1781 - John Paul Jones arrives in Philadelphia. to assume command of his promised ship, the *America*, but Congress instead gives it to the French.

March 15, 1781-Battle of Guilford Courthouse, Greensboro, N.C.

March 15, 1781 - A British fleet and a French fleet engage in a ferocious battle off the Chesapeake Cape. The French prevail, but the British escape.

April-May 1781 - The British lose Forts Watson, Motte, Granby, Galphin and the Americans also take Fort Ninety-Six after the British evacuate South Carolina.

May 31-June 5, 1781- British-held Fort Cornwallis, Georgia surrenders.

June 20, 1781 - The British evacuate Richmond. Soon after, they abandon Williamsburg for Yorktown to await reinforcements to thwart Lafayette.

July 17, 1781 - Battle of Quimby Bridge, South Carolina.

August 8, 1781 - Following a heavy battle between the USS *Trumbull* and three British warships, the *Trumbull* (final U.S. frigate still afloat) is lost.

August 30, 1781 - A French fleet arrives off Yorktown, Virginia from Haiti with an additional 4,000 French troops to bolster the Americans.

September 8, 1781 - The Battle of Eutaw Springs, South Carolina.

September 5-11, 1781- A French fleet defeats a British armada off Yorktown.

September 9-11, 1781 - Additional French fleets arrive at Yorktown, Virginia.

September 11, 1781 - A British fleet embarks from Yorktown for New York.

September 6, 1781- British seize Fort Griswold, Connecticut and begin to kill the Americans incl. wounded. Other British troops burn New London.

September 26, 1781 - General Washington's force arrives at Yorktown, Va..

September 28-October 19, 1781- The Americans, bolstered by the French, initiate the siege of Yorktown, Virginia. The British surrender on 19 October.

Oct. 30, 1781- Major General Benjamin Lincoln becomes Secretary at War.

October 24, 1781 - A British fleet which had earlier arrived with General Henry Clinton at Yorktown, but too late to support Cornwallis, returns to N.Y.

November 5, 1781-John Hanson is elected President of the United States in Congress, holding the office for one year as presiding officer of Congress.

November 1781 - An American contingent is attacked at Hayes Station, South Carolina. The British burn the blockhouse and its defenders.

November 17, 1781 - Battle of Cloud's Creek, S.C. - Two Americans survive.

December 1, 1781 - American and British cavalry clash at Dorchester, S.C.

January 5, 1782 - The British abandon Wilmington, N.C.

May 4, 1782 - The Battle of John Town (South Carolina).

May 1782 - Sandusky Expedition - Regulars and militia under Colonel Crawford engage Indians near Fort Henry (W. Va.). Crawford is burned at the stake.

July 11, 1782 - U.S. troops engage the British near Savannah; it is evacuated.
August 19, 1782 - British-Loyalists and Indians overwhelm Kentuckians.
November 10, 1782 - A force including Virginia Marines under George Rodgers Clark attacks the Shawnee for their recent strike against Blue Licks, Kentucky. This is the final battle on land during the War for Independence.
December 14, 1782 - The British abandon Charleston, South Carolina.
February 14, 1783- England declares an end to all hostilities with America.
March 10, 1783 - The USS *Alliance* and a new vessel the *Duc De Luzon*, engage two British warships, the *Alarm* and the *Sybil*. The *Duc De Luzon* is too slow placing the *Alliance* in peril, but another French vessel appears and the British disengage, ending the final sea battle of the War for Independence.
September 3, 1783- The United States and England sign the Treaty of Paris.
September 24, 1783-Congress directs General Washington to decrease the size of the army: "As he shall deem proper and expedient." The army is disbanded; it retains a force of 600 men (one Infantry Regiment and one Artillery battalion remain in service) to safeguard West Point, and other posts. Following the close of the war, the Marine Corps and Navy are also disbanded.

Post Revolution - Quasi War (undeclared war with France)

November 2, 1783 - General George Washington issues his Farewell speech to the U. S. Army at Rocky Hill, New Jersey.
December 23, 1783 - George Washington resigns as Commander-in-Chief.
March 8, 1775 - Henry Knox is elected Secretary at War by Congress. He remains in the office beyond the time of the Articles of Confederation into the period governed by the Constitution, making him the first Secretary of War.
June 3, 1785 - Congress allows the sale of the *Alliance*, the sole ship in the navy.
July 1785 - The U.S. schooners *Maria* and the *Dauphin* are captured by Tripoli Pirates. Tripoli demands ransom for the Americans.
November 30, 1785 - The U.S. insists that England abandon Forts Detroit, Michilimackinac, Niagara and Oswego (Northwest Frontier).
August 31, 1786 -January 25, 1787 (Shay's Rebellion) - A crowd of weapon-carrying citizens appears at a court session in Northampton, Massachusetts.
1787 - 1790 - An American sea captain, Robert Gray (former naval officer during American Revolution) leads an expedition to China. From the Orient he sails west arriving in Boston, Massachusetts on August 10, 1790 to become the first American to circumnavigate the world. His vessel, the *Columbia,* flew the Stars and Stripes on her first cruise around the world.
July 13, 1787- The U.S. establishes the Northwest Ordinance (N.W. Territory).
September 17, 1787- The U. S. Constitution is born; nine states must ratify it.
December 7, 1787 - Delaware becomes the 1st state in the Union.
December 12, 1787 - Pennsylvania enters the Union to become 2nd state.
December 18, 1787 - New Jersey enters the Union to become the 3rd state.
January 2, 1788 - Georgia enters the Union to become 4th state.
January 9, 1788 - Connecticut becomes the 5th state to enter the Union.
February 6, 1788 - Massachusetts becomes the 6th state to enter the Union.
March 24, 1788 - Rhode Island declines to ratify the Constitution.
April 28, 1788 - Maryland enters the Union to become the 7th state.
May 23, 1788 - South Carolina enters the Union to become the 8th state.
June 21, 1788 - New Hampshire enters the Union to become the 9th state.
June 25, 1788 - Virginia enters the Union to become the 10th state.
July 26, 1788 - New York enters the Union to become the 11th state.
April 30, 1789 - George Washington is inaugurated as first President of the U.S.
June 8, 1789- James Madison proposes "Bill of Rights" to Congress (House).
August 7, 1789 - Congress establishes The Department of War. Henry Knox, at present the Secretary at War since 1785, becomes the first Secretary of War.
September 24, 1789 - Congress establishes the Supreme Court, the position of Attorney General, thirteen district courts and three ad hoc circuit courts.

September 25, 1789 - Congress introduces the Twelve Amendments to the Constitution. The first ten will be ratified (Bill of Rights) during 1791.
November 21, 1789 - North Carolina enters the Union (twelfth state).
May 26, 1790- The U.S. establishes the Territory southwest of the River Ohio.
May 29, 1790 - Rhode Island enters the Union, becoming the 13th state.
July 16, 1797 - Congress moves the capital from New York to Philadelphia.
August 4, 1790 - Congress authorizes the purchase of ten boats to act against smugglers. The Fleet ("Revenue Marines" and or "Revenue Cutter Service") later (1848) becomes the Coast Guard. During 1796, the Cutter Service receives larger vessels with more firepower. Alexander Hamilton who urged the purchase of the fleet, is considered the father of the Coast Guard.
March 3, 1791 - Congress enacts the "Whiskey Act."
March 4, 1791 - Vermont enters the Union to become the 14th state.
July 25, 1791 - General Anthony Wayne occupies Forts Miamis & Detroit. He brings the U.S. Flag to the Great Lakes region, in place of the British flag..
November 4, 1791 - General St. Clair sustains a disastrous defeat (loses about 637 killed and 261 wounded-half of his army by surprise attack) at the hands of Indians under Little Turtle near present day Fort Wayne, Indiana. The survivors retire leaving dead and wounded behind. The Indians lose less than fifty braves.
December 15, 1791 - The Bill of Rights (10 Amendments) becomes effective.
1792 - Robert Gray, the 1st American to circumnavigate the globe discovers the mouth of the Columbia River (N.W. Territory), the second largest river in the U.S., following the Mississippi. The river is named after Gray's ship, the *Columbia* His discoveries lay the foundation of U.S. claim to Oregon Territory.
May 8, 1792 - Congress passes the first act calling for a uniform Militia.
June 1, 1792 - Kentucky enters the Union to become the 15th state.
February 1, 1793 - France declares war on England, the Netherlands and Spain. The U. S. remains neutral. France (King Louis XVI and his wife Marie Antoinette had been executed on 31 Jan.) is run by a revolutionary government.
March 4, 1793 - George Washington begins his second term as President of U.S.
July 16-17, 1794 - "Whiskey Rebellion" (Penna.) - Citizens oppose the tax.
March 27, 1794 - Congress authorizes the rebuilding of the U. S. Navy.
June 1794 - The United States Navy is reestablished.
August 20, 1794 - Battle of Fallen Timbers, Ohio (Chief Turkey Foot).
May 1, 1795 - The American Flag is changed from 13 stars and 13 stripes to 15 stars and 15 stripes (admission of Vermont (1791) and Kentucky (1792).
June 24, 1795 - The Senate ratifies the Jay Treaty. The terms include England's withdrawal from the Northwest Territory (by June 1796).
September 5, 1795 - The U. S. signs a treaty with Algiers (includes tribute).
November 8, 1795 - The U. S. signs a truce with Tunis (includes tribute).
June 1, 1796 - Tennessee enters the Union to become the 16th state.
September 19, 1796 - George Washington's Farewell Address (published).
November 15, 1796 - France suspends diplomatic relations with the U.S.
March 4, 1797 - John Adams is inaugurated as 2nd President of the U.S.
June 10, 1797 - The U. S. and Tripoli sign a peace treaty (includes tribute).
June 24, 1797 - Congress passes a law calling for an army of 80,000 men.
August 28, 1797 - The U. S. signs a new treaty with Tunis (includes tribute).
April 3, 1798 - The Department of the Navy is initiated by act of Congress. The first Secretary of the Navy is Benjamin Stoddert.
April 7, 1798 - The Mississippi Territory is organized.
May 28, 1798 - President John Adams directs the American Fleet to capture any French Ships interfering with U.S. commercial shipping.
July 2, 1798 - President Washington is recalled from retirement and reappointed Commander-in-Chief of the Army in anticipation of war with France.
July 11, 1798 - The United States Marine Corps is re-established by Congress.
November 16, 1798 - The *Baltimore,* a U.S. ship, is halted in search of British deserters. On the 20th, a French ship seizes the USS *Retaliation*.
February 9, 1799 - Congress forbids U. S. Ships from entering French ports.

Also, the USS *Constellation* defeats the *Insurgente*, a French warship.
December 14, 1799 - George Washington dies at Mount Vernon in Virginia.
May 7, 1800 - The Territory of Indiana is established.
April-September 1800 - A U.S. naval squadron under Captain John Barry focuses on attacking French vessels in the West Indies (Quasi War).
May 11, 1800 - Marines and Sailors aboard the USS *Constitution* transfer to the *Sally* (a detained ship). They surprise and capture a French privateer, the *Sandwich* and the Spanish fort at Puerto Plata (Dominican Republic is seized.
September 30, 1800 - An agreement (Treaty of Morfontaine, Convention of 1800), terminates the hostilities between the U.S. and France (Quasi War).
February 3, 1801 - Congress, following the close of the Quasi War with France, directs that the Navy sell all, but fourteen vessels. Within two weeks Tripoli declares war against the U.S. and it again lacks warships.
March 4, 1801 - Thomas Jefferson is inaugurated as third President of the U. S.
May 1801 - The Bashaw of Tripoli demands more tribute from the U.S.
June 1, 1801 - A U.S. naval squadron, transporting Marines, embarks to terminate the tribute demands of the pirates in Tripoli.
June 10, 1801 - Tripoli declares war against the United States.
February 6, 1802 - Congress declares war on Tripoli.
June 22, 1802 - Morocco declares war against the United States.
July 4, 1802 - West Point becomes the site of the U. S. Military Academy.
March 1, 1803- Ohio is admitted to the Union as the 17th state.
October 31, 1803 - The USS *Philadelphia* is captured off Tripoli.
December 20, 1803 - The U. S. takes possession of the Louisiana Territory.
February 16, 1804 - The USS *Intrepid* led by Stephen Decatur sails into Tripoli, recaptures the USS *Philadelphia* and sets her afire.
March 26, 1804 - The Territory of Orleans is established.
May 14, 1804-September 23th 1806 - An expedition led by Meriwether Lewis and William Clark departs St. Louis to explore the new lands to reach the Pacific.
August-September 1804 - A U.S. naval squadron bombards Tripoli.
1805 - An expedition led by an army officer Zebulon M. Pike departs St. Louis to attempt to discover the mouth of the Mississippi River and to conclude treaties with the Indians in the area. The 20-man team travels about 2,000 miles to reach Leech Lake, Minnesota, but fails to reach the headwaters of the river. During 1806, Pike leads another expedition and reaches Colorado (Pike's Peak). He fails to make it to the peak, but the mountain is later named in his honor.
January 11, 1805 - Territory of Michigan is organized (taken from Indiana).
March 4, 1805 - Thomas Jefferson begins his second term as President of U.S.
April 25, 1805 - U.S. Marines and a mercenary force led by Lt. Presley O'Bannon capture Derne, Tripoli. The Marines raise the Stars and Stripes, the first time the American flag is raised over a captured fort in the Old World.
March 3, 1805 -The Louisiana-Missouri Territory is established.
June 4, 1805 - The U. S. and Tripoli sign a treaty ending the Barbary Coast War.
September 23, 1806 - The expedition team led by Lewis and Clark arrives back in St. Louis from their journey to the Pacific Ocean.
January 17, 1807 - Aaron Burr (Vice President under Thomas Jefferson), accused of treason, is seized in the Mississippi Territory at McIntosh Bluff, Alabama. He is later acquitted, but before he can be tried on charges of having murdered Alexander Hamilton, he flees the U.S.
July 2, 1807 - British Warships are ordered to leave U.S. waters.
April 17, 1808 - France (Napoleon Bonaparte) issues the Bayonne Decree ordering the capture of all American Ships entering French and Italian ports. This follows Napoleon's Milan Decree of the previous December.
July 16, 1808 - The Missouri Fur Company is founded in St. Louis, Missouri.
November 10, 1808 -Osage Indians cede land (Missouri and part of Ark.) to U.S.
July 1809 - Tecumseh (Shawnee) and his brother Prophet begin to organize the other Indian tribes (confederacy) against U.S. expansion (westward).
February 3, 1809 - The Territory of Illinois is organized.

March 4, 1809 - James Madison is inaugurated as the 4th President of the U.S.
Mar. 23, 1810- Rambouillet Decree - Permits seizure of U.S. ships (Fr. ports).
June 23, 1810 - The Pacific Fur Trading Co. is founded by John Astor; during April 1811, a post is opened at Astoria, at the mouth of the Oregon River.
September 30, 1809 - Treaty of Fort. Wayne - Gov. William H. Harrison and the Indians (Indiana); U.S. acquires tracts of Indian land along Wabash River.
September 26, 1810 - Americans residing at Spanish Fort of Florida rebel, capture the garrison at Baton Rouge, and seek annexation to the United States. The area remains a republic only for a short time, October 27th, 1810, when President Madison annexes the land for the United States joining it with the Territory of Orleans (State of Louisiana in 1812).
February 2, 1811 - Russian settlers arrive at Bodega Bay near San Francisco.
April 12, 1811 - Americans establish the initial permanent settlement in Northwest at Fort Astoria on the Columbia River.
November 7, 1811 - The Battle of Tippicanoe, Indiana Territory (Indians).

War of 1812

March 12, 1812 - U.S. troops take control of Amelia Island off Georgia.
March 18, 1812 - U.S. troops advance into Florida ("Patriot's War").
April 1812- The Indians initiate attacks against settlers (Northwest Territory).
April 30, 1812 - Louisiana enters the Union as the 18th state. After Louisiana becomes a state, the remainder of the Territory purchased from France is called the Missouri Territory (all of Louisiana Purchase except Louisiana).
June 4, 1812 - Missouri is organized into a U.S. Territory.
June 18, 1812 - The United States declares war on England (War of 1812). At this time, the English hold more than 8,000 Americans as prisoners.
July 2-30, 1812 - The Navy is heavily engaged with the British Royal Navy.
July 12, 1812 - A U.S. force invades Canada, but it retreats by 8 August.
August 15, 1812 - A small contingent of Americans is ordered to abandon Fort Dearborn (Chicago). Soon afterwards, the troops are massacred by Indians.
August 16, 1812 - Detroit surrenders without a fight to the British. General William Hull and his command are captured and transported to Montreal. By September, General William H. Harrison is made commander, northwest army.
August 19, 1812 - The USS *Constitution* defeats the HMS *Guerriere*.
September-October 1812 - Kentucky volunteers initiate a campaign against the Kickapoo and Peoria Indians in Illinois, but the venture is unsuccessful.
September 11, 1812 - A 20-man Marine contingent and Georgia Militia, while escorting a wagon train, are ambushed by Seminole Indians at Twelve Mile Swamp. One man is scalped and six others are wounded, and one of the latter, Captain John Williams USMC, succumbs from his wounds.
October 13, 1812 - Battle of Queenston Heights, Ontario Canada.
October 17-18, 1812 - The USS *Wasp* defeats and captures the HMS Frolic.
October 25, 1812 - The USS *United States* defeats the HMS *Macedonian*.
December 26, 1812 - England blockades the Chesapeake and Delaware Bays.
December 29, 1812 - The USS *Constitution* under Captain William Bainbridge defeats the HMS *Java* and earns the nickname, "Old Ironsides."
December 1812 - During this first year of hostilities with Great Britain, the U.S. Navy has seized more than 300 British ships.
January 21, 1813 - Battle of Raisin River (Lake Erie) - A British-Indian force engages Kentucky Militia. About 500 Kentuckians are captured and about 100 killed, many of the latter are massacred by the Indians.
April 16, 1813 - The Spanish surrender Fort Charlotte, at Mobile (Alabama).
April 27, 1813 - The Americans attack and capture York (Toronto), the capital of upper Canada. General Zebulon M. Pike is killed when a powder magazine explodes. Pike's Peak, Colorado is named after General Pike.
May 1813 - The British extend the sea blockade from New York to Savannah.
May 6, 1813 - The "Patriots War," which had commenced on 18 March, 1812

when Americans crossed into Florida, ends this day.

May 1-9, 1813 - Fort Meigs' (northwestern Ohio) garrison raises a cheer of jubilation after the British abandon their siege on 9 May.

May 26-27, 1813 - Battle of Sacketts Harbor, Lake Ontario (New York).

June 6, 1813 - Battle of Stony Creek (New York).

August 2, 1813 - The Battle of Fort Stephenson - The U.S. Army repels a British-Indian attack at Fort Stephenson on the Sandusky River (Ohio).

August 30, 1813 - Fort Mims Massacre (near Mobile, Alabama) - The fort is attacked by Indians under Red Eagle (William Wetherford).

September 10, 1813 - Naval Battle of Lake Erie (Commodore Oliver H. Perry).

September 18, 1813 - The British evacuate Fort Detroit (Chicago).

October 1813 - Commodore David D. Porter lands at Nukahiva, in the Pacific, founding the first American overseas Naval Base. (Madisonville).

October 4, 1813 - Volunteers move to Fayetteville, Tennessee to serve with General Andrew Jackson against the Creeks, for the recent massacre at Fort Mims.

October 5, 1813 - The Battle of the Thames (Lake Erie). Shawnee Chief, Tecumseh an ally of the British is killed during this battle.

November 3, 1813 - Tennessee Militia battles Indians at Talishatchie, Alabama.

November 9, 1813 - U.S. troops battle Indians at Talladega, Alabama.

November 11, 1813 - The Battle of Chrysler's Farm near Ogdensburg, N.Y.

November 29, 1813 - A U.S. force under General John Floyd attacks Creek Indians at Autosee near "Hickory Ground" Creek Territory.

December 13, 1813 - Indians attack Lewistown and Tuscarora, New York.

December 18, 1813 - The British seize Fort Niagra (Youngstown New York).

December 29-30, 1813 - Buffalo, New York is burned by the British.

January 22- 24 and 27, 1814 - The Tennessee Militia is defeated by Indians at Emuckfaw, Enotachopco Creek and Calibee Creek, respectively.

April 6, 1814 - Napoleon is overthrown; this frees British troops for duty in U.S.

February 14, 1814 - The British, following a pursuit of more than one year, corner the USS *Essex,* the final U.S. ship in the Pacific at Valparaiso, Chile and on 28 March, it is destroyed. One of the survivors is a young boy of 12, named Davey Farragut, later Admiral David Farragut.

March 1814 - An U.S. force (about 4,000 troops under Gen. James Wilkinson is stymied by 200 British and Canadian troops in Canada at LaColle Mill.

March 24, 1814 - Colonel Winfield Scott is promoted to Brigadier General and given command at Buffalo, New York. Also, Major General Jacob Brown replaces General James Wilkinson as Commander in Niagra, New York.

March 27, 1814 - Battle of Horseshoe Bend (Creek Indians) Alabama - The Tennessee Militia under General Andrew Jackson and General John Coffee vanquish the Creeks. This victory ends the Indian resistance, terminating the "Creek War." Sam Houston is wounded during this battle.

April 1814 - The Royal Navy blockades the New England ports.

May 6, 1814 - The British destroy Fort Oswego, New York.

June 1814 - The USS *Wasp* and her Marine detachment attack and capture six British warships, the last being the HMS *Reindeer* on the 28th (North Atlantic).

July 2, 1814 - Battle of Fort Erie (Canada) - U.S. forces attack the British.

July 5, 1814 - Battle of Chippewa (Lake Erie vicinity). The gray uniforms worn by the cadets at West Point are in honor of this battle.

July 22, 1814 - The U.S. concludes a treaty with the Delaware, Miami, Seneca, Shawnee and Wyandot Indian tribes. One term of the treaty calls for the tribes to declare war against the British.

July 25, 1814 - Battle of Lundy's Lane (Niagra Falls). This is one of the biggest battles of the war. Generals Winfield Scott and Jacob Brown are wounded.

August 2-September 21, 1814 - The British Siege of Fort Erie. The Stars and Stripes prevails. Following the siege, the British retire towards Chippewa.

August 3, 1814 - American sharpshooters at the Niagra River compel a British force to abort an invasion of Buffalo, New York.

August 4, 1814 - The Battle of Michilimackinac Island (Great Lakes).

August 9, 1814 - Treaty of Ft. Jackson - Creeks cede large amount of territory in Georgia and Mississippi Territory to U.S. (About two thirds).
August l9-25, 1814 - The Battle of Bladensburg (Maryland). U.S. troops (mostly militia) collapse. Marines and Sailors hold the line for several hours.
August 24, 1814 - The British enter the capital, Washington, D.C., without opposition. The British burn buildings including the White House. On the following day, a terrible storm forces the British to abandon the city.
August 30, 1814 -A British fleet arrives at Alexandria, Virginia.
August 1814 - The U.S.. Navy continues to rattle the British fleets. The *Peacock* raids England and Ireland. Aided by the ship's Marines, several vessels are seized. The USS *Adams* and *Wasp* also attack British ships off Europe.
September 2-5, 1814 - A small U.S. fleet battles the British on the Potomac.
September 11, 1814 - Naval Battle of Lake Champlain.
September l2-l4, 1814 - The Siege of Fort McHenry (Maryland) - The British are repulsed and Baltimore is saved. The Star Spangled Banner is written by Francis Scott Key during the bombardment of the fort. On the 15th, General Ross, the British commanding officer, killed during the ground fighting, is transported (encased in a barrel of Jamaican rum) to England aboard the HMS *Royal Oak*. An article on Key's untitled poem is published in the *American* (Baltimore) on 21 Sept. under the headline, "Defence of Fort McHenry."
September 17, 1814 - U.S. artillery within Fort Erie (Canada) bombards English positions. By the 21st, the English lift their siege.
September 25-26, 1814 - The USS *Armstrong*, commanded by Capt. Samuel Reid, refuses a surrender demand (Azores). It delays a fleet, transporting 14,000 troops, that is en route to bolster the British at New Orleans.
November 5, 1814 - U.S. General George Izard destroys Fort Erie, Canada and orders all American troops to move out of Canada.
November 7, 1814 - General Andrew Jackson captures Pensacola, Florida.
December 2, 1814 - General Andrew Jackson's force arrives in New Orleans.
December 24, 1814 - Treaty of Ghent - It ends the War of 1812.
January 8, 1815 - Battle of New Orleans - (after the close of hostilities). The British tactics of forward attack cause many casualties. The British lose more than 2,000 killed or wounded. The Americans under General Andrew Jackson, aided by pirates under Jean Lafitte, sustain only 13 casualties during the initial battle and a total of about 100, killed or wounded. The sharpshooters from Kentucky and Tennessee and U.S. Army artillery devastate the British as they attack in formation during an early morning fog. The battle was fought after the close of hostilities, but neither side is aware of the termination of the war.

Post War of 1812

March 3, 1815 - The United States declares war against Algiers.
June 30, 1815 - Algeria signs a treaty with the U.S., ending tribute payments.
July 26, 1815 - A U.S. fleet convinces Tunis to sign a peace agreement.
July - Sept. 1815 - Treaties of Portage des Sioux (Indians Old Northwest).
August 7, 1815 - A U.S. fleet secures a treaty with Tripoli.
December 11, 1816 - Indiana is admitted to the Union as the 19th state.
March 3, 1817 - The Mississippi Territory is subdivided, part forming a new territory, the Alabama Territory.
March 4, 1817 - James Monroe is inaugurated fifth President of the U. S.
April 7, 1817 - General Jackson's troops capture the Spanish Fort at St. Marks.
June 1817 - An expedition led by Major Stephen Harriman Long departs St. Louis heading for Minnesota. It concurs with an earlier suggestion by Zebulon Pike that a fort be established (Minneapolis). The party passed through Green Bay and operated around the Great Lakes. After remaining in the area around St. Anthony's Falls, Long returns to St. Louis , reaching there on 15 August.
December 10, 1817 - Mississippi is admitted to the Union as the 20th state. Also,

the Territory of Alabama is organized (taken from Mississippi).

December 23, 1817 - A combined operation including the Army, Navy and Marines, tightens the noose on the pirates holding Amelia Island, Florida.

April 4, 1818 - Congress designates the U.S. Flag to remain 13-striped, with the addition of stars only for new states on 31 March. President James Monroe signs the bill this day.

May 24, 1818 - U. S. forces capture the Spanish garrison at Pensacola, Florida ending the Seminole Indian War. Another war will ignite and last until 1843.

December 3, 1818- Illinois is admitted to the Union as the 21st state.

1819 - Major Stephen H. Long leads an expedition to explore the region between the Missouri River and the South Platte, Arkansas and Canadian Rivers (Colorado and New Mexico). During 1820, Long arrives at Pike's Peak and another huge mountain, the latter being named Long's Peak (Colorado).

February 22 1819 - Adams-Onis Treaty - Spain cedes East Florida to U.S.

March 2, 1819 - Arkansas is formed as a U.S. Territory.

December 14, 1819 - Alabama is admitted to the Union as the 22nd state.

March 15, 1820 - Maine is admitted to the Union as the 23rd state.

October 1820 - U.S. warships and Marines anchor off S. America and remain there for 3 years during the rebellion against Spanish rule.

March 5, 1821 - James Monroe is inaugurated to his second term as President.

July 17, 1821 - The Floridas (East and West) are ceded to the U. S. by Spain.

August 10, 1821 - Missouri is admitted to the Union as the 24th state.

September 4, 1821 - Russia claims U.S. Pacific coast north of 51st parallel (also claimed by U.S. and England); includes Oregon and British Vancouver.

March 30, 1822 - The Territory of Florida is formed.

December 12, 1822 - U.S. recognizes Mexico's independence (from Spain).

December 22, 1822 - The West Indies Squadron (U. S. Navy) is established by Congress for the purpose of eradicating piracy in the Mediterranean Sea.

April 30, 1823 - Major Stephen Harriman Long departs Philadelphia on a new expedition. The party moves to Ft. Wayne, Indiana. From there the expedition travels the Mississippi River to the St. Peter's River to find the source of the latter. Afterwards, Long is to locate the source of the Red River and follow it north to the border with Canada (49th Parallel). He is to conspicuously display the Stars and Stripes and then return to Philadelphia via the Great Lakes. The party arrives at Fort St. Anthony (later Fort Snelling), Minnesota on 2 July.

April 17, 1824 - U.S. and Russia sign a treaty in which Russia reduces its claims on the U.S. Pacific coast from north of the 59th parallel to 54 ° 40'.

November 1824 - A U.S. naval squadron arrives at Fajardo, Puerto Rico to demand an apology for a recent insult to the American flag.

March 4, 1825 - John Quincy Adams is inaugurated as 6th President of U. S.

July 4, 1826 - Presidents John Adams (age 91) and Thomas Jefferson (age 83), each succumb on this the 50th anniversary of the Declaration of Independence.

November 15, 1827 - The Creeks cede the balance of their lands in west Georgia.

February 7, 1832 - U.S. Marines and Sailors assault Qualla Battoo, Sumatra.

March 4, 1829 - Andrew Jackson is inaugurated as 7th President of U. S.

July 4, 1831 - James Monroe, the fifth President of the U. S. succumbs.

March 24, 1832 - Creeks cede their territory east of the Mississippi River to U.S.

April 6 -August 2, 1832 - "Black Hawk War," Wisconsin (Sauk and Fox).

October 14, 1832 - Chickasaws cede their lands (east of Mississippi R) to U.S.

May 1, 1832 - An expedition departs Fort Osage for the Columbia River; the Oregon Trail (Independence, Missouri to the river becomes main route (Oregon).

March 4, 1833 - Andrew Jackson begins his second term as President of U.S.

January 30, 1835 - President Andrew Jackson survives an assassination attempt.

Dec. 28, 1835 - Seminoles ambush U.S. Soldiers between Fort Brooke, and Fort King (108 killed-2 survive) and at Withlacoochie, Florida (Starts Seminole Wars).

December 29, 1835 - Cherokees cede all their land east of Mississippi River.

January 3, 1836 - American Texans dispatch a resolution to Mexico City, requesting annexation to the United States.

February 23-March 6, 1836 - Siege of the Alamo (San Antonio, Texas). The defenders including Davy Crockett, Jim Bowie and William Travis are outnumbered about 20-to-1. After the fall of the Alamo, Santa Anna orders the bodies of the defenders to be stacked, soaked with oil and burned.
March 2, 1836 - Texas adopts a Declaration of Independence from Mexico.
March 17, 1836 - Texas adopts a constitution.
March 27, 1836 - More than 300 Texans under Captain Fannin at Goliad, Texas are surrounded. They surrender to the Mexican army only to be shot.
April 20, 1836 - The Wisconsin Territory is established (from Michigan).
May 19, 1836 - Comanches raid Parker's Fort, Tex.- 5 women & children seized.
June 15, 1836 - Arkansas is admitted to the Union as the 25th state.
September 1836 - Texans vote affirmatively on annexation by the U.S.
Oct. 22, 1836 - Sam Houston is inaugurated as 1st president, Republic of Texas.
November 21, 1836 - Marines skirmish with Indians at Wahoo Swamp, Florida.
January 26, 1837 - Michigan is admitted to the Union as the 26th state.
January 27, 1837 - A U.S. contingent (Soldiers and Marines) engage Indians in the vicinity of Hatchie-Lustee, Florida. An agreement to end the Seminole War is signed during March, but a treaty is never consummated.
March 4, 1837 - Martin Van Buren is inaugurated as 8th President of the U.S.
October 1837 - Osceola, the Seminole leader is captured while under a "white flag." He is placed in Ft. Marion (later Castillo de San Marcos), St. Augustine, Florida and later transferred to Ft. Moultrie, S.C.; he lives in Officer's quarters until his death (January 30 1838). A U.S. military salute is fired over his grave.
June 12, 1838 - The Territory of Iowa (from Wisconsin Territory) is formed.
August 9, 1838 - Three U.S. vessels (Wilkes Exploring Expedition) embark for the Fiji and Gilbert Islands; the expedition returns during July 1842.
October 1838 - Cherokees remaining in Georgia evicted (Trail of Tears).
October 12, 1838 - Texas withdraws its request for annexation to the U. S.
September 25, 1839 - The Republic of Texas signs a peace treaty with France.
March 9, 1840 - Comanches arrive (San Antonio) for a peace parley. They return two captives (abused women) and a fight erupts (Council House Fight).
April 16, 1840 - Marines and Sailors battle Indians along Florida's east coast.
August 6, 1840 - Comanches raid Victoria, Texas and massacre some settlers.
August 10-12, 1840 - Battle of Plum Creek - Texans against Comanches.
November 13, 1840 - England signs treaty with Republic of Texas.
December 1840 - November 1841 - Soldiers, Sailors and Marines begin a campaign to eliminate Indians in the Everglades. Not one Seminole is detected.
March 4, 1841 - William Henry Harrison is inaugurated ninth President of the U.S. He dies of pneumonia on April 4th. John Tyler, his Vice President, assumes the Presidency, being sworn in on April 6th as the tenth President.
May 1842 - John Fremont begins expedition to Rocky Mountains (Wyoming); he makes several other subsequent westward expeditions.
September 11, 1842 - San Antonio, Texas, is captured by the Mexican Army.
August 14, 1843 - The 2nd Seminole War in Florida ends (without a treaty).
June 1843 - The Texans and the Mexicans, still clashing with each other since the siege of the Alamo (1836), conclude a truce.
November 29, 1843 - Marines and Sailors debark at Greenville, Liberia to terminate the slave trade and piracy in the area.
April 22, 1844 - President John Tyler submits a treaty (accept annexation of Texas) to the Senate, but it is rejected (8 June 1844).
Dec. 12, 1844 - Anson Jones becomes the 2nd president of the Republic of Texas.
December 14, 1843 - Marines and Sailors retaliate against Africans on the Ivory Coast. King Crack-o is slain and the town is burned.
March 3, 1845 - Florida is admitted to the Union as the 27th state.

Mexican War Era

March 4, 1845 - James K. Polk is inaugurated as 11th President of the U. S.
March 28, 1845 - Mexico breaks diplomatic relations with the United States.

May 28, 1845 - General Zachary Taylor's force enters Corpus Christi, Texas.
July 4, 1845 - Texas accepts the dictated terms of American statehood.
October 10, 1845 - The U.S. Naval Academy opens at Annapolis, Maryland.
December 2, 1845 - President James K. Polk addresses Congress, emphasizing America's claim to all of Oregon (Known as the "Polk Doctrine").
December 29, 1845 - Texas is admitted to the Union as the 28th state.
January 13, 1846 - General Zachary Taylor advances to a position in Texas near the Rio Grande River after negotiations with Mexico break off.
April 11, 1846 - Mexico demands that the U.S. withdraw from the Rio Grande or face armed conflict; it is rejected by General Zachary Taylor.
April 25, 1846 - A contingent of U.S. Cavalry is attacked and surrounded by Mexicans. General Taylor informs Washington that the conflict has started.
May 3, 1846 - General Zachary Taylor arrives at Point Isabel, Texas to protect U.S. supplies there. During his absence from Ft. Texas (Ft. Taylor), the garrison refuses to surrender, despite a prolonged bombardment; 2 troopers killed.
May 7, 1846- General Taylor issues the order to march on Matamoros, Mexico.
May 8, 1846 - The Battle of Palo Alto (Texas).
May 9, 1846 - The Battle of Resaca De La Palma (Texas).
May 13, 1846 - Congress approves a Declaration of War against Mexico. The war further divides the North (anti) and the South (pro).
May 18, 1846 - American Soldiers cross the Rio Grande River unopposed, occupy Matamoros, Mexico and hoist the Stars and Stripes over the city.
June 14, 1846 - Americans, who had settled in California, declare independence from Mexico ("Republic of California," also known as the "Bear Republic").
July 7-29, 1846 - On the 7th, a U.S. fleet arrives in Monterey and claims California. The Marines raise Old Glory atop the Custom House. On the 9th, Sailors and Marines seize Yerba Buena (present day San Francisco) without incident; soon after San Diego is captured by the USS *Cyane*.
August 1846 - American troops capture Los Angeles without opposition.
August 13, 1846 - Commodore David Stockton in a message to Washington: "The U. S. flag is flying from every commanding position in territory of California."
August 15, 1846- Col. Stephen Kearny announces the annexation of N. Mexico.
August 17, 1846 - Americans occupy Sante Fe, New Mexico without incident. Also, Commodore D. Stockton declares the annexation of California.
September 23, 1846 - Mexicans recapture Los Angeles.
December 6, 1846 - Battle of San Pasqual (California).
November 16, 1846 - General Zachary Taylor seizes Saltillo, Mexico.
December 25, 1846 - U. S. troops defeat Mexican Cavalry (El Paso, Texas).
December 28, 1846 - Iowa is admitted to the Union as the 29th state.
January 8, 1847 - Battle of the San Gabriel River (California).
January 10, 1847 - Los Angeles is recaptured. Old Glory is raised at the spot Captain Gillespie USMC, was forced to surrender three months earlier.
January 19th, 1847 - Bent Massacre, New Mexico (Pueblo Indians).
February 3, 1847- The Battle of Pueblo de Taos, New. Mexico (Pueblo Indians).
February 22-23, 1847 - The Battle of Buena Vista, Mexico.
February 28, 1847 - The Battle of Rio Sacramento (Mexico) - Americans under Colonel Alexander Doniphan while en route to capture Chihuahua, Mexico.
March 9, 1847 - The Army (10,000 troops under General Winfield Scott) lands near Vera Cruz, initiating the 1st amphibious landing of the U.S. Army.
March 29, 1847 - The Mexicans at Vera Cruz (city of the True Cross) lay down their arms. Soon after, the Stars and Stripes is hoisted over the city.
April 18, 1847- Battle of Cerro Gordo, Mexico (General Winfield Scott).
August 20, 1847 - After defeats at Contreras and Churubusco (San Antonio, Texas), Mexico seeks a truce. Also, two cannon previously lost are recovered and now stand at West Point: "Lost without dishonor, recovered with glory."
August 24, 1847- General Winfield Scott and Santa Anna agree on an armistice.
Late August 1847 - A U.S. wagon-train is fired upon in Mexico City.
September 6, 1847 - Mexico rejects the U. S. demands for a settlement.

September 8, 1847 The Battle of Molino del Rey (Mexico).
September 12, 1847 - The U.S. bombards Chapultepec.
September 13, 1847 - The Battle of Chapultepec (Mexico). U.S. Marines seize the national palace (Halls of Montezuma) and hoist the Stars and Stripes. Robert E. Lee and Ulysses S. Grant participate at this battle.
September 13-14, 1847 - The U.S. Army marches into Mexico City.
November 29, 1847 - Some settlers in Oregon are slain by Indians.
January 24, 1848 - John Marshall discovers gold in the American River near Sacramento, California, initiating the California Gold Rush.
February 2, 1848 - The U. S. and Mexico sign the Treaty of Guadalupe Hidalgo. The treaty cedes Texas, California, portions of Arizona and New Mexico to the U. S. and some of Colorado, Wyoming, Nevada and Utah.
May 29, 1848 - Wisconsin is admitted to the Union as the 30th state.
August 14, 1848 - The United States establishes the Oregon Territory.
March 3, 1849 - The Minnesota Territory is organized by the United States.
March 4, 1849 - Zachary Taylor is inaugurated as 12th President of the U.S.
July 9, 1850 - President Zachary Taylor succumbs. Vice President Millard Fillmore becomes the 13th President of the U.S.
September 9, 1850 - California becomes the 31st state. Also, New Mexico and Utah become territories.
July 23, 1851 - Treaty of Traverse des Sioux- Sioux give up land (Minn.-Iowa).

Civil War Era

March 2, 1853 - The U.S. forms the Washington Territory.
March 4, 1853 - Franklin Pierce is inaugurated as 14th President of the U.S.
July 8, 1853 - A U.S. fleet under Commodore Matthew C. Perry (brother of Commodore Oliver Hazard Perry) arrives at Yedo, Harbor, Japan to open up trade. He returns again (March 1854) to consummate the Treaty of Kangawa.
May 30, 1854 - The Territories of Kansas and Nebraska are established with the option of choosing or not choosing slavery. The establishment of these two Territories in essence, repeals the "Missouri Compromise Act of 1850."
June 1854 - The army begins campaigns against the Apaches in New Mexico.
October 22, 1854 - The Army establishes Ft. Larned along the Santa Fe Trail.
March 1855- Congress authorizes the 1st and 2nd U.S. Cavalry Regiments.
June 1855 - Mescalero Apaches sign a treaty ending their war with the U. S.
March 4, 1857 - James Buchanan is inaugurated as 15th President of the U.S.
July 20, 1857 - A U.S. Army unit is ambushed near Devil's River, Texas.
September 11, 1857 - Mountain Meadow Massacre - About 100-120 settlers emigrating to California are slaughtered in Utah by a group of malcontents (Indians and Mormons) led by John D. Lee. Later, Lee is later caught and hanged.
1857 - An American sea captain, Peter Duncan claims Navaza (Navassa Island) in the Caribbean Sea (between Haiti and Jamaica) for the United States.
April 22- May 11, 1858 - Texas Rangers and Indian Scouts en route to Oklahoma are attacked on 11 May by Comanches. Chief Iron Jacket is killed.
May 6th, 1858 - Battle of Fort Walla Walla (Washington Territory).
May 11, 1858 - Minnesota becomes the 32nd state.
September 1858 - Troops under Colonel Steptoe battle Indians near the Snake River near Fort Walla Walla, Washington Territory.
October 1st, 1858 - The U.S. 2nd Cavalry engages Comanches (Oklahoma).
February 14, 1859 - Oregon is admitted to the Union as the 33rd state.
October 16-18, 1859 - John Brown (abolitionist) raids Harper's Ferry, Va.
April 1860 - October 1861 - Pony Express operates (delivers mail) between Missouri and California. Service ends due to arrival of telegraph service.
November 6, 1860 - Abraham Lincoln is elected President of the U. S.
Dec. 20, 1860 - South Carolina secedes from Union; it reenters 9 July, 1868.
January 9th, 1861 - Mississippi secedes from Union; it reenters Feb. 23, 1870.
January 10th, 1861 - Florida secedes from Union; it reenters June 25, 1868.
January 11, 1861- Alabama secedes from Union; it reenters July 13, 1868.

January 19, 1861 - Georgia secedes from Union; it reenters July 21, 1868, but its Congressman is unseated 3/5/1869. Georgia is then readmitted July 15, 1870.
January 26, 1861 - Louisiana secedes from Union.; it is readmitted July 9, 1868.
January 29, 1861 - Kansas is admitted to the Union as the 34th state.
February 1, 1861 - Texas secedes from the Union; it reenters March 30, 1870.
February 9, 1861 - Jefferson Davis is elected 1st President (Confederate States).
February 13th-14th, 1861 - Siege of Apache Pass (Chiricahua Apaches).
February 18, 1861 - Jefferson Davis is inaugurated President of the Confederate States. The ceremony takes place at Montgomery, Alabama, the site of the Confederate capital. Later, the capital is moved to Richmond, Virginia.
February 25, 1861 - The Confederates evacuate Nashville, Tennessee.
February 28, 1861 - The Territory of Colorado is established.
March 2, 1861- Territories of Dakota & Nevada are established (from Utah).
March 4, 1861 - Abraham Lincoln is inaugurated 16th President of the U.S.
April 12, 1861 - Confederates fire upon Fort Sumter, SC, to open the Civil War.
April 13, 1861 - Union Major Robert Anderson surrenders Fort Sumter, S.C.
April 17, 1861 - Virginia secedes from Union; it reenters Jan. 26, 1870.
May 6, 1861 - Arkansas secedes from Union; it reenters June 22, 1868.
May 10, 1861 - Union troops seize control of Camp Jackson, Illinois.
May 18, 1861 - Union naval vessels bombard Sewall's Point, Virginia.
May 20, 1861 - North Carolina secedes from Union; it reenters July 4, 1868.
May 24, 1861 - The Union occupies the plantation of Robert E. Lee and his wife Mary. It is later transformed into Arlington National Cemetery.
June 8, 1861 - Tennessee secedes from Union; it reenters July 24, 1866.
June 10, 1861 - Confederate troops attack Union lines at Big Bethel, Virginia.
June 14, 1861 - Confederates abandon Harper's Ferry, Virginia (later West Va.).
June 17, 1861 - Union Loyalists in Western Virginia (In Convention) vote to secede from Virginia, a Confederate state, to form an independent state.
July 5, 1861 - Battle of Carthage, Missouri- About 12 other clashes occur here.
July 11, 1861 - Battle at Rich Mountain (West Virginia).
July 18, 1861 - Union and Confederates clash at Blackburn's Ford, Virginia.
July 21, 1861 - First Battle of Bull Run (Manassas), Virginia.
July 26, 1861 - Confederates are repelled at Fort Fillmore, NM, but on the following day, about 400 Union troops are captured there.
August 2, 1861 - The Union abandons Fort Stanton, New Mexico.
August 10, 1861 - Battle of Wilson's Creek (Springfield, Missouri).
August 23, 1861 - The Cherokee Indian nation joins the Confederacy.
August 29, 1861 - Forts Hatteras & Clark, North Carolina surrender to Union.
September 4, 1861 - Confederates occupy Columbus, Kentucky.
September 10, 1861 - Battle of Carnifex Ferry (Virginia).
September 12-13, 1861 - Battle of Cheat Mountain (West Virginia).
September 12-20, 1861 - Battle of Lexington, Missouri (Main battle 18-20).
September 27th, 1861 - Apaches attack the town of Pinos Altos (Arizona).
October 9, 1861 - Union repels Confederates at Santa Rosa Island, Florida.
October 16, 1861 - Lexington, Missouri recaptured by Union.
October 21, 1861 - Battle of Ball's Bluff (Leesburg, Virginia).
November 7, 1861 - Battle of Port Royal (South Carolina).
November 7, 1861 - Battle of Belmont (Missouri and Columbus Kentucky).
November 9, 1861 - Battle of Fry Mountain (Piketown), Kentucky.
December 13, 1861 - Battle at Buffalo Mountain, Camp Alleghany, W. Virginia.
January 19-20, 1862 - Union and Confederates clash at Mill Springs (Logan's Crossroads) and Fishing Creek, Kentucky.
February 7-8, 1862 - Roanoke, Island, N.C. is seized by the Union.
February 14-16, 1862 - Battle of Fort Donelson (Tennessee).
March 3, 1862 - Union troops seize Fort Clinch (Fernandina, Florida). Also, Confederate General Stonewall Jackson is defeated at Kernstown, Virginia.
March 6-8, 1862 -Battle of Pea Ridge (Arkansas). Cherokees participate.
March 8-9, 1862 - Naval Battle - The Monitor and the Merrimac (*Virginia*).
March 26-28, 1862 - Battle of Apache Pass (Glorietta), Santa Fe, NM.
April 1862 - "The Great Locomotive Chase." Union troops attempt to seize and

destroy railroad tracks between Chattanooga Tennessee and Atlanta, Georgia.
April 5-May3, 1862 - Union Siege of Yorktown, Virginia.
April 6-7, 1862- Battle of Shiloh (Pittsburg Landing),Tennessee.
April 8 - 1862 - The Union seizes Island # 10, Tennessee.
May 3, 1862 - Confederates evacuate Yorktown, Virginia.
May 5, 1862 - Union and Confederates clash at Ft. Magruder (Williamsburg, Va.).
May 8, 1862 - Battle of Bull Pasture, Virginia.
May 23, 1862 - Battle of Front Royal (Virginia).
May 15, 1862 - Fort Darling (Conf. Naval Academy), Va., repels Union ships.
May 27, 1862 - Battle of Hanover Court House (Virginia).
May 29-31, 1862 -Conf. batteries clash with Union gunboats (Acquia Creek, Va.).
May 31-June 1, 1862 - Battle of Seven Pines (Virginia).
June 3-5, 1862 - Fort Pillow (Fort Wright), Tennessee falls to the Union.
June 9, 1862 - Battle of Port Republic, Virginia.
June 16, 1862 - Battle of Secessionville (Fort Lamar), S.C. - Saves Charleston.
June 26-July 2, 1862 - The Seven Days' Battle (Va.) - Includes Cold Harbor, Mechanicsville, Peach Orchard, White Oak Farm, Glendale, Frazier Farm, Savage Station and Gaine's Mills.
July 12, 1862 - Congress authorizes the Congressional Medal of Honor.
July 15th, 1862 - Battle of Apache Pass, Arizona (Apaches).
July 17, 1862 - Congress authorizes President Lincoln to create National Cemeteries "for the soldiers who shall die in the service of the country."
August 9, 1862 - Battle of Cedar Mountain (Slaughter Mountain), Virginia.
August 13, 1862 - Union and Confederates clash at Clarendon, Arkansas.
August 22, 1862 - Sioux Indians attack Fort Ridgely, Minnesota.
August 23, 1862 - Santee Sioux attack New Ulm, Minnesota.
August 27, 1862 - Battle at Bull Run Bridge, Virginia.
August 27-28, 1862 - Union and Confederates clash at Kettle Run, Virginia.
August 28-30, 1862 - 2nd Battle of Bull Run (Manassas). Heavy fighting erupts at Groveton and Gainesville, Va. on the 28th-29thand culminates on the 30th.
August 30, 1862 - Battle at Richmond, Kentucky.
September 1, 1862 - Battle of Britton's Lane (near Jackson, Tennessee).
September 1, 1862 - Battle of Chantilly (Ox Hill), Virginia.
September 2, 1862 - Battle of Britton's Station, Tennessee.
September 12-15, 1862 - The Confederates seize Loudon Heights, Virginia, Maryland Heights, Maryland and Harper's Ferry, West Virginia.
September 14, 1862 - Battle of Crampton's Gap (Turner's Gap), S. Mtn., Md.
September 17, 1862 - The Battle of Antietam (Sharpsburg), Maryland.
September 18, 1862 - Battle of the Yellow Medicine River (Sioux).
September 19-20, 1862 - Heavy fighting develops at Iuka, Mississippi.
September 22, 1862 - The "Emancipation Proclamation." President Lincoln frees the slaves in the Confederate states.
October 8, 1862 - The Battle of Perryville (Kentucky).
October 20-22, 1862 - Confederates capture Loudon, Kentucky.
November 28, 1862 - Battle of Cane Hill, Arkansas.
December 7, 1862 - Battle of Prairie Grove (Arkansas).
December 12, 1862 - USS Cairo is sunk (1st ship sunk by electronic device).
December 13, 1862 - Battle of Fredericksburg (Virginia).
December 20, 1862 - Confederates attack Union lines (Holly Springs, Miss.).
December 27, 1862 - Union ships attack Haine's Bluff (Miss.) on the Yazoo.
December 28-29, 1862 - Heavy fighting occurs at Chickasaw Bayou, Miss.
December 30, 1862 - Battle at Parker's Crossroads, (Red Mound) Tennessee.
December 31, 1862 - January 2, 1863 - Battle of Murfreesboro.(Tennessee).
January 11, 1863 - The Union seizes Fort Hindman, Arkansas.
January 17, 1863 - U.S. Cavalry engages Indians (Lava Beds, California).
January 29, 1863 - Battle of Bear River - The 3rd California Infantry engages Shoshone Indians under Chief Bear Hunter in the Utah Territory.
February 24, 1863 - The U. S. splits New Mexico Territory (forms Ariz. Terr.).
March 3, 1863 - Congress authorizes the Territory of Idaho.
March 8, 1863 - Confederates evade Union troops and capture General Edwin H.

Stoughton and 35 Union troops at Fairfax Court House, Virginia.
March 16, 1863 - Union fleet halted near Steele's Bayou, saving Vicksburg.
March 17, 1863 - Battle of Kelly's Ford, Virginia.
April 4, 1863 - General Grant launches fourth attack against Vicksburg, Miss.
April 17, 1863 - Union troops depart LaGrange, Tn. en route to Baton Rouge, La.
April 28-29, 1863 - Union forces attack Grand Gulf, in front of Vicksburg.
May 1, 1863 - Battle of Port Gibson (Magnolia Thompson, Mississippi).
May 2, 1863 - Col. Grierson arrives at Baton Rouge, La. from LaGrange, Tenn.
May 1-4, 1863 - The Battle of Chancellorsville (Virginia).
May 14, 1863 - Union and Confederates clash at Jackson, Mississippi.
May 16, 1863 - Battle of Champion Hills or Baker's Creek, Mississippi.
May 17, 1863 - Battle of Big Black River Bridge, Mississippi.
May 27-July 9, 1863 - Union siege (48 days) of Port Hudson (Louisiana).
June 9, 1863 - Skirmishing occurs at Beverly Ford and Brandy Station, Va.
June 15, 1863 - After fight at Winchester, the Union moves to Harper's Ferry.
June 20, 1863 - West Virginia is admitted to the Union as the 35th state.
July 1-3, 1863- The Battle of Gettysburg (Pennsylvania).
July 3-4, 1863 - Confederate Surrender of Vicksburg (Mississippi).
July 10-Sept. 6, 1863 - Siege of Fort Wagner, Morris Island (includes Batteries Gregg & Wagner), S.C. - Union uses "Swamp Angel,"(long-range cannon).
August 8, 1863 - Robert E. Lee's resignation letter is denied by President Davis.
August 12-23, 1863 - Fort Sumter, S.C. repels Union attacks.
August 21, 1863 - Quantrill's Raiders attack Lawrence, Kansas.
September 7, 1863 - Fort Wagner, South Carolina falls to the Union.
Sept. 9, 1863 - The Union seizes Cumberland Gap & Chattanooga, Tenn.
September 19-20, 1863 - The Battle of Chickamauga (Georgia).
October 14, 1863 - Clashes occur at Broad Run and Bristoe Station, Virginia.
October 26, 1863 - The Union seizes Brown's Ferry near Chattanooga, Tenn.
October 28-29, 1863 - The Union opens a supply line from Ala. to Chattanooga.
November 6, 1863 - Battle of Droop Mountain- Averell's Raid (W. Virginia).
November 17-December 3, 1863- Confederate Siege of Knoxville (Tennessee).
November 19, 1863 - President Lincoln delivers his Gettysburg Address.
November 23, 1863 - General Burnside informs Grant he can hold Knoxville for 10 or 12 days and if not relieved he would be forced to surrender or retreat.
November 24, 1863 - Battle of Lookout Mountain (Battle Above the Clouds).
Nov. 25, 1863 - Battle of Missionary Ridge. (Ends Siege of Chattanooga).
November 27, 1863 - Sam Davis (young Conf. Scout) is hanged as a spy.
December 10-14, 1863 - A clash occurs at Morristown (Bean's Station), Tenn.
February 17, 1864 - The CSS *Hunley* initiates submarine warfare by sinking the USS *Housatonic* in Charleston harbor.
February 20, 1864 - Battle of Olustee - (only major battle fought in Florida).
April 8-9, 1864 - Battle of Sabine Cross Roads and Pleasant Hill (Louisiana).
April 12, 1864 - Massacre at Fort Pillow (Tennessee).
April 15-16, 1864 - Union and Confederates clash heavily at Camden, Arkansas
May 5, 1864 - The Union repels a Confederate attack against New Bern, N.C.
May 5-6, 1864 - The Battle of the Wilderness (Virginia).
May 5-9 1864 - Heavy fighting occurs at Rocky Face Ridge, Ga. and includes clashes at Dug Creek Gap, Buzzard's Roost, Mill Creek Gap and Tunnel Hill.
May 8-21, 1864 - The Battle of Spotsylvania (Virginia).
May 9-10, 1864 - The Battle of Cloyd's Mountain (Virginia).
May 11, 1864 - Battle at Yellow Tavern, Va.-Conf. Gen. J.E.B. Stuart killed here.
May 12-16, 1864 - Heavy fighting at Drewry's Bluff (Ft. Darling), Virginia.
May 13-15, 1864 - Union and Confederate forces battle at Resaca, Georgia.
May 15, 1864 - Battle of New Market (VMI Cadets participate) Virginia.
May 25-June 4, 1864 - Union and Confederate forces clash at Dallas, Burned Hickory, Pumpkin Vine Creek, Pickett's Mill, Allatoona Hills and New Hope Church (dubbed Hell Hole), Georgia.
May 26, 1864 - The Territory of Montana is established.
May 27, 1864 - Battle of Pickett's Mill (Georgia).
June 3, 1864 - The Battle of Cold Harbor (Virginia).

33

June 9-30, 1864 - Fighting erupts at Pine Mtn., Golgotha, Culp's House, Powder Springs and at Kennesaw Mountain (27 June).
June 10, 1864 - The Battle of Brice's Cross Roads (Mississippi).
June 22, 1864 - Battle of Kolb's Farm, Georgia.
June 23, 1864 - Battle at Weldon Railroad Stat., Va. (5,000 Union casualties).
June 25, 1864 - Battle of Staunton River Railroad Bridge (Southside, Virginia).
June 27, 1864- The Battle of Kennesaw Mountain (Georgia).
July 22, 1864 - The Battle of Atlanta (Georgia).
July 24, 1864 - Confederate cavalry routs a Union force at Winchester (Virginia.).
July 29-30, 1864 - Union attempts to destroy Macon RR, south of Atlanta, Ga.
July 30, 1864 - Battle of Petersburg (Va). Rebels hold until April 2, 1865.
August 1, 1864 - Near Atlanta, Union General Stoneman is captured at Sunshine Church and Union General E. M. McCook's force escapes encirclement.
August 5, 1864 - Union fleet under David Farragut enters Mobile Bay.
August 25, 1864 - Union and Confederate troops clash at Ream's Station, Va.
August 31- Sept.1, 1864 - Union takes Macon & Western RR, isolating Atlanta.
September 2, 1864 - General William T. Sherman's troops enter Atlanta, Ga.
September 19-22, 1864 - Clashes occur at Winchester & Fisher's Hill, Va.
September 23, 1864 - Confederates attack Union positions at Athens, Alabama.
September 26-27, 1864 - Battle of Pilot Knob (Fort Davidson, Missouri).
September 27, 1864 - Confederates attack Pine Knob, Missouri.
Sept. 28-30, 1864 - Union seizes Ft. Harrison, Va; Rebels retain Ft. Gilmore, Va.
October 9, 1864 - Union continues to evict Confederates from the Shenandoah Valley; a heavy skirmish occurs at Strasburg (Fisher's Hill), Virginia.
October 13, 1864 - Comanches raid the area near Fort Belknap, Texas.
October 15, 1864 - Confederates attack Glasgow, Missouri.
October 18-19, 1864 - Battle of Winchester (Cedar Creek)- Sheridan's Ride.
October 19, 1864 - A 22-man Confederate unit raids St. Alban's, Vermont.
October 31, 1864 - Nevada is admitted to the Union as the 37th state.
October 31, 1864 - Navy warships attack and capture Plymouth, North Carolina.
Autumn 1864 - Union forces seize Camp Moore, Louisiana.
November 8, 1864 - President Lincoln is re-elected as President of the U. S.
November 16, 1864 - General William T. Sherman departs Atlanta, Georgia for Savannah, completing his "March to the Sea" on 22 December.
November 29, 1864 - Colorado State Militiamen attack an Indian reservation near Fort Lyon. The attack devastates the tribe, mostly women and children. Chief White Antelope is killed, but Chief Black Kettle escapes. Chief Black Kettle raises both a white flag and the U.S. flag, but the troops still fire.
Nov. 30, 1864 - Battle of Franklin (Tenn.); 6 Conf. Generals killed; 3 wounded.
December 13, 1864 - The Battle of Fort McAllister (Georgia).
December 14, 1864 - Union cavalry clashes with Confederates at Bristol, Tenn.
December 15-16, 1864 - The Battle of Nashville (Tennessee).
December 22, 1864 - Sherman's troops enter Savannah (March to the Sea.).
December 24-25, 1864 - The Union is repulsed at Fort Fisher, North Carolina.
January 11, 1865 - Robert E. Lee informs the Confederate Secretary of War that his supplies are nearly expended, having enough only for two-days.
January 13-15, 1865 - The Battle of Fort Fisher (North Carolina). On the 15th, a sign appeared: "Wanted, flag bearer for the 97th Pennsylvania Volunteer Regiment! This day, our regimental flag received 107 bullet holes and one canister shot while approaching Confederate-held Ft. Fisher."
January 16, 1865 - Confederates abandon Fort. Caswell (Capewell River, NC.).
February 17, 1865 - Union troops occupy Columbia, Georgia.
February 18, 1865 - Confederate-held Fort Sumter, South Carolina. surrenders.
March 4, 1865 - Lincoln is inaugurated to his 2nd term as President of the U. S.
March 5, 1865 - Union and Confederate troops clash at Staunton and Charlottesville, Va. Many Confederates seized, but General Jubal Early escapes.
March 6, 1865 - Battle of Natural Bridge (Tallahassee, Florida).
March 8-10, 1865 - Confederates attack Union lines at Wilcox's Bridge, N.C.
March 11-23, 1865 - Union troops under Sherman take Fayetteville, Goldsboro,

and Columbus Georgia; Sherman has moved 425 miles in 50 days.
March 18, 1865 - The Confederate Congress convenes for the final time.
March 19-21, 1865 - Battle of Bentonville (North Carolina).
March 20, 1865 - Stoneman's Raid - General Stoneman's Union Cavalry operates between Jonesboro, Tennessee and North Carolina.
March 22-April 24, 1865 - General James Wilson's raid (Tenn. to Alabama).
March 24-25, 1865 - The capture of Fort Steadman (at Petersburg, Va).
March 26-April 8, 1865 - Union Siege of Spanish Fort (Alabama).
March 31-April 1, 1865 - Heavy fighting erupts at Dinwiddie Courthouse, Five Forks and Berryville, Virginia.
March 31-April 9, 1865 - Union Siege of Fort Blakely (Alabama).
April 2, 1865 - Petersburg, Va., under siege since May 1864, falls to Union.
April 3, 1865 - The Union occupies Richmond, Virginia, the Confederate capital.
April 2-6, 1865 - The Battle of Sailor's Creek, Virginia (Harper's Farm).
April 6, 1865 - Union cavalry defeats Gen. Nathan B. Forrest at Selma, Alabama.
April 9, 1865 - General Ulysses S. Grant accepts the surrender of Confederate General Robert E. Lee at Appomattox Court House, Virginia.
April 11, 1865 - Union forces occupy Forts Huger and Tracy, Mobile Bay, Alabama, terminating the siege of Mobile. On the 14th, five Union vessels in Mobile Bay are sunk by Confederate torpedoes.
April 14-15, 1865 - President Lincoln is assassinated (Good Friday, 14th) at Ford's Theater (Washington, D.C.), watching the play, "Our American Cousin." He dies on the 15th. Vice .President Andrew Johnson is sworn in as 17th President.
April 16, 1865 - News of Lincoln's death reaches Fort Warren. Fifteen Confederate Generals, held there, each send personal regrets to General Grant.
April 26, 1865 - General Joseph Johnston surrenders at Durham, N.C. Negotiations with General Sherman had begun on the 21st.
May 4, 1865 - General Richard Taylor surrenders his forces to General Edward Canby; this ends organized Southern resistance east of the Mississippi.
May 10, 1865 - Confederate President Jefferson Davis is captured at Irwinsville, Georgia and transported to Fort Monroe, Virginia; later he is pardoned.
May 12, 1865 - Union troops in Texas occupy Palmetto Ranch on the Rio Grande; on the 13th, they clash with Confederates (last active battle of the war).
May 27, 1865 - The USS *Sultana* transporting freed Union prisoners sustains an explosion (common occurrence with steamships). More than 1,500 die.
November 10, 1865 - Confederate. Captain Henry Wirz, commandant of Andersonville, Prison is hanged for crimes including murder.

Post Civil War And Indian Campaigns

July 1866 - The U.S. expands westward and the rails now move through Indian Territory. The army increases its forces to guard the trains.
December 21, 1866 - The Sioux attack a lumber train, commanded by Captain Brown, near Fort Kearny, Wyoming. Eighty-one men under Captain Fetterman (Fetterman's Folly) move out to reinforce and encounter about 2,000 Sioux.
March 1, 1867 - Nebraska is admitted to the Union as the 37th state.
March 30, 1867 - The U.S. buys Alaska from Russia. On October 18 1867, Marines officially unfurl the Stars and Stripes at Sitka, Alaska.
June 24, 1867 - Pawnee Indians attack Custer's forces at the Republican River.
August 2, 1867 - Wagon Box Fight - Fort Kearny, Wy. (Sioux) Sgt. Sam Gibson: "Thanks to God and General Sherman, we were armed with the new weapon."
July 25, 1868 - The Territory of Wyoming is established.
Sept.-Oct. 1868 - The Cavalry begin campaigns in Kansas & Colorado.
October 17-27, 1868 - Battle of Beecher's Island, Colorado (600 Cheyenne, Sioux and Arapahoe (Roman Nose) against scouts under Colonel George Forsyth.
November 12, 1868 - The Army begins its winter campaign against the Sioux. Sheridan and Custer leave Fort Hays (Kansas) for the Oklahoma Panhandle.
November 1868 - Battle of Black Kettle Island (Oklahoma Panhandle).

March 4, 1869 - Ulysses S. Grant is inaugurated as 18th President of the U.S.
May 10, 1869 -The Union Pacific Railroad (east from Nebraska) links with the Central Pacific Railroad (west from Pacific) at Promontory Summit, Utah.
April 30, 1871 - Grant Massacre- Civilians raid Apache camp (Fort Grant, AZ).
May 18, 1871 - Wagon Train Massacre (Texas near Fort Richardson).
June 9-11, 1871 - Five U.S. warships anchor off the coast of Korea waiting about 10 days for a Korean apology for the massacre of a U.S. Survey team. None comes. The Sailors and Marines land and overwhelm three forts.
November 1872 - The Modoc Indians, deeply entrenched in the lava beds of northern California, initiate an uprising along the California-Oregon boundary.
December 27-28, 1872- Battle of Skull Cave, Arizona (Apaches).
April 6, 1873 - A treaty is signed with the Apaches (Camp Verde, Arizona).
April 11, 1873- General Edward R. S. Canby, while under a white flag of truce, is murdered by the Modoc Chief, Captain Jack and his warriors.
August 8-11, 1873 - U.S. Cavalry engages Sioux at the Yellowstone River.
October 3, 1873 - Modoc Chiefs Captain Jack, Boston Charley, Black Jim and Schonchin are hanged on the Parade Field of Fort Klamath, Oregon.
July 20, 1874 - General Sheridan is authorized to wage war against the Indians.
August 30, 1874 - Colonel Nelson Miles' command engages Kiowa and Comanches that had left their reservation in the Antelope Hills of Oklahoma.
September 12, 1874- Buffalo Wallow Fight (Texas) - Four enlisted men and two army scouts engage 125 warriors (Comanche and Kiowa).
September 24-27, 1874 - U.S. troops attack a camp of the Cheyenne, Kiowa and Comanches, located in the Palo Duro Canyon, near Amarillo, Texas.
April 28, 1876 - Battle of Blowout (Fort Hartsuff, Nebraska).
June 17, 1876 - Battle of the Rosebud (Powder River, Montana) - Shoshone and Crow Indian Scouts fight with General Crook against Sioux & Cheyenne.
June 25-27, 1876- The Battle of the Little Big Horn (Montana) - General Custer's Last Stand. About 225 men (7th Cavalry) against 2,500 Sioux and Cheyenne. The command is killed (200 discovered naked and mutilated).
July 17, 1876 - Battle of Warbonnet Creek, Nebraska (Cheyenne). William F. Cody "Buffalo Bill" becomes a national hero after this battle near Fort Kearny.
August 1, 1876 - Colorado is admitted to the Union to become the 38th state.
September 9, 1876 - U.S. troops defeat Indians under Crazy Horse in Dakota Ter.
January 8, 1877- Battle of Wolf Mountain, Montana (Sioux and Cheyenne).
March 4, 1877- Rutherford B. Hayes is inaugurated 19th President of the U.S.
May 7, 1877 - The Sioux attack the 2nd Cavalry at Little Muddy Creek, Montana.
Spring 1877 - September 30, 1877 - The Nez Perce Indian War breaks out in the Idaho Valley. It ends during September when the U.S. 2nd Cavalry and 5th Infantry intercept Chief Joseph at Bear Paw Mountain, Montana. The clashes include the Battle of White Bird Canyon (17 June) and at Clearwater on 11-12 July. At the latter, the U.S. 4th Artillery is equipped with Gatling Guns.
May 30, 1878- Chief Buffalo Horn raids Southern Idaho until his death on 8 June. Subsequently, his followers move to Steen's Mountain, Oregon.
July 8, 1878 - Battle of Birch Creek, Oregon (Umatila).
July 13, 1878 - U.S. troops engage Indians under Chief Egan (Oregon).
September 4, 1878 - Battle of Clark's Fork River, Montana (Bannocks).
September 1878- Northern Cheyenne attempt to leave the reservation in Oklahoma to return to their lands (Montana). U.S. troops initiate pursuit.
January 9, 1879 - Cheyenne, led by Chief Dull Knife break out of prison in an attempt to reach the Canadian border and join Chief Sitting Bull.
May 29, 1879 - The Cavalry clashes with Indians in Mimbres Mountains., N.M.
September 4, 1879 - October 1880 - Victorio's War - (Mimbres Apaches).
September 18, 1879 - Battle of Las Animas Canyon, New Mexico (Apaches).
September 29 - October 5, 1879 - U.S. troops battle a Ute war party near the White River Agency, Milk River, Colorado. A massacre had occurred here and among those killed was Nathan Meeker (Mount Meeker is named after him).
April 1, 1880 - The 2nd Cavalry engages Indians at O'Fallon's Creek, Montana.

May 4, 1880 - The 9th U.S. Cavalry engages Indians near Fort Tularosa, N.M.
March 4, 1881 - James A. Garfield is inaugurated as 20th President of the U.S. He is assassinated on September 19, 1881. Vice President Chester A. Arthur assumes the office, becoming the 21st President of the United States.
July 19, 1881- Chief Sitting Bull surrenders to the Army at Ft. Buford, S. Dakota.
August. 16, 1881 - The 9th Cavalry battles Indians (Cuchillo Negro Mtns. NM)
August 30, 1881 - Nakaidoklini (medicine-man) is arrested at Cibicu Creek, Ariz. After sunset, Apaches attack and Nakaidoklini is then killed by his guard.
July 17, 1882 - Battle of Big Dry Fork(Apaches), Arizona.
March 1883- Apaches raid southern Arizona and New Mexico.
May 15, 1883 - U.S. troops attack Apaches in the Sierras (Mexico).
May 17, 1884 - The Territory of Alaska is established.
1885 - Throughout this year, the U.S. Navy and U.S. Marines are often dispatched to Columbia, South America during periods of political turmoil.
March 4, 1885 - Grover Cleveland is inaugurated as 22nd President of the U.S.
June 8, 1885 - Apaches attack an army patrol (Guadalupe Canyon, AZ).
November 1885 - Apaches under Josanie attack civilians and the Indian Reservation near Fort Apache, Arizona.
January 10-11, 1886 - A U.S. force attacks Geronimo (Sierra Madre Mountains.).
September 4, 1886 - Geronimo surrenders for the third and final time.
October 28, 1886 - The Statue of Liberty, a gift from France, is dedicated.
November 14, 1888 -Troops aboard the USS *Nipsic* land at Apia, Samoa to protect American interests and to deter Germany from seizing the island.
March 4, 1889 - Benjamin Harrison is inaugurated 23rd President of the U.S.
November 2, 1889 - North and South Dakota join Union as 39th & 40th states. A 39-star flag was unofficially prepared, but simultaneous entry prevents its use.
November 8, 1889 - Montana is admitted to the Union as the 41st state.
November 11, 1889 - Washington is admitted to the Union as the 42nd state.
May 2, 1890 - The Territory of Oklahoma is established.
July 3, 1890 - Idaho is admitted to the Union as the 43rd state.
July 10, 1890 - Wyoming is admitted to the Union as the 44th state.
December 15, 1890 - Chief Sitting Bull is killed by Indian policemen. The remaining Sioux flee and follow Chief Big Foot. The U.S. Cavalry pursues.
December 29, 1890 - Battle of Wounded Knee - The 7th Cavalry attempts to disarm Sioux under Chief Big Foot (final major battle with Indians).
July 1891 - U.S. troops land at Buenos Aires, Argentina (political turbulence).
January 1, 1892 - Ellis Island, New York opens to receive immigrants.
January 1893 - Marines are sent to Hawaii during a period of political strife.
March 4, 1893 - Grover Cleveland is inaugurated as the 24th President of the U.S. (His second, but non-consecutive term). He also served from 1885-1889.
July 1894 - U.S. naval forces embark for Korea to protect American interests.
January 4, 1896 - Utah is admitted to the Union as the 45th state.

Spanish American War Era

March 4, 1897 - William McKinley is inaugurated as 25th President of the U.S.
January 15, 1898 - The USS Maine enters Havana harbor in Cuba.
February 15, 1898 - The USS *Maine*, a battleship is rocked by a tremendous explosion while in Havana Harbor. The exact cause of the explosion is never discovered. The incident leads to war between the U.S. and Spain.
April 19, 1898 - Congress adopts a joint resolution declaring Cuba free from Spain, and a demand of the withdrawal of Spanish forces from Cuba.
April 24, 1898 - Spain declares war on the U. S. The U.S. reciprocates.
May 1, 1898 - Naval Battle of Manila Bay (Philippines) - Admiral Dewey: "You may fire when ready, Gridley." The Spanish fleet is devastated.
June 24, 1898 - Battle of Las Guasimas (Cuba).
June 30, 1898 - The U.S. seizes Guam from Spanish. Marines raise Old Glory.
July 1, 1898 - Battle of Kettle Hill-San Juan Hill (Cuba).
July 4, 1898 - Naval Battle of Santiago Harbor (Cuba).

July 4, 1898 - Americans place Old Glory on Wake Island (unoccupied) an island in the Pacific near Japan and claim it for the United States.

July 17, 1898 - The Spanish surrender at Santiago, Cuba. The Stars and Stripes replaces the Spanish colors which had flown over Cuba for 382 years.

July 27, 1898 - U.S. Marines attached to the USS *Dixie* debark at Playa del Ponce, Puerto Rico against no opposition and hoist the Stars and Stripes.

August 9, 1898 - Spain accepts U. S. peace terms. On the 12th, the treaty is signed by the French ambassador, as representative for Spain, ending the war.

August 13, 1898 - The Spanish surrender Manila (Philippines).

October 5, 1898 - The Chippewa Indians stage an uprising in Minnesota.

Dec. 10, 1898 - Treaty of Paris- ends Spanish American War. Guam, Philippines and Puerto Rico are ceded to U.S.; Cuba receives its independence.

January 1899 - The U.S. declares the Philippines a possession.

February 4, 1899 - Philippine rebels attack a U.S. outpost. The rebels will raise opposition against the U.S. until 1902 (Philippine Insurrection).

Apr. 1, 1899-Natives (Samoa) strike U.S.-British; 3 Marines receive M. of Honor.

Twentieth Century

April 30, 1900 - The Territory (district) of Hawaii is established. The official designation as territory becomes effective August 24, 1912.

May - August 1900 - The Boxer Rebellion, China (U.S. and allied troops).

August 6, 1900 - Marines and Army artillery repulse Chinese cavalry (Yangtsun).

September 6, 1901 - President William McKinley is assassinated. He succumbs on 12 September. Vice President Theodore Roosevelt assumes the office to become the 26th President of the United States on 14 September.

November 1901 - Battle of Samar, Philippines - Marines retaliate against Moros tribesmen for massacre (28 September) of Company, C, 9th Infantry, USA.

May 20, 1902 - U.S. forces depart Cuba as its 1st president is sworn into office.

July 4, 1902 - President Theodore Roosevelt formally announces the end of the Philippine Insurrection. The Moros tribes do not totally end their resistance.

December 17, 1903 - Orville and Wilbur Wright complete four successful flights (of short duration) by plane in the vicinity of Kitty Hawk, North Carolina.

July 6, 1905 - A contingent of Marines and Sailors arrives at Paris, France to retrieve John Paul Jones's remains; he died there after the American Revolution.

April 18, 1906 - San Francisco, California sustains a devastating earthquake.

March 27, 1907 - Marines are dispatched to Honduras to quell a rebellion.

November 16, 1907 - Oklahoma joins the Union to become the 46th state.

December 16, 1907 - President Theodore Roosevelt dispatches the Great White Fleet (16 Battleships) on a tour of the world.

March 19, 1908 - The U.S. post at Midway Island in the Pacific, established during April 1904, is disbanded; the Marines embark for Honolulu, Hawaii.

October 1, 1908 - The automobile is introduced (Model T) by Henry Ford.

March 3, 1909 - The House Naval Appropriation Committee prevents an attempt by President Teddy Roosevelt to remove all Marines from Naval Warships.

March 4, 1909 - William Howard Taft is inaugurated as 27th President of U.S.

April 6, 1909 - Admiral Robert E. Peary and Matthew Henson reach the North Pole (latitude 90 ° north). Some Eskimos are among the party.

May 1910 - Marines are dispatched to Nicaragua (period of political unrest). The Marines and Sailors will continue to intervene here until 1933.

February 15, 1911 - The Revenue Cutter Service (later Coast Guard) receives Fort Trumbull, New London, Connecticut as a base.

March 7, 1911 - President W. Taft deploys troops along the Mexican border.

March 13, 1911 - A contingent of Marines, drawn from eleven warships of the Atlantic Fleet, arrives at Guantanamo, Cuba.

April 13, 1911 - Five Americans are captured at Agua Prieta, Mexico.

January 6, 1912 - New Mexico is admitted to the Union as the 47th state.

February 14, 1912 - Arizona joins Union (48th state) Continental U. S.

May 25, 1912 - Marines embark for Guantanamo, Cuba to defuse a rebellion.
August 24, 1912 - Hawaii officially becomes the Territory of Hawaii.
March 4, 1913 - Woodrow Wilson is inaugurated as the 28th President (U.S.).
April 6, 1914 - Sailors attached to the USS *Dolphin* are arrested by Mexican troops at Tampico, Mexico while attempting to intercept German arms.
April 11, 1914 - Mexico severs diplomatic relations with the United States.
April 20, 1914 - President Wilson, infuriated by Mexico, addresses Congress, seeking permission to use armed force against Mexican General Huerto.
April 21-23, 1914 - A U.S. Naval Fleet debarks Marines at Vera Cruz, Mexico. They seize the city and hold it until relieved by U.S. Army contingents.
June 28, 1914 - Archduke Ferdinand (heir to Austro-Hungarian throne) and his wife Sophia are assassinated in Serbia. The murders ignite World War I.
July 1914 - In Mexico, civil war erupts. The U.S. remains neutral.

World War I Era

July 28, 1914- The Austro-Hungarian government declares war against Serbia.
August 4, 1914 - England declares war against Germany. Also, Germany invades Belgium, declares war on Russia and drives towards France.
August 15, 1914 - The Panama Canal opens under control of the U.S.
November 23, 1914 - American troops stationed in Mexico are withdrawn.
January 25, 1915 - Alexander G. Bell and Thomas A. Watson initiate the first transcontinental telephone call (from New York to San Francisco).
January 28, 1915 - The U.S. Cutter Service becomes the U.S. Coast Guard.
May 1, 1915 - A U.S. vessel, the *Gulflight* is sunk by a German warship.
June 28, 1915 - Marines arrive at Haiti and remain there for nineteen years.
July 25, 1915 - The *Leelanow*, a U.S. vessel is sunk by a U-boat.
September 16, 1915 - The United States and Haiti sign an agreement to establish a Haitian Constabulary under the supervision of the Marine Corps.
November 8 - 17, 1915 - Battles of Forts Selon and Berthol, Haiti - Marines vs. Bandits (8th). The Battle of Fort Riviere, Haiti (Marines) on 17 November.
January 10th, 1916 - Eighteen American engineers are executed in Mexico.
March 9th, 1916 - General Pancho Villa and a force of 500-1,000 men attack Columbus, New Mexico. A U.S. force later enters Mexico to capture Villa.
June 1, 1916 - Marines land in the Dominican Republic to eliminate bandits.
July 1-September 15, 1916 - Battle of the Somme- The British sustain 614,000 casualties; the Germans sustain 650,000. It ends in a stalemate.
July 3rd, 1916 - Battle of Guayacanas, Dominican Republic (Marines).
October 1916 - A German submarine arrives off New England. Subsequently, it sinks 9 allied ships off the New England coast. The U.S. does not retaliate.
November 20, 1916 - Rebel-held Fort San Francisco de Macoris falls to the United States Marines (Dominican Republic).
Nov. 29, 1916 - U. S. declares "Military Occupation of Dominican Republic.
January 17, 1917 - The U. S. purchases the Virgin Islands from Denmark.
February 3, 1917 - A U.S. vessel, the *Housatonic* is sunk by a U-boat.
February 5th, 1917 - The U.S. Expedition force is withdrawn from Mexico.
March 17, 1917 - A revolution occurs in Russia. The Czar abdicates.
March 31, 1917 - The U.S. officially takes control of the Virgin Islands.
April 2nd, 1917 - During the past few weeks, four more U.S. vessels, each flying the Stars and Stripes, have been sunk by German U-Boats.
April 6th, 1917 - The United States declares war on Germany.
August 25, 1917 - The 82nd Division, later the 82nd Airborne Division is activated. It will serve with the First Army in France during WW I.
November 1917 - The Germans initiate trench raids against the American 6th Infantry, the unit which had paraded in Paris on July 4th.
1917-1918 - The U.S. Coast Guard engaged in the protection of cargo and transport vessels during the hostilities (World War I).
May 28th, 1918 - A contingent of the U.S. 1st Division, with the aid of French tanks and artillery, captures the German-held town of Cantigny.

June 6-25, 1918 - Battle of Belleau Wood - Following the battle, the Marine commander states: "Woods now U. S. Marine Corps entirely." The victory saves Paris. A French officer suggests that the Marines retreat and an officer responds: "Retreat Hell. We just got here." The battle historically changes the Marine Corps. The Germans give the Marines a new name, "Devil Dogs."
June 28, 1918 - U.S. Marines land in Vladivostok, Russia to guard U.S. consulate.
July 4, 1918- General John Pershing notes that 1 million Yanks are in France.
July 15th-August 5th, 1918 - Battle of the Marne.
July 18th-August 5th, 1918 - The Second Battle of the Marne.
July 30, 1918 - The First Marine Aviation force lands in Brest, France.
August 13th, 1918 - The 3rd Army joins the British offensive (Amiens Salient).
August 18th-September 18th, 1918 - The U.S. 27th and 30th Divisions participate with the British Third Army in actions in Picardy.
September 2nd, 1918 - Voormezeele, Belgium is captured by the Americans.
September 12th, 1918 - The Allied Offensive against St. Mihiel begins. The U.S. First Army is composed of about 665,000 troops (I, IV and V Corps).
September 12th, 1918 - Battle of Vignuelles (France).
September 15, 1918 - The 82nd Division seizes Hill 128, north of Vandieres.
September 25th, 1918 - 1st Lieut. Edward Rickenbacker, Army Air Corps, 94th Aero Squadron, encounters seven enemy planes. Rickenbacker attacks and shoots down two of the enemy planes and chases off the remainder.
September 25th-November 11th, 1918 - The Battle of the Meuse Argonne.
October 1, 1918 - Marines join the offensive at Blanc Mont, Champagne, France.
October 24th-November 4th, 1918 - The Battle of Vittono-Veneto.
Oct. 31, 1919- Marines attack Cacos (Haiti). Charlemagne Peralte, the rebel leader is slain.
November 8th, 1918 - American troops occupy the area overlooking Sedan, the site of a devastating French defeat during 1870. The American offensive at Meuse Argonne is abruptly halted to permit the French to move up and take Sedan.
November 11th, 1918 - World War I, ceases according to a whim of the allies at the 11th hour of the 11th day of the 11th month.
December 1, 1918 - The 2nd Division & 4th Marine Brigade enter Germany.
January 1919 - During a power struggle between the Bolsheviks (Reds) and the "White" Russians, the White Russians received support from the allies including England and the U.S. (Archangel Expedition). The Reds prevail.
May 1919 - The American Legion is officially founded in St. Louis, Missouri.
June 28, 1919 - The Treaty of Versailles is signed, ending World War I.
August 28, 1919 -The Coast Guard comes under the Treasury Department.
Nov. 11, 1919 - American Legion calls for the deportation of Communists.
November 19, 1919 - The Senate defeats ratification of the Versailles Treaty.
November 1919 - One hundred soldiers (from Michigan) who had lost their lives in Russia (Archangel Expedition) arrived in Detroit for re-interment.
May 20, 1920 - Congress (by resolution) declares an end to World War I.
March 4,1921 - Warren G. Harding is inaugurated as 29th President of the U.S.
January 1921 - The bodies of 45,000 U.S. troops are exhumed from their graves at Romagne, France & other cemeteries for return to the U.S. for burial.
July 2, 1921 - Congress declared an end to World War I. President Harding signs the joint resolution. Germany, Austria and Hungary sign during August.
July 21, 1921 - To demonstrate air power, U.S. planes attack and sink two ships, the USS *Alabama* (decommissioned) and a captured German vessel. Colonel William Mitchell, USA, an advocate of air power pushed for the test.
September 4, 1922 - The 1st transcontinental flight (Pablo Beach, Florida and San Diego, California), completed in under 24 hours, is flown by Lieutenant James N. Doolittle. The flight covers 2,163 miles (air time is 21 ½ hours).
August 2, 1923 - President Warren G. Harding succumbs. Vice President Calvin Coolidge is sworn into office on 3 August (becomes 30th President).
November 4, 1924 - Calvin Coolidge is elected President of the U.S. He had initially assumed office upon the death of President Harding on 3 August, 1923.

March 4, 1925 - Calvin Coolidge is inaugurated as 30th President of the U.S.
February 16, 1926- Coast Guard Academy is founded (New London, Conn.).
May 8-9, 1926 - U.S. Navy Commander Richard E. Byrd & Machinist Floyd Bennett complete the 1st flight (1,545 miles) over the North Pole in a Fokker.
July 2, 1926- The Army Air Service becomes the Army Air Corps.
February 9, 1927- Marines aboard the USS *Pecos* debark in Shanghai, China.
May 20-21, 1927 - Charles A. Lindbergh, piloting the *Spirit of St. Louis*, completes the first non-stop flight between New York and Paris, France.
March 4, 1929 - Herbert Hoover is inaugurated as 31st President of the U.S.
October 29, 1929- The Stock Market crashes; the "Great Depression" follows.
March 3, 1931 - The Star Spangled Banner, written by Francis Scott Key during 1814 (bombardment of Fort McHenry), becomes the National Anthem.
September 18, 1931 - The Japanese march into Manchuria (World War II).
July 28-29, 1932 - The Army, under the personal command of General D. MacArthur, expels World War I veterans (Bonus Army) from Washington.

World War II Era

Nov. 11, 1932 - Tomb of the Unknown Soldier is dedicated at Arlington National Cemetery, Virginia.
February 25th, 1933 - The United States Navy launches its 1st aircraft carrier. The vessel is christened the USS *Ranger* in honor of John Paul Jones' ship.
March 4, 1933 - Franklin D. Roosevelt is inaugurated 32nd President of U.S.
April 19, 1933 - The United States goes off the gold standard.
June 15, 1934 - Congress passes the National Guard Act, placing the Guard under jurisdiction of the Army during a national emergency or in time of war.
August 1-15, 1934 - The U.S. ends its occupation of Haiti (began in 1915).
November 3, 1936 - President Franklin Roosevelt is reelected (2nd of 4 terms).
July 2, 1937 - Amelia Earhart (1st woman to fly across the Atlantic) and her co-pilot Fred Noonan crash in the Pacific and both are lost.
December 12, 1937 - Japanese planes sink the USS *Panay* (Yangtze River).
March 1938 - Mexico seizes U.S. and British oil companies.
March 12, 1938 - German troops move into Austria.
April 6, 1939 - England and France agree to guarantee Poland's independence.
May 13, 1939 - The *Squalus* (submarine) sinks during a training dive. Twenty-six men are lost, but rescue teams save thirty-three crewmen.
September 1, 1939 - Germany invades Poland.
September 3, 1939 - France and Great Britain declare war against Germany.
September 4, 1939- A U-boat sinks the *Lusitania* with Americans aboard.
September 5, 1939 - President Roosevelt issues two proclamations (Neutrality), for both the Atlantic and Pacific areas. He also initiates naval patrols.
September 17, 1939 - The Russians invade Poland.
November 30, 1939 - The Russians invade Finland.
January 1940 - Battle of the Atlantic - Germany begins to sink allied vessels. U-boats cost the Allies about 500,000 tons in only a few months.
April 9, 1940 - Germany invades Norway and Denmark
April 5, 1940 - The U.S. launches the carrier, USS *Wasp*.
May 10, 1940 - Germany invades Belgium and Luxembourg.
May 15, 1940 - The Dutch Army (Netherlands) surrenders to Germany.
May 28, 1940 - Belgium surrenders to Germany.
June 1, 1940 - The U.S. Navy launches the battleship *Washington*(BB-56) at the Philadelphia Navy Yard; it is the first battleship launched since 1921.
June 5, 1940 - Germany invades France.
July 10, 1940 - Battle of Britain - Air war between England and Germany.
June 15-17, 1940 - Russia seizes Lithuania (15th), Latvia & Estonia (17th).
June 22, 1940 - France capitulates to Germany and signs an armistice.
July 8, 1940 - America, following the fall of France to Germany, dispatches Marines to Martinique, a French possession to prevent German occupation.
September 3, 1940 - The U.S. transfers fifty destroyers to England.

September 16, 1940 - The "Selective Service Act (Draft)" is initiated. At this time, the army possesses less than 50 machine guns, only 235 artillery pieces and a total of 10 light and 8 medium tanks. Congress had begun to strip the defenses after the close of World War I. Troops use stove pipe for cannon and bags of flour for bombs during training and empty beer cans are used as shells.

September 27, 1940 - Germany, Japan and Italy sign the Triparte Treaty. By 20 November, Hungary and Rumania join the alliance.

September 29, 1940 - The U.S. Navy & Marines arrive at Midway Island in the Pacific to establish defensive positions in the event of hostile actions by Japan.

October 16, 1940 - Sixteen million Yanks register for the draft.

October 28, 1940 - Italy invades Greece.

February 19, 1941 - The Coast Guard establishes the Coast Guard Reserve.

March 30, 1941 - The U.S. seizes Danish, German & Italian vessels in U.S. ports.

April 6-June 1, 1941- Germany takes Yugoslavia on 17 April & Greece on 23 April. Crete falls on 20 April-1 June.

June 1, 1941 - The U.S. Coast Guard initiates patrols near Greenland.

June 12, 1941 - The U. S. Navy calls up all reservists (except those deferred).

June 22, 1941 - Germany invades Russia.

July 7, 1941- Marines move to Iceland to prevent German occupation.

July 29, 1941 - The Japanese (with French permission) move into Indo China.

July 30, 1941 - Japanese planes attack the USS *Tutuila* at Chunking, China.

August 1941 - General MacArthur requests reinforcements (Philippines).

September 1, 1941 -The Navy takes responsibility for guarding allied convoys (Trans-Atlantic) between Iceland to a point off Argentina.

September 17, 1941 - The Navy escorts its first British Convoy to England.

September 24, 1941 - Japan orders its spies (Consular General) to report on U.S. ships at Pearl Harbor. Responses are sent to Japan and the information is intercepted and decoded on 10 Oct., but Admiral H. Kimmel is not informed.

September 27, 1941 - The United States launches its first Liberty Ship, the *Patrick Henry*, at Baltimore, Maryland.

September 1941 - German U-boats sink two American steamships off Iceland.

October 19, 1941 - German U-boats sink a U.S. ship (*Lehigh*) off Africa.

October 21, 1941 - The Navy initiates its war patrols with two submarines.

October 31, 1941 - The *Reuben James* a U.S. destroyer is sunk by a U-boat.

November 6, 1941 - The Navy seizes a German ship, posing as a U.S. vessel.

November 10, 1941 - The United States Navy accompanies its first troop convoy (British troops) on a voyage from Halifax to the Far East.

November 14, 1941 - Japan orders its Consular General in Hawaii to report twice a week on ships at Pearl Harbor. The message is intercepted and decoded in Washington, on 3 December, but it is not given to Admiral H. E. Kimmel.

November 27, 1941 - It is determined that the available army planes can only pursue 15 miles from shore. Consequently, Marine Fighter Squadron 211 is dispatched to Midway, Johnston, Palmyra and Wake Islands in case of a Japanese attack. Admiral Halsey's carriers transport the planes. It is requested that the army relieve the Marines on Midway and Wake, but the army has no guns available; the Marines would have to leave their weapons and none are available at Pearl.

December 2, 1941 - An American ship, the *Dunboyne,* becomes the 1st merchant vessel to receive a naval armed guard.

December 7, 1941 - The Japanese launch a sneak attack against Pearl Harbor.

December 8, 1941 - The U.S. declares war against Japan.

December 8, 1941 - Japanese planes attack the U.S. forces in the Philippines.

December 9, 1941 - Japanese planes attack Guam and Wake Island.

December 10, 1941 - Japan seizes Guam and invades the Philippines. Radio-man George Tweed, USN, evades capture for the duration; when the U.S. returns, he signals the warships and sends them the positions of the enemy guns.

December 10, 1941 - The USS *Triton* damages a Japanese warship; it becomes the first submarine to launch a torpedo attack during the war.

December 11, 1941 - Germany and Italy declare war on the United States. The

U.S. reciprocates. This compels Hitler to fight a two-front war.

December 11, 1941- Marines (388 men) repulse a Japanese invasion of Wake and Wilkes Islands. Attacks continue, but Wake holds until 23 December when the remaining 85 men are ordered to surrender by their naval commander.

December 28, 1941 - The Navy authorizes the establishment of the Seabees. Their motto: "We build. We Fight." Although they usually are older than the troops, often they are in harm's way. The Seabees shadow the Marines in the Pacific. More than 300,000 Seabees serve during World War II on 300 islands.

December 31, 1941-Jan. 1, 1942 - U.S. and Filipino troops head for Bataan.

1942 - The U.S. constructs eight airfields between Great Forks, Montana and Fairbanks, Alaska. U.S. pilots (many women) ferry 8,000 planes to Fairbanks. A Russian pilot takes the plane from there to Russia to avoid facing the Luftwaffe.

January 24, 1942 - Naval Battle of Makassar Strait (Java Sea).

January 29, 1942 - A German submarine sinks the Coast Guard cutter, *Alexander Hamilton*, off Iceland; it is the 1st U.S. warship sunk (during war).

February 1942 - Submarine Division 53, at Panama, receives orders to move to Australia, a trip of 12,000 miles. The vessels have no air conditioning.

February 1, 1942 - U.S. Warships bombard the Marshall & Gilbert Islands.

February 4, 1942-Naval Battle of Madoera Strait near Borneo.

February 8, 1942 - The submarine *Shark* which reported damages from attack on the previous day is not responsive to orders. She is considered the first sub sunk by a surface ship in the war. If lost by other causes, the USS *Perch* lost on March 3, 1942, would become the first submarine sunk by a surface ship.

March 25, 1942 - The 82nd Division (Infantry) is activated under Generals Omar Bradley and Matthew Ridgway; it becomes 82nd Airborne on August 15.

April 9, 1942- Bataan, Philippines falls to Japanese. Old Glory is ripped down.

April 18, 1942- Admiral Bill Halsey's carriers launch B-25s that bomb Tokyo.

May 1, 1942- General Joe Stilwell is driven from Burma. Stilwell is the U.S. commanding officer in Burma, but he has never had any U.S. combat troops. Old Glory returns to Burma during 1944. Stilwell is forced to walk to India. En route, he declines an offer to purchase a large number of elephants.

May 4-8, 1942- Battle of the Coral Sea (fought by opposing planes- fleets make no contact). The *Lexington* is lost, the *Yorktown* damaged. Australia is saved.

May 6, 1942- Allied troops in the Philippines surrender to the Japanese. More than thirty percent of Japanese-held prisoners die during their confinement.

May 15, 1942 - The U.S. Women's Auxiliary Corps (WAAC) is founded.

June 2-6, 1942- Naval Battle of Midway (turning point in war). U.S. prevails.

June 6-7, 1942 - Japanese land at Attu and Kiska (Aleutian Islands) Alaska as part of a diversionary tactic to draw U.S. carriers at Midway out of position.

June 11, 1942 - German submarines lay mines in Delaware Bay and off Boston.

June 12, 1942 -. The Army Air Corps bombs Ploesti, Rumania. Some pilots, are forced to land in Turkey. They are interned.

June 13, 1942 - Eight German spies are put ashore, four at Long Island and four at Ponte Vedra Beach, Florida. All eight are captured by 27 June.

July 30, 1942 - The U.S. Navy Women Reserve (WAVES) is established.

August 7th, 1942 - The First Marine Division invades Guadalcanal (first U.S. offensive of war). U.S. Army troops (164th Infantry) arrive on 13 October.

August 8, 1942 - Naval Battle of Savo Island, Solomons; Four U.S. cruisers are lost. The Marines become isolated on Guadalcanal.

August 19, 1942 - The British invade France, but the landing at Dieppe fails. Six thousand British and Canadian troops land; about 4,600 are killed, wounded or captured. The Canadian 2nd Division sustains about 3,300 casualties. Fifty U.S. Rangers accompany this mission; 6 Rangers are wounded and 7 are lost.

August 24, 1942-Naval Battle of Eastern Solomons.

August 24, 1942- Army and Navy forces land at Adak, Alaska unopposed.

August 1942- March 1943 - Battle for New Guinea- U.S. (709th Airborne and 43rd U.S. Engineers) and Australians (Milne Force) are attacked on 26 August.

September 1, 1942 - Seabees aboard the *Betelguese* arrive at Guadalcanal.

September 12-14, 1942- Battle Edson's Ridge (Bloody Ridge), Guadalcanal, Solomons. Colonel Edson's Marines repel 12 attacks and save Henderson Field.
September 28, 1942 - The 126th Regiment, USA arrives at New Guinea.
October 11-12, 1942-Naval Battle of Cape Esperance, Guadalcanal.
October 23, 1942 - Operation Torch - The U.S. Army heads for North Africa.
October 26-27th, 1942-Naval Battle Santa Cruz, Guadalcanal, Solomons.
November 4-December 4, 1942 - Carlson's Patrol (Guadalcanal). Marines operate behind enemy lines and disrupt communications and destroy supplies.
November 8-11, 1942- North Africa Invasion- French resistance ends by 11th.
November 12-15, 1942-Naval Battle of Guadalcanal - The five Sullivan brothers are all lost when the USS *Juneau* is sunk.
November 23, 1942 - Women (SPARS) are admitted to the Coast Guard.
November 30, 1942-Naval Battle of Tassafaronga, Guadalcanal, Solomons.
1942 - 1944 - General John R. Deane, USA, during 1942 refuses permission for engines to be shipped to Russia, but the Russians call Harry Hopkins at the White House; the shipment is released. The Russians also receive enormous amounts of graphite and aluminum tubes (used for cooking uranium) and 13,000 pounds of a secret ingredient, thorium (shipped out of Newark Airport during 1942). By the end of 1944, Russia receives 1,300 diesel engines.
January 20-23, 1943 - The U.S. 25th Division and the Army-Marine Division press to eliminate the final resistance on Guadalcanal.
January 22, 1943 - The Papua Campaign (New Guinea) ends. About 7,000 Japanese have been buried by the Australian-American troops.
January 29, 1943 - Mrs. Ruth Cheyney Streeter is commissioned a major in the United States Marine Corps Women's Reserve and becomes its director.
February 1, 1943 - The Soviet Purchasing Committee (New York) through the help of Herman H. Rosenberg (Chematar Inc) procures 220 pounds of uranium oxide, 220 lbs. of uranium nitrate and 25 lbs. of uranium metal.
February 7, 1943 - The Japanese (13,000) abandon Guadalcanal. On 9 February, General Alexander Patch, USA declares the total defeat of the Japanese there.
February 14, 1943 - In North Africa, a German offensive drives the allies back at Faid and Kasserine Pass, but the ground is regained by the 25 February.
March 1-4, 1943 - Naval Battle of the Bismarck Sea, New Guinea.
March 6, 1943 - Following the poor showing of the U.S. II Corps at Kasserine Pass, Tunisia, North Africa, General George S. Patton becomes its new commander, replacing General Fredendall. Patton's orders from Eisenhower: "Rehabilitate the American forces and prepare them for the attack."
March 8, 1943 - Army officers (Lend-Lease), catch the Russians smuggling "black suitcases" (about 50 at a time) out of the U.S. as "personal luggage." The Russians receive help (White House); the bags get "diplomatic immunity."
March 13, 1943 - The U.S. prepares for an offensive (Tunisia) scheduled for the 17th. Patton's order:"Find them...Attack Them...Destroy them."
March 18, 1943 - In North Africa, Rangers and the U.S. 1st Division seize El Guettar without incident. Also, Allied planes bomb Vegesack, Germany.
March 26, 1943 - The Naval Battle of Komandorski Island (North Pacific).
Spring 1943 - The Navy organizes teams called Navy Combat Demolition Teams, formed by volunteers from the Seabees (Naval Construction Battalions) for the purpose of clearing beach obstacles prior to an invasion.
April 3, 1943 - German planes bomb Gafsa, Tunisia during an ongoing meeting between U.S. and British commanders. The British had told the U.S. that the skies were clear of the enemy and U.S. complaints were unfounded.
April 8, 1943 - General George S. Patton announces that his troops had won the battle of El Guettar after 22 days of fighting.
April 18, 1943 - U.S. planes down General Yamamoto's plane near Guadalcanal. Also, an air operation (Flax) intercepts German fighters and transport planes. The Germans lose 50-70 transports and 16 escort planes.
April 21, 1943 - The British hit resistance in Tunisia, North Africa. Gen. Bradley

quips to Gen. William Kean: "Lets radio Monty and ask if he wants us to send him a few American advisors to show him how to get through those hills."
April 26, 1943 - General Douglas MacArthur issues the third plan for capture of New Britain, New Guinea and New Ireland.
April 29, 1943- The U.S. 1st Division advances in Tunisia (Mousetrap valley).
May 1943 - The Japanese allow American prisoners in Manchuria to bury their dead, 150 men laying in the barracks due to the frozen ground.
May 7, 1943 - General Patton states: "road to Bizerte (Tunisia) is wide open."
May 9, 1943 - U.S. accepts surrender of all German troops in its sector (Tunisia). The officers are well dressed prompting General Harmon to remark to Bradley: "You'd have thought the *******s were going to a wedding."
May 11, 1943 - U.S. troops (7th Division) invade Japanese-held Attu, Alaska.
May 30, 1943 - Japanese resistance ends on Attu, in the Aleutians (Alaska). Engineers under Major James Bush repel the final attack.
June 10, 1943 - President Roosevelt instructs Eisenhower: "ensure that North Africa does not come under the domination of DeGaulle (Charles)." A message from Roosevelt to Churchill: "If DeGaulle should move into French West Africa, I would be impelled to send naval and ground forces into Dakar."
June 10, 1943 - Army officers (Lend-Lease) at Great Falls Montana discover the Russians shipping out chemicals for making an atom bomb.
June 12, 1943 - The U.S. Eighth Air Force attacks the German Kiel Submarine Works; 22 of 60 B17s are lost. Another 102 planes strike Bremen. The Eighth Air Force never aborts a mission due to the enemy (for duration).
June 21-22, 1943 - The 4th Marine Raider Battalion (21st) and the 103rd Infantry, 43rd Div. (22nd) land on Segi Point (New Georgia) to prevent Japanese occupation.
June 29-30, 1943- The U.S. invades the Central Solomons, the Trobriands and New Guinea to eliminate resistance at Rabaul (Army and Marine operation).
July 3, 1943 - A bill establishing the Women's Army Corps (WAC) is signed into law. The WAACs (established May, 1942) are given a choice to enter the army as a member of the WAC or a return to civilian life. A contingent of WACs would, this month, depart for England to support Eighth Air Force.
July 4, 1943 - The U.S. Navy turns back the 6th and final daylight attempt by the Japanese to land reinforcements on Kolombangara, New Georgia.
July 6, 1943 -The Naval Battle of Kula Gulf, Solomons.
July 8, 1943 - U.S. B24s from Midway strike the Japanese on Wake Island. The U.S. military captured there were transferred to prison camps; several Marines were decapitated during the voyage. The American civilians are retained.
July 9-11, 1943 - Invasion of Sicily (Italy). More than 2,000 ships participate. Thousands of paratroopers (British and the 82nd and 101st U.S. A/B Divisions) also participate. Patton's 3rd Army lands at several locations.
July 12, 1943 - Naval Battle of Kolombangara (2nd battle of Kula Gulf) New Georgia, Solomons. The Japanese during darkness get 1,200 troops ashore; it is the final time Japanese destroyers get troops ashore at New Georgia.
July 15, 1943 - General Matthew Ridgway (Airborne) pauses next to a blind soldier during heavy fighting in Sicily. The soldier yells: "Who's that?" Ridgway retorts: General Ridgway." The blind soldier: "Oh, glad to see you."
July 22, 1943 - The U.S. 7th Army under Patton takes Palermo, Sicily.
July 24, 1943 - U.S. Eighth Air Force (208 planes) strikes Norway.
July 30, 1943 - The Japanese execute two Marines and one Sailor on charges of stealing an item (unknown) at the prison camp in Manchuria.
Summer 1943 - Army officers spot more "diplomatic suitcases" being shipped from the U.S. to Russia and they discover that the Russians have copies of patent information (tanks, planes etc.), supplied by the U.S. patent office.
August 1, 1943 - Bombers (8th Air Force and Northwest Air Force) launch an air strike against Ploesti, Romania; 54 planes are lost, 41 in action. By September, 50,000 U.S. airmen fly missions to destroy the facilities there and deliver 27,000

tons of bombs; the Russians walk into the facility (Sept.) Thanks to the Air Corps.
August 2, 1943 - A Japanese destroyer rams the PT 109 off the Solomons; the crew, including John F. Kennedy (later President Kennedy), is rescued.
August 5, 1943 - Munda Airfield, New Georgia falls to the U.S. XIV Corps.
August 6, 1943 - Naval Battle of Vella Gulf, Solomons.
August 17, 1943 - Regimental Combat Team 7, 3rd Division, Seventh Army rolls into Messina, terminating the Sicily campaign. Messina, Sicily surrenders. General Lucius Truscott instructs General Eagles to go into Messina to oversee the Americans already there (and quips): "To see that the British did not capture the city from us after we had taken it." General Patton arrives at 1000 hours and later greets British General Bernard "Monty" Montgomery when he arrives.
August 22, 1943 - General Patton Order # 18 (Sicily): "Soldiers of the 7th Army: born at sea, baptized in blood and crowned in victory in the course of 38 days of incessant battle and unceasing labor you have added a glorious chapter to the history of war...Your fame shall never die." On the following day, Pvt. Kuhl (slapped by Patton) visits General Patton who states: "I did it namely to make you mad at me so you would regain your manhood."
August 1943 - At this time, U.S. airmen and pilots forced to drop into Yugoslavia are saved by either the Partisans (Communists) under Josip Broz Tito or the Chetniks under General Draza, both of whom are at war with each other. By November, Roosevelt and Churchill end support for Draza to support only Tito, the Bolshevik. The Chetniks (Serbs) continue to save Americans.
September 2, 1943 - U.S. planes again bombard enemy positions in Italy.
September 8, 1943 - General Dwight D. Eisenhower announces an armistice with Italy; Italian ships and planes surrender at specific locations.
September 9, 1943 - Invasion of Italy by General Mark Clark's Fifth Army. General Patton is without a command due to the "slapping incident" in Sicily.
September 13, 1943 - 82nd Airborne troops arrive in Italy to bolster 5th Army.
September 15-19, 1943 - British forces land on the boot of Italy and attempt to advance. The British Broadcasting Co., always attempting to undercut the U.S., reports: "General Montgomery is dashing up the Italian Boot to rescue the Fifth Army (U.S.) which is preparing to evacuate the beachhead."
September 16, 1943 - General Mark Clark regarding Fifth Army in Italy: "Our Beachhead is secure and we are staying."
September 22, 1943 - General Mark Clark becomes incensed when he receives a censorship message from British General Alexander's headquarters that states: "Play up Eighth (British) Army progress. The Americans may be mentioned."
October 1, 1943 - Admiral Bill Halsey's forces at this time have sunk about 598 enemy barges (past three months). Also, British troops accompanied by U.S. Rangers and paratroopers enter Naples. British General Alexander asks Clark to "Tell the press that the British had entered (Naples) first." General Mark Clark sends a message to his wife: "I give you Naples for your birthday."
October 5, 1943 - The Navy attacks (surface and air) Wake Island.
October 6, 1943 - The Naval Battle of Vella La Vella, Solomons.
October 6, 1943 - Again, the Navy bombards Wake Island. The Japanese retaliate and later blindfold the U.S. civilian captives, tie their hands behind their backs, make them kneel (their backs to the sea) and then execute them.
October 10, 1943 - The Eighth Air Force strikes Munster, Germany. German fighters knock out 30 fortresses. In one group, 12 of 13 planes are lost.
October 14, 1943 - The Eighth Air Force, without fighter support, attacks targets in Germany. About 291 B-17s and some B24s strike Schweinfurt; 60 planes are lost and of these, 30 are shot down and 600 airmen are missing.
October 17, 1943 - Marine Fighter Squadron 214, attacks Kahili. The Japanese lose 20 planes in the dog fight. Pappy Boyington's squadron loses none. Between 12 Sept.1943-3 January, 1944, Boyington singlehandedly downs 26 planes.
October 24, 1943 - The recently commissioned submarine, USS *Dorado* is reported missing and presumed to be sunk, the 2nd and final sub sunk in the

Atlantic. It departed New London on 6 October, but never arrived at Panama.
November 1, 1943 - Invasion of Bougainville, Solomons (3rd Marine Division).
During the invasion, the Naval Battle of Empress Bay erupts; the enemy is
repulsed. On the 2nd, 100 planes attack during "Colors and 12 are shot down.
November 7-10, 1943-Battle of Piva-Trail-2nd Marine Raider Bn. & 9th Marines.
November 12, 1943 - The Japanese withdraw their carriers from Rabaul.
November 20-23, 1943 - Invasion of Tarawa and Makin (Gilberts). Task Force
52 (165th Infantry & 3rd Battalion 105th Infantry and 193rd Tank Battalion)
invades Makin. The 2nd Marine Division assaults Tarawa. General Holland
Smith, USMC: "...The reason this battle was won was that these great American
men were determined that their nation would not go down in defeat."
November 5, 1943 - About 100 planes launch the first strike against Rabaul (New
Britain). Five enemy cruisers and two destroyers are damaged. Ten U. S. planes
are lost. Japan radio: "In an air raid against Rabaul the much vaunted reinforced
enemy (U.S.) air force suffered the loss of 200 out of 230...The shooting down of
90 % of the total air strength represents a new world record."
November 25, 1943 - Naval Battle of Cape St. George, Bismarcks, New Ireland.
Late 1943 - An American officer (Lend-Lease) reports that Russia has received
non-war supplies against the rules and these include lipstick, cigarettes, perfume,
bank vaults, women's jewelry and an amusement park (3 billion dollars worth).
December 8-16, 1943 - The Battle of San Pietro, Italy (U.S. 5th Army).
December 15, 1943 - Naval Battle of Arawe Peninsula, Bismarcks, New Britain.
December 26, 1943-Jan.16, 1944- Naval Battle of Cape Gloucester (Bismarcks).
December 26, 1943 - The Americal Division begins to relieve the 3rd Marine
Division at Bougainville, Solomons.
January 20, 44-May 18, 1944 - Battle of Monte Cassino, Italy (U.S. 5th Army).
January 22, -May 18, 1944- Invasion of Anzio, Italy and its siege by the
Germans (U.S. VI Corps under General John Lucas and one British division).
January 30, 1944- U.S. Rangers (two Battalions) are wiped out at Cisterna, Italy.
January 31-Feb. 8, 1944- Battle of Kwajalein, Marshalls (Army-Marines).
February 15, 1944 - Allied planes level the Benedictine monastery (founded 560
A.D.) at Cassino (Italy); the attack provides more cover for the Germans.
February 16, 1944-Germans attack Anzio beachhead (Italy); it is repulsed (20th).
February 18, 1944-Invasion of Enegbi Island, Marshalls (22nd Marines and an
Army Cannon company). On the 19th, the U.S. invades Eniwetok, Marshalls
(Regimental Combat Team 106, USA, supported by the 22nd Marines).
February 20, 1944 - The U.S. Strategic Air Force launches a week-long mission
that sends more than 1,000 planes against targets in Germany.
February 23, 1944- A bomb strikes U.S. WAC area near Kingston (England).
February 24, 1944 - Merrill's Marauders move to take Myitkyina, Burma.
February 27-Mar. 1, 1944 - Battle of Los Negros (Admiralties). The 1st, 5th and
12th Cavalry Regiments participate.
March 4-9, 1944-Battle of Walawbum, Burma (Merrill's Marauders).
April 22, 1944-Battle of Hollandia, New Guinea (U.S. 24th and 41st Divisions).
May 11-18, 1944 - Main II Corps offensive against Gustav Line, Anzio, Italy.
May 17-18, 1944 - Merrill's Marauders attack Myitkyina airstrip (Burma).
Myitkyina airfield falls to the allies on 4 August. On August 10, Merrill's
Marauders are disbanded, without fanfare nor decoration. During the grueling
campaign, General Merrill sustained two heart attacks. The Marauders were the
first U.S. troops in Burma since 1942 when General Stilwell was driven out, and
they were the only U.S. force standing between India and the Japanese in Burma.
May 23, 1944 - U.S. VI Corps (Anzio) attacks towards Cisterna, Italy.
May 27, 1944-Invasion of Biak, N. Guinea (U.S. 41st Division).
May 29, 1944 - The USS *Block Island* (escort carrier) is sunk off the Canary
Islands. Six men are killed by the initial explosion, but no other injuries occur.
Rescuers save 951 others. The destroyers *Barr, Ahrens & Paine* participate.
May 31, 1944 - The Destroyer Escort *England* (recently destroyed 5 of 6 Japanese
submarines assigned the task of spotters to protect the Pelew Islands, makes

47

contact with the RO-105 on the 30th and sinks it this day.

June 1, 1944 - British General Alexander informs General Clark that "if any help is needed, the entire British Eighth Army could be thrown into the fight (for Rome)." Clark responds. He tells Alexander that Fifth Army could handle the job and: "Fifth Army troops, not Allied troops would enter the city."

June 4, 1944 - Rome falls to U.S. 5th Army. Also, U.S. forces capture the German U-boat, 505, the first enemy warship captured by the U.S. since the War of 1812; the Nazi ensign is lowered and replaced by the Stars and Stripes.

June 6, 1944 - Invasion of Normandy, France (D-Day). More than 5,000 transports carry 150,000 Allied troops. Also, the 82nd and 101st Airborne are dropped prior to the landing. Pathfinders (paratroops) arrive earlier to mark the landing spots.

June 12, 1944 - The U.S. and its allies continue to advance towards Cherbourg, by first seizing the Cotentin peninsula, France.

June 15-July 7, 1944 - Battle of Saipan, Marianas (2nd and 4th Marine Divisions, supported after the invasion by 27th U.S. Infantry Division).

June 17, 1944 - General Holland M. Smith, USMC, and General Arthur M. Hopper (Army XVI Corps) establish headquarters on Saipan.

June 19-20, 1944 - Naval Battle of the Philippine Sea ("The Great Turkey Shoot"). The U.S. gains total air supremacy over the Marianas.

June 21, 1944 - The German commander at Cherbourg, France, while the U.S. VII Corps closes upon the town: "I empower all leaders of whatever rank to shoot at sight anyone who leaves his post because of cowardice."

July 3, 1944 - A German buzz-bomb (VI) strikes the quarters of U.S. troops and WACs in London. The WACs assist the wounded. During the war, sixteen WACs receive the Purple Heart (most caused by V-I bombs).

July 4, 1944 - In Normandy, the American Generals include the Germans in the annual festivities (all posts firing a 48-gun salute). General Eisenhower tells General Leonard Gerow to point the guns at the Germans. Gerow asks: "Just 48 guns?" Eisenhower retorts: "No, hell no!....We'll fire every gun in the army." At precisely 12 noon, 1,100 guns commence fire (4th of July salute).

July 6, 1944 - General George S. Patton establishes the headquarters of Third Army (VIII, XII and XV Corps, and a French armored division) at Nehou, France.

July 7, 1944 - B29s bomb Kyushu Island, Japan (2nd attack against Japan).

July 11, 1944 - U.S. and allies attack Po River bridges and Leghorn in Italy.

July 14, 1944 - The first contingent of WACs arrive in France at Normandy. They begin working the switchboards (recently abandoned by the Germans).

July 18, 1944 - The U.S. XIX Corps attacks St. Lo., France.

July 20, 1944 - A plot to assassinate Adolph Hitler fails.

July 21-August 11, 1944 - Invasion of Guam, Marianas (3rd Marine and 77th Divisions). The ships receive unexpected signals from a U.S. sailor on the island.

July 1944 - WACs arrive in China-Burma-India Theater.

July 24-August 1, 1944 - Invasion of Tinian, Marianas (2nd and 4th Marine Divs.

July 31, 1944 - The submarine *Parche* engages a group of enemy vessels and sinks two and it shares credit with the submarine *Steelhead* on the destruction of a third. The captain of the *Parche*, "Red Ramage,"receives the Medal of Honor.

August 14-15, 1944 - Invasion of Southern France (Patton's 3rd Army).

August 17, 1944 - St. Malo, France falls to U.S. 3rd Army.

August 25, 1944 - U.S. troops advance to Paris, but they are held up to allow the French to enter first. Later, the U.S. 4th Division enters to restore order.

August 30, 1944 - Patton's 3rd Army is forced to halt its advance to the Siegfried Line due to lack of gas. His supply is given to British General Montgomery.

September 1, 1944 - In Italy, the V Corps drives Germans across the Arno River.

September 2, 1944 - The U.S. VII Corps drives into Belgium heading for Brussels.

September 2, 1944 - Lt. George Bush (later President George H. Bush) and two crewmen, John Delaney and Ted White, are hit near the Bonin Islands. White and Delaney are ordered to bail out first; both are lost. Japanese forces attempt to capture Bush after he bails out, but U.S. forces save him (Bush's 50th mission).

Sept. 4, 1944 -U.S. 1st and 3rd Armies attack toward the Ruhr & Saar.
September 8, 1944, German V-2 bombs strike London.
September 15, 1944- Invasion of Peleliu, Palaus Islands (1st Marine Division).
September 15, 1944- Invasion of Morotai, Dutch East Indies (T.F. Tradewind).
September 17, 1944- Invasion of Angaur, Palaus Islands (81st Division).
September 17, 1944 - Operation Market Garden - British and U.S. troops move against Arnhem, Holland for British 2nd Army. The mission fails, but the U.S. takes its targets (82nd A/B (James Gavin) & 101st A/B (Maxwell Taylor).
October 20, 1944- Invasion of Philippines (General MacArthur returns). This is an Army operation. The Marines supply some air support and some artillery.
October 23-26, 1944 - The Naval Battle of Leyte Gulf, Philippines.
October 25, 1944 - The Naval Battles of Samar and Engano, Philippines.
November 28, 1944 - The submarine *Scabbardfish* sinks the Japanese submarine I-365 off Japan. Sasaki, the lone survivor, is saved by the "*Scabby.*"
Dec. 16-26, 1944-Ardennes, Battle of Bulge, Siege of Bastogne (France).
December 19, 1944 - The U.S. halts the German armor units at the Salm River.
December 23-24, 1944 - The Belgium vessel *Leopoldville* is sunk in the English Channel. The crew abandons ship, leaving troops aboard. More than 800 men of the U.S. 66th Division are lost while en route to Cherbourg, France.
December 17, 1944 - The 82nd and 101st A/B Divisions rush to the Ardennes.
December 26, 1944 - General George Patton (3rd Army) breaks the siege at Bastogne. Gen. McAuliffe declined an earlier surrender demand stating: "Nuts."
January 9, 1945 - Invasion of Luzon, Philippines. (Army).
February 16, 1945 - Invasion of Corregidor (Philippines) (U.S. Army).
February 19, 1945 - Invasion of Iwo Jima, Volcano Islands, North Pacific (3rd, 4th, and 5th Marine Divisions. The 147th Infantry Regiment arrives on 20 March to assume responsibility for the island.
February 23, 1945 - Old Glory is raised atop Mount Suribachi, Iwo Jima. Admiral Chester Nimitz later states: "Uncommon valor was a common virtue."
March 24, 1945 - General Patton's 3rd Army crosses Rhine River (Germany).
April 1, 1945 - Invasion of Okinawa (1st and 6th Marine Divisions and the XXIV Corps' 7th and 96th Infantry Divisions).
April 6, 1945-Kamikazes attack U.S. fleet at Okinawa (Fleet that came to stay).
April 7, 1945- The Naval Battle of the East China Sea.
April 7, 1945 - B-29s, protected 1st time by Land-Based Planes, strike Japan.
April 12, 1945 - President Roosevelt dies during his 4th term (1933-1945). Vice President Harry Truman takes the oath to become 33rd President of U.S.
April 1945 - U.S. takes Schweinfurt, Germany; it sends a German flag with a note to Eighth A. F.: "Rainbow Division has revenged your losses at Schweinfurt."
May 7, 1945- The Germans surrender at Rheims, France. A separate ceremony is staged on the following day for the Russians; Eisenhower does not attend.
June 22, 1945 - Old Glory is officially raised on Okinawa.
July 4, 1945 - U.S. troops occupy their zone in Berlin as the cold war begins to further chill and Soviet intent becomes crystal clear.
July 16, 1945- U.S. explodes the 1st atom bomb (Almogordo, New Mexico).
July 16-August 23, 1945 - The USS *Indianapolis* embarks from the States (16th) and delivers a secret cargo (atom bomb) to Tinian (July 26). Later, while en route from Guam to the Philippines the *Indianapolis* is sunk (30th) by the Japanese sub I-58. The "Indy," is not immediately missed. On 16 August, survivors are found; 900 men lost incl. 30 Marines; 15 officers & 301 men incl. 9 Marines are saved.
July 22, 1945 - The U. S. officially raises the Stars and Stripes in Berlin. The flag used for the ceremony is the same one that flew over the Capitol on December 7th, 1941 and it was raised after the fall of Rome. From Berlin, the flag will be transported to General MacArthur to be flown over Tokyo.
August 6-9, 1945-The U.S. drops an Atomic Bomb on Hiroshima and Nagasaki Japan on the 6th and 9th respectively. On the 7th, Russia declares war on Japan.
August 14, 1945-Japan capitulates (three years, eight months and seven days since the attack against Pearl Harbor on December 7, 1941).

September 2, 1945- The Japanese officially sign the surrender document on the deck of the USS *Missouri* in Tokyo Bay. The Stars and Stripes that flew over the capital on December 7, 1941 is hoisted for the ceremony. General Wainwright, one of the "Battling B******'s* of Bataan is there to observe.

Post World War II

September 7, 1945 - U.S. advance troops arrive in South Korea to counter Russian troops that had arrived earlier in North Korea.
December 9, 1945 - Germany - General George S. Patton is injured in a vehicle crash (dies 21 Dec.); he notes: "This is a hell of a way for a Soldier to die."
January 20, 1946 - President Harry S Truman by Executive Order establishes a Central Intelligence Group, later Central Intelligence Agency (CIA).
March 21, 1946 - The U.S. Strategic Air Command is established.
July 4, 1946 - The Philippines receives its independence from the U.S.
1947 - The U.S. Navy forms its 1st offensive Underwater Demolition Teams (UDTs). They become very active when the Korean War erupts during 1950.
February 17, 1947 - Communist-dominated countries (Iron-Curtain) in Europe begin receiving broadcasts from the Voice of America (radio).
May 1947 - In response to Soviet boasts of superior air and military power in Germany, and after a flight over Berlin by Soviet planes, the U.S. displays its Air Force. A fighter group passes over Berlin in a formation that spells U.S.
July 2, 1947 - Tension continues to build in Germany between the Soviets and the allies. The U.S. sends B-29s over Berlin, giving the Russians a view of the Stars and Stripes from their positions on the ground.
July 26, 1947 - The Department of War, (established 1789), becomes Department of the Army (Unification Act). The official seal of the War Office, initiated during May, 1789, remains the official seal of the Department of the Army and it remains as part of the Army Flag.
September 18, 1947 - The Army Air Corps becomes the U.S. Air Force.
October 10, 1947 - The Army Transport *Honda Knot* arrives at San Francisco, bearing the first contingent of U. S. war dead (WWII) to be returned home.
April 10, 1948 -The Soviets halt passenger trains moving out of Berlin.
June 12, 1948 - Congress establishes the Women's Army Corps, as a separate corps of the army. Later during 1978, the Women's Army Corps is dissolved.
June 18-24, 1948 -The Soviets halt U.S. rail movements heading for Berlin.
June 21-26, 1948 - The Russians create a blockade of Berlin (land and sea) By the 26th, the U.S. and England institute an airlift (Operation Vittles).
June 24, 1948 - At 0600, the Soviets halt all rail traffic departing West Berlin.
July 25, 1948 - General Curtis LeMay's C-47s land in Berlin to bypass the Soviet blockade and deliver the first airlifted supplies for the besieged city.
August 4, 1948 - The Soviets complete the land and water blockade of Berlin.
January 20, 1949 - Harry S Truman is inaugurated 33rd President of the U. S.
April 4, 1949 - In Washington, D.C., the North Atlantic Treaty Organization (NATO) is established (mutual defense pact as a deterrent against Communism). Recently, a large spy system operating in the U.S. and other free nations had been discovered to confirm a Communist conspiracy.
May 3, 1949 - North Korean troops launch a raid which brings them to the vicinity of Kaesong in the Republic of South Korea. The raids continue.
May 4, 1949 - The Soviets relent and agree to lift the blockade of Berlin.

Korea Conflict ("Forgotten War") Era

June 29, 1949 - The final contingents of U.S. troops depart Korea.
August 3, 1949 - Congress passes legislation designating June 14, as National Flag Day and President Harry Truman signs it into law.
August 24, 1949 - NATO is organized for the security of Western Europe.
June 25-June 28, 1950 - N. Korea invades South Korea (ignites Korean War).

June 29, 1950 - The North Koreans seize Seoul, the capital of South Korea.
June 30, 1950 - President Harry S Truman authorizes a naval blockade of Korea and the bombing of particular targets in Korea above the 38th Parallel.
June 30, 1950 - Korea - A U.S. Task Force (later named Task Force Smith), arrives in Korea (the first U.S. combat troops to arrive). In conjunction, about 10,000 Seabees will be called to service during this conflict.
July 2, 1950 - General D. MacArthur orders a Marine Combat Team to Korea.
July 3, 1950 - The USS *Valley Forge* launches jets (1st air attack of the war).
July 4, 1950 - Battle of Osan (1st contact between U.S. and Communists).
July 9, 1950 - General W. Walker opens Eighth Army Headquarters at Taeju.
July 10, 1950 -By this time, U.S. planes, supported by Australian planes, clear the skies of North Korean aircraft and gain air supremacy for the U.S.-U.N.
July 12, 1950 - By this time, N. Korean forces hold about half of South Korea.
July 19-20, 1950 - The Battle of Taejon, Korea (Eighth Army).
July 20, 1950 - General Walton Walker's order (Korea): "Stand and fight or die."
August 1, 1950 - Eighth Army deploys below the Naktong at Pusan Perimeter (25th Division at Masan, 24th Division at Miryang, 1st Cavalry at Miryang).
August 2, 1950 - First Provisional Marine Brigade arrives at Pusan, Korea.
August 3, 1950 - Battle of Chindong-ni (Korea).
August 3, 1950 - Marine planes launch their initial mission over Korea.
August 5-6, 1950 - North Koreans attack Eighth Army at the Naktong. The 1st Marine Brigade advances to Chinju to support the army forces.
August 7, 1950 - U.S. B-29s bombard P'yongyang the capital of N. Korea.
August 7-15, 1950 - Task Force Kean initiates the 1st U.S. offensive (Korea).
August 15, 1950 - 1st Marine Brigade moves to Miryang to support the 24th Div.
August 16, 1950 - Heavy fighting occurs at the Naktong Bulge (Korea).
August 19, 1950 - The North Korean offensive against Taegu is halted. By the 20th, Marines and the 24th Division clear enemy bridgehead near Taegu.
September 1, 1950 - U.S. counterattack (1st Provisional Marine Brigade) to intercept a second North Korean crossing of the Naktong River.
September 15, 1950 – The First Marine Division invades Inchon (Korea).
September 16, 1950 - Eighth Army is divided into two corps, I and IX Corps.
September 17, 1950 - Marines seize Kimpo airfield and move toward Seoul.
September 19, 1950 - U.S. forces recapture Waegwan, South Korea.
September 25, 1950 - Marines and Army infantry recapture Seoul, S. Korea.
September 27, 1950 - Marines hoist the Stars and Stripes over Seoul, S. Korea.
October 1, 1950 - South Korean troops (vanguard) cross into North Korea.
October 7, 1950 - The 1st Cavalry Division advances into North Korea.
October 19, 1950 - Pyongyang, the capital of N. Korea falls to Eighth Army.
October 23, 1950 - By this day, North Korean forces have been driven into the mountains to a point about 50 miles from Manchuria.
Oct. 26, 1950- S. Korean troops move to Manchurian border at the Yalu River.
October 27-28, 1950 - The Chinese maul units of the S. Korean 6th Division.
October 28, 1950 - The 1st Marine Division moves from Wonsan (East Korea) and advances towards the Manchurian border.
November 1, 1950 - A plot to assassinate President Harry S Truman fails.
November 2, 1950 - Battle at Unsan (Eighth Army).
November 3, 1950 - Marines make contact with the Chinese. Fighting continues near Sudong until the 7th. This is the first Chinese loss to U.S. troops.
November 5, 1950 - Chinese forces encircle nearly the entire 1st Marine Division in northeastern Korea, but the Marines fight their way out of the trap.
November 6, 1950 - The Joint Chiefs of Staff are told by General MacArthur that huge numbers of Chinese threaten the destruction of his forces.
November 10, 1950 - Marines (175th birthday) advance (Chanjgin Reservoir).
November 23, 1950 - U.S. forces treated to Turkey dinners (Thanksgiving Day). The offensive to drive to the Yalu River is to begin on 24 November.
November 24, 1950 - Elements (17th Regiment) of the 7th U.S. Division advance to the Yalu River. This is the only American unit to reach the river.
November 25, 1950 - The Chinese attack (2nd-phase offensive) and devastate the

ROK II Corps (central Korea). The loss endangers Eighth Army's flank.
November 26, 1950 - Eighth Army, posted above the Chongchon River sustains a heavy Chinese attack, forcing General Walker to withdraw by the 27th.
November 28, 1950 - A Chinese force attacks the Marines and the U.S. 7th Division at their lines (Chosin Reservoir); the Yanks fight their way to Yudam-ni.
November 29, 1950 - A 260-man contingent led by Marine Major R. R. Myers repulses a Chinese attack that saves the Marine perimeter at Hagur-ri.
December 1, 1950 - The First Marine Division begins its breakout from Yudam-ni on a 56-mile march over frozen Korean ground. The Marines, units of the 7th Division and the British 41st Royal Commando unit receive air support.
December 5, 1950 - The 1st Marine Division, subsequent to evacuating its wounded, fights its way to Koto-ri, arriving there on the 7th.
December 8, 1950 - The First Marine Division, the 41st Royal Commando and contingents of the U.S. 7th Division depart Koto-ri en route to Hungnam.
December 15, 1950 - The last units (1st Marine Div.) embark for Pusan.
December 15, 1950 - By this date, the Chinese pressure compels General Walker to withdraw Eighth Army and the ROK Army below the 38th Parallel.
December 18, 1950 - The 1st Marine Division is committed to eliminate Communist guerrillas (10th North Korean Division) in the vicinity of Masan.
December 23, 1950 - General Walton Walker is killed by accident in Korea while riding in a jeep. He is succeeded by General Matthew Ridgway.
December 24, 1950 - On Christmas Eve, X Corps completes its evacuation by sea from Hungnam. The operation to abandon N. Korea began on 12 December.
December 31, 1950 - Chinese launch their 3rd offensive (New Year's).
1950 - The IPR (Institute of Pacific Relations), as early as the mid-1930's, according to the Internal Security Subcommittee of the U.S. Senate, has been dominated by pro-Communists and pro Soviet sympathies. Also, the Reece committee, called to investigate tax-exempt foundations notes: "... nor does the point need to be labored that the loss of China to the Communists may have been the most tragic event in our (U.S.) history, and one to which the foundation-supported Institute of Pacific Relations heavily contributed."
January 3-4, 1951 - Eighth Army abandons Seoul on the 3rd. On the 4th, Inchon and Kimpo airport are demolished to prevent use by the Communists.
January 17, 1951 - The Chinese reject a recent U.N. peace proposal. On the 22nd, the Chinese present a counter proposal, which is rejected by the U.S.
January 25, 1951 - Eighth Army initiates an offensive towards the Han River.
January 28, 1951 - The Communists depart Masan, S. Korea and head north.
February 11, 1951 - The Chinese launch a fifth offensive; it ends on the 17th.
February 17, 1951 - Battle of Chipyong-ni (Korea).
February 21, 1951 - IX and X Corps initiate an offensive (Operation Killer).
February 28, 1951 - Communist resistance below the Han River is eliminated.
March 7, 1951 - Eighth Army initiates Operation Ripper. The IX and X Corps bolt the Han River and drive into northward (Korea).
March 11, 1951 - American forces (1st Cavalry, 2nd Division and the 1st Marine Division) continue to gain ground in central Korea near Hongchon.
March 14-15, 1951 - The Eighth Army retakes Seoul (Korea).
March 31, 1951 - U.S. forces (2nd time) cross the 38th Parallel into N. Korea.
April 5, 1951 - Operation Rugged is initiated (Korea).
April 11, 1951 - General Douglas MacArthur is fired by President Truman. He is succeeded by General Matthew Ridgway. On the 19th, General MacArthur addresses a Joint Session of Congress to close out his military career.
April 22-28, 1951 - The Communists begin the fifth-phase offensive. An attack against IX Corps' flank is repelled (23rd), by the 1st Marine Division.
April 27, 1951 - Chinese offensive against left flank of IX Corps is halted.
May 9, 1951 - About 300 planes of the Fifth Air Force and elements of the 1st Marine Air Wing strike enemy positions near the Yalu (Korea).
May 23, 1951 - Marines counterattack near the Hwachon reservoir (Korea).
May 26-28, 1951- By the 28th, most Communists are pushed out of South Korea.

June 1, 1951 - The First Marine Division advances against North Korean units east of the Hwachon Reservoir. It drives towards the "Punch Bowl."

July 5, 1951 - The Chinese Communists propose a peace conference to the U.S. It is accepted by General Ridgway. The two sides meet in Kaesong.

August 1, 1951- The 1st Marine Division begins an attack in the Punchbowl.

August 22, 1951- Communists quit peace talks (Kaesong); begin again Oct. 25.

September 2-15, 1951 - Battle of Heartbreak Ridge (U.S. 2nd Division), Korea.

September 2, 1951 - Battle of Bloody Ridge (2nd U.S. Division), Korea.

September 20, 1951 - Marine helicopters transport a full company of Marines to the front (eastern mtns. Korea), the 1st mission lifting a full unit to combat zone.

September 21, 1951 - Marines take hill (central front) held by 2,000 troops.

November 12, 1951 - General Matthew Ridgway orders a suspension of offensive action. He directs his forces to construct a sturdy defense.

December 29, 1951 - January 2, 1952 - The Communists reject two separate peace proposals by the U.N. during peace talks at Panmunjom. While the talks are stalled, an attack is launched against a Chinese-held hill near Korangop.

January 1, 1952 - The Communists are greeted with fanfare. Air attacks and an artillery bombardment are initiated (Korea). They terminate on 31 January.

May 7, 1952- Gen. Francis Dodd, is seized by POWs (Koje-do) & freed on 11th.

March 25, 1952 - The 1st Marine Division redeploys on Eighth Army's left flank (western front). There is not much activity as peace talks continue.

May 1, 1952 - An Air Force bomber flying over Arizona drops (test) an atomic bomb near Yucca Flat, Arizona. Ground troops are in nearby foxholes.

June 6-14, 1952 - U.S. establishes eleven patrol camps (occupied by 45th Div.).

July 25, 1952 - Puerto Rico becomes the first commonwealth of the U. S.

August 11, 1952 - The 1st Marine Division battles the Communists for control of "Bunker Hill." The fight continues sporadically until year's end.

August 22, 1952 - The Army purchases 25,000 armored vests.

September 11, 1952 - During an operation near Korean airport K-2, six separate planes sustain a breakdown (instrument) and crash into a mountain. All pilots are instantly killed. During September (excluding Air Force), the Navy and Marine pilots drop 6,200 tons of bombs, 6,100 rockets and 1,700,000 rounds of ammo.

October 1952 - The Marine 1st Aircraft Wing flew 3,765 sorties.

September - Nov., 1952 - Navy & Marines (excl. Air Force) flew 28,102 sorties.

December 5, 1952 - Dwight D. Eisenhower (President elect), keeping his word, visits Korea to try to bring an end to the war, ongoing since June 1950.

January 16, 1953 - U.S. sustains 128,971 casualties since start of hostilities.

January 20, 1953 - Dwight D. Eisenhower is inaugurated 34th President of U.S.

March 5, 1953 - Joseph Stalin (Soviet Premier) dies. Cold War tensions ease.

March 25, 1953 - The Communists seize an outpost (Hill 266) in Korea.

April 9, 1953 - Marines lose Carson Hill near Panmunjom, but recapture it.

April 11, 1953 - The Communists and the U.N.-U.S. agree to a prisoner (sick and wounded) exchange. The transfer occurs on the 20th at Panmunjom, Korea.

May 8, 1953 - Uncle Sam (U.S.) announces it is providing the French with $60 million to use during the Indo China War. More U.S. dollars will follow.

May 28, 1953 - The Chinese assault five outposts of the 25th Division.

June 10, 1953 - The ROK forces near Kumsong come under attack.

June 15, 1953 - U.S. I Corps is attacked; ends 30 June.

June 19, 1953 - The Communists and the U.S.-U.N. agree to an armistice pact. And two American spies, Julius and Ethel Rosenberg, are executed for treason.

July 13, 1953 - Chinese attack (ROK's left flank and IX Corps' right flank).

July 27, 1953 – An armistice is signed (Korea); however, no peace agreement is signed. The armistice remains in effect. U.S. troops remain in South Korea.

Post Korea and Vietnam War Era

1950-1953 - The U.S. lost about 1 plane for every 14 lost by the Communists.

August 17, 1953 - In Vietnam, the U.S. begins to evacuate 200,000 civilians from Hanoi and Haiphong and bring them into southern Vietnam.

January 21, 1954 - The U.S. launches the 1st atomic submarine , the *Nautilus*.
May 7, 1954 - The Viet Minh (Communists) defeat the French at Dien Bien Phu. On 20 July, peace is reached, ending the French Indo Chinese War. During the 55-day siege, the 16,000-man French garrison sustains 6,000 casualties and 10,000 captured. Vietnam is divided (North & South); the French move south.
January 1, 1955 - The U.S. initiates direct assistance to S. Vietnam in accordance with a recent pact (Dec. 23 1950) to provide support Vietnam's military. During April, U.S. advisors (MAAG) begin to train South Vietnamese.
January 28, 1955 - Congress gives President Eisenhower authority to defend Formosa (Taiwan) and the Pescadores Islands; Eisenhower is also authorized to use the military if the Chinese Communists attack.
April 29, 1955 - Civil war breaks out in South Vietnam in opposition to the U.S.-backed regime of (Ngo Dinh Diem.
July 7, 1955 - Communist China agrees to provide aid to North Vietnam.
July 18, 1955 - The Soviet Union agrees to provide aid to North Vietnam.
April 28, 1956 - The French Military High Command in Vietnam is disbanded. French forces embark for home. The Stars and Stripes which had defended South Korea against Communism, now begins to help South Vietnam.
May 21, 1956 - The Air Force drops an H-bomb over an uninhabited island of the Bikini Atoll (Pacific), the initial testing, an aerial drop of the H-bomb.
June 12, 1956 - The U.S. subsequent to Executive Order # 10670 issued by President Dwight D. Eisenhower, officially adopts the U.S. Army flag.
July 30, 1956 - "In God We Trust" becomes the national motto of the U.S.
December 2, 1956 - Fidel Castro, for the second time invades Cuba. His force of slightly more than eighty men is defeated, but Castro escapes to the hills and initiates a guerrilla movement against the regime of Fulgencio Batista.
March 9, 1957 - President Eisenhower receives authorization from Congress to support the Middle East states with their efforts to fend off Communism.
December 17, 1957 - The U.S. tests an intercontinental ballistic missile, about three months after the Russians (Soviet Union) had tested one.
1958 - Congress passes Public Law 529, declaring 1 May, as Loyalty Day.
January 31, 1958 - The U.S. sends its first satellite (*Explorer* 1) into orbit. The Army launches it from Cape Canaveral, Fla. This follows the launching of a Russian (Soviet Union) satellite (*Sputnik* I) during the previous October.
March 17, 1958 - The U.S. launches its first solar-powered satellite (*Vanguard*).
March 27, 1958 - Nikita Khrushchev, having outmaneuvered his rivals, becomes the sole leader of the Soviet Union, bringing the Communist nation back into one-man rule, which was eliminated when Joseph Stalin succumbed.
July 15, 1958 – Marines land in Lebanon in request for support during a time of turbulence between Christians and Moslems. More Marines   and Army units including 24th and 29th A/B Brigades, 82nd Airborne Division follow. No armed force by the U.S. becomes necessary. A withdrawal is begun during mid-August.
July 23, 1958 - The USS *Nautilus* (nuclear powered submarine) commanded by Commander William R. Anderson embarks from Pearl Harbor, Hawaii initiating Operation Sunshine; it takes the U.S. flag to the N. Pole. The *Nautilus* is the first ship to reach the geographic North Pole 90° North (1115 hours on 3 August).
January 3, 1959 - Alaska is admitted to the Union as the 49th state.
March 3, 1959 - The U.S. launches its first probe into deep space (*Pioneer* 4).
April 1959 - The U.S. introduces its first 7 astronauts, each a military jet test pilot who will participate in the Mercury Project (initiated the previous year).
May 28, 1959 - The U.S. launches *Jupiter*, a space capsule (sub-orbital) that transports two primate astronauts (monkeys) named Able and Baker.
July 1959 - Fidel Castro, leader of Cuba declares his allegiance to Marxism, causing friction in relations between the U.S. and Cuba.
August 21, 1959 - Hawaii is admitted to the Union as the 50th state.
May 1, 1960 - A U.S. spy plane (U-2) is shot down over Soviet territory. The pilot, Gary Powers is captured. Initially, the U.S. denies the existence of such a

plane. It was unknown that the Russians had captured the pilot. During February 1962, Powers is returned to the U.S. in exchange for a Russian spy.
May 5, 1960 - The U.S. decides to send more military advisors to South Vietnam.
July 9, 1960 - Marines aboard the *Wasp* are deployed in the Congo. Also, the USS *Thresher* is launched; 13 more Thresher class (nuclear) submarines follow.
July 14, 1960 - The U.S. informs the Russians that the Monroe Doctrine of 1823 remains in effect regarding the U.S. mandate against manipulation by foreign states in the Western Hemisphere. Russian advisors are flooding Cuba.
January 3, 1961 - The United States severs diplomatic relations with Cuba.
January 20, 1961 - John F. Kennedy (first Catholic) is inaugurated as the 35th President of the United States. During his first year in office, the army's Special Forces (Green Berets) expands from less than 2,000 to about 9,000.
January 31, 1961 - The Stars and Stripes goes into Space (*Mercury-Redstone* 2), transporting Ham, a chimpanzee.
February 1-8, 1961- U.S. forces aboard the USS *Hermitage* assist in the evacuation of U.N. troops (Guineans) from the Congo (Africa).
April 17, 1961 - A force of about 1,400 anti-Castro Cubans embarks from the U.S. to overthrow the Cuban Communist government of Fidel Castro. The mission, backed by the CIA, fails. U.S. troops are not involved.
May 5, 1961 - President John F. Kennedy announces the possibility of providing aid to S. Vietnam in its struggle with the Communist government of North Vietnam. Also, the U.S. launches its first manned suborbital space flight (*Mercury-Redstone* 3), manned by Navy Commander Alan B. Shepherd Jr.
June 12, 1961 - President John F. Kennedy orders that the Stars and Stripes be flown 24 hours a day over the Iwo Jima Memorial at Arlington, Virginia.
July 21, 1961 - The U.S. launches another space capsule (*Mercury-Redstone* 4), a suborbital flight manned by Virgil Grissom, 2nd American in space.
August 2, 1961 - President Kennedy proclaims an all out effort to save South Vietnam from Communism. The U.S. intensifies its support for the South.
August 12-13, 1961 - The Communists close the border with West Berlin to keep East Germans from escaping; they construct a wall along the border.
November 16, 1961 - Following inroads by the Communists, the U.S. decides to provide more aid to South Vietnam. President Kennedy increases the number of U.S. advisors from 1,000 to about 16,000 within two years.
December 11, 1961 - U.S. Army helicopter contingents arrive in South Vietnam.
1962 - U.S. Navy establishes SEAL Teams (formed from existing UDT). Seal Team One operates in the Pacific, Seal Team Two in the Atlantic.
February 1962 - U.S. advisors in S. Vietnam come under fire from Communist forces and receive authorization to return fire (about 4,000 advisors in Vietnam).
February 10, 1962 - Gary Powers (Air Force pilot) shot down over the Soviet Union on May Day 1960, is exchanged for a Soviet spy, Colonel Rudolf Abel.
February 20, 1962 - The Stars and Stripes goes into space with Lt. Col. John Glenn, USMC, aboard the 1st manned U.S. space craft *(Mercury-Atlas* 6) "*Friendship* 7." Glenn becomes the 1st American to orbit the earth (3 times).
April 9, 1962 - U.S. Marines begin to arrive in Vietnam. On the 15th, a Marine helicopter squadron arrives in the Mekong Delta near Soc Trang and begins operations from an abandoned air base used by the Japanese during WW II.
May 12, 1962 - The U.S. dispatches air, ground and naval forces to Vietnam.
May 17, 1962 - U.S. Marines land in Thailand to support the government against Communist pressure. They remain through the latter part of July.
May 24, 1962 - The U.S. launches its fourth astronaut, M. Scott Carpenter, into space (*Mercury-Atlas* 7) in the "*Aurora*." He orbits the earth three times.
October 3, 1962 - The U.S. launches its 5th manned space trip. Walter M. Schirra, Jr., USN, orbits the earth six times in the *Sigma* 7 (Mercury-Atlas 8).
October 27, 1962 - President Kennedy announces that Cuba has Soviet missiles capable of striking the U.S. He orders a naval blockade of Cuba. The Navy firmly stands. On 2 November, Kennedy announces that the missiles will be

dismantled. U.S. forces had prepared for hostilities. Marines embarked for Guantanamo The incident brought the world close to a nuclear confrontation.
November 20, 1962 – The U.S. naval blockade of Cuba ceases following an agreement with the Soviet Union to dismantle the missiles installed in Cuba.
November 15, 1962 At this time about 16,000 U.S. troops are in South Vietnam.
January 2, 1963 - Vietnam - Battle of Ap Bac. (U.S. advisors present).
April 1963 – The USS *Thresher*, a nuclear-powered submarine with its crew of 129 men, sinks (cause unknown) off the New England coast. This is the 2nd submarine lost during the Cold War. The *Cochino* sank due to a fire (1949).
May 15-16, 1963 - L. Gordon Cooper makes the final (sixth flight) (Mercury-Atlas 9) Mercury project flight. He orbits the earth 22 times in *Faith 7*.
June 20, 1963 - General William Westmoreland succeeds General Paul D. Harkins as Commander-in-Chief, U.S. Military Assistance Command in Vietnam.
July 28, 1963 - U.S. announces that 5,000 more troops will head for Vietnam.
November 22, 1963 - President John F. Kennedy is assassinated. Vice President Lyndon Baines Johnson assumes the office. He takes the oath as 36th President while aboard Air Force 1, en route from Dallas to the capital.
January 9-10, 1964 - A confrontation regarding the flying of the Stars and Stripes and the Panamanian flag occurs in Panama between a mob and U.S. troops in the Canal Zone. Four soldiers are killed and seventeen civilians die.
July 28, 1964-U.S. Lunar probe (*Ranger 7*) succeeds. Photos are returned to earth.
August 2, 1964 - The USS *Maddox* is attacked (Gulf of Tonkin, Vietnam).
August 4, 1964 - Enemy PT boats attack U.S. vessels off Vietnam.
August 5, 1964 - U.S. planes attack enemy bases in North Vietnam.
August 7, 1964 - Congress passes the "Gulf of Tonkin Resolution," giving President Johnson authority to take steps to deter attacks against U.S.
November 1, 1964 - Communist guerrillas launch a mortar attack on Bien Hoa, a U.S. base; it destroys planes, damages others and inflicts casualties.
February 7, 1965 - The U.S. base at Pleiku is attacked by the Viet Cong. On the following day, planes (Air Force and South Vietnamese) attack enemy positions in North Vietnam in retaliation for the deaths of about eight Americans and the wounding of more than 75. Coincidentally, while American bombs were descending upon Hanoi, Soviet Premier Nikita Khrushchev was there visiting.
March 2, 1965 - North Vietnam comes under heavy air attack (Rolling Thunder).
March 8, 1965 - The 3rd Battalion, 9th Marines debarks at Danang, Vietnam, the first ground troops to arrive. About 20,000 U.S. advisors are already there.
March 23, 1965 - The U.S. launches its first Gemini mission (*Gemini 3*), manned by astronauts Virgil Grissom (2nd flight) and John W. Young.
May 3, 1965 - The 173rd Airborne Brigade arrives in Vietnam.
April 1965 - U.S. forces land in the Dominican Republic to ensure the safety of Americans and to prevent a possibility of a Communist coup. Marines land on 28 April, trailed by units of the 82nd A/B, and other Army and Air Force personnel.
June 3, 1965 - The U.S. launches its 2nd Gemini flight (*Gemini 4*), manned by James A. McDivitt and Edward H. White, the first American to walk in space.
June 18, 1965 – B52 bombers strike enemy positions in S. Vietnam (1st strike).
June 26, 1965 General William Westmoreland receives authorization to commit his U.S. troops to battle when necessary (Vietnam).
June 27, 1965 - Airborne troops (173rd Brigade) initiate an offensive against the Viet Cong positions northeast of Saigon, South Vietnam.
July 1, 1965 - Enemy guerrillas attack Da Nang airfield (South Vietnam).
July 1965 - By the latter part of the month, Washington decides to commit the 1st Cavalry Division to Vietnam and to boost the forces there to 175,000.
August 18, 1965 - The Marines commence their initial offensive (Operation Starlite) on the Van Tuong Peninsula, just south of the Chu Lai airstrip.
August 21, 1965 - The 3rd U.S. Gemini flight (*Gemini 5*) is launched, and manned by L. Gordon Cooper (2nd) and Charles Conrad.
September 7, 1965 - Marines begin Operation Piranha (Batangan Peninsula).
October 27, 1965 - U.S. forces initiate an offensive (Ia Drang Campaign). Also,

the Viet Cong, using boats, attack China Beach. Only a few of the enemy penetrate, but they destroy helicopters and severely damage a hospital.

November 13, 1965 - The 3rd Battalion, 3rd Marines lands near Hoi An (Quang Nam Province) and begins a 3-day search mission. Also, a Viet Cong Regiment seizes Hiep Duc, but South Vietnamese troops retake it.

November 22, 1965 - The North Vietnamese 18th Regiment attacks Thach Tru, held by South Vietnamese Rangers, bolstered by destroyers and Marine planes.

December 4, 1965 - The fourth Gemini space capsule (*Gemini* 7), manned by Frank Borman and James A. Lovell, is launched. It remains in space until 18 December and while in orbit, *Gemini* 6, rendezvous with it.

December 8-16, 1965 - Operation Harvest Moon is launched in the Queson valley above Hiep Duc. The Marines on the ground receive support from B52s which commence their first four raids in support of Marines (Vietnam).

December 15, 1965 - The U.S. launches its fifth Gemini space capsule (*Gemini* 6), manned by Walter M. Schirra (2nd) and Thomas P. Stafford. This flight links with *Gemini* 7, the latter having been launched on 4 December.

December 24, 1965 - On Christmas Eve, following talks in Washington, the air raids against enemy targets (Vietnam) halted to coincide with diplomatic moves.

January 31, 1966 - U.S. planes reinitiate bombing raids in Vietnam.

March 4, 1966 - Battle of Quang Ngai city (Vietnam).

March 9, 1966 - Despite air-support, a Special Forces camp at A Shau near the Laotian border is destroyed following a two-day assault. On the 11th, helicopters evacuate survivors, including twelve of the original seventeen Green Berets.

March 16, 1966 - The 6th Gemini space capsule (*Gemini* 8) is launched, (Neil Armstrong & David R. Scott); a space docking with *Agena* 8, is aborted.

May 1, 1966 - Artillery bombards enemy targets in Cambodia.

June 3, 1966 - The seventh Gemini space capsule (*Gemini* 9) manned by Thomas P. Stafford (2nd) and Eugene A. Cernan is launched.

June 15, 1966 - Battle of Hill 488 (Vietnam).

June 29, 1966 - U.S. planes bombard Hanoi, North Vietnam.

July 15, 1966 - Task Force Delta (8,000 Marines and S. Vietnamese troops) moves against a North Vietnamese Division (324B) at Cam Lo below the DMZ.

July 18, 1966 - The 8th Gemini space capsule (*Gemini* 10) manned by John W. Young (2nd) and Michael Collins is launched; completes the 1st orbital docking.

Aug. 10, 1966 - The U.S. launches Lunar Orbiter 1. It returns photos to earth.

September 12, 1966 - The ninth Gemini space capsule (*Gemini* 11) manned by Charles Conrad Jr. (2nd) and Richard F. Gordon is launched.

November 11, 1966 - The final (tenth) Gemini capsule (*Gemini* 12) is launched into space, manned by James A. Lovell and Edwin "Buzz" Aldrin Jr.

1967 - The U.S. Navy renames the Naval Operations Support Groups. They become Naval Special Warfare Groups (NSWGs).

January 8, 1967 - Operation "Cedar Falls," commences. U.S. and S. Vietnamese forces north of Saigon attack to reduce enemy controlled area ("Iron Triangle").

January 27, 1967 - Three astronauts are killed in their space capsule (*Apollo* 1) during a pre-flight test when a fire takes their lives in what would have been the initial Apollo mission. Lt. Commander Roger Chafee, Lt. Colonel Virgil "Gus" Grissom and Lt. Colonel Edward H. White II, succumb.

February 2, 1967 - Operation Gadsden - The elements of the 4th and 25th U.S. Infantry Division operate near the Cambodian border.

February 12, 1967 - The Marines initiate Operation Stone, south of Da Nang.

February 22, 1967 - Operation Junction City, biggest war operation to date.

March 16, 1967 - The Communists ambush a Marine contingent near enemy-held Hill 861, just northwest of Khesahn. Fighting in this area continues as the Communists focus on evicting the Americans from the airstrip.

May 8, 1967 - The Marine garrison at Con Thien comes under attack.

May 18, 1967 - The 9th Marines advances into the southern part of the DMZ.

June 8, 1967 - The USS *Liberty*, an intelligence gathering vessel flying the Stars and Stripes is attacked by Israeli aircraft and torpedo boats in international waters off the Sinai Peninsula during the "Israeli Six Day War." The ship sustains severe damage and 34 crewmen are killed; 75 others are wounded. Israel claims the attack was accidental. The U.S. takes no retaliatory action, but many believe the attack was intentional to eliminate the interception of Israeli intelligence.

June 1967 – July 1967 - In the Marine sector, heavy fighting develops at Que Son (11-day contest) and Khesahn, the latter a prime target due to its airstrip.

July 23, 1967- Puerto Rico votes to become a U.S. commonwealth, not a state.

September 1967 - Communists launch attacks against far-strung U.S. positions near the Cambodian and Laotian borders, including an isolated Marine garrison (Conthien), south of the border with North Vietnam.

September 13-16, 1967 - Operation Coronado 5, Mekong Delta (9th Division).

October 4, 1967 - The Marines terminate the Communist siege of Con Thien.

November 1967 - The Communists attack in the vicinity of Dakto (Vietnam).

December 30, 1967 - The Communists announce at Hanoi that they will begin negotiations with the U.S. once the bombing raids against N. Vietnam halt. However, all the while, the Communists prepare to launch a major offensive.

December 31, 1967 - As of this date it is estimated that the Communists have lost about 90,000 killed (this year). Also, by this date the U.S. has determined that more than 40,000 enemy troops are forming to attack Khesahn.

January 20, 1968 - Battle of Khesahn (2nd), (77 day siege against Marines).

January 23, 1968 - The USS *Pueblo,* commanded by Lloyd M. Bucher, an intelligence vessel is seized by the North Koreans. The crew, originally 83 men, is released on 22 December, amidst a large U.S. military build-up in the region. One of the captives dies from wounds (during capture) while held. The crew is forced to sign documents stating that they had penetrated N. Korean waters. North Korea keeps the vessel as a propaganda tool. The U.S. makes no effort to re-seize it. As of 2001, the crew and others urge the U.S. to get it back or halt giving North Korea food. Actions of spy John Walker add to the intelligence loss.

January 30-31, 1968 - Tet Offensive - The Communists about 70,000 strong initiate an offensive that strikes across South Vietnam from just below the DMZ at Saigon to Camau. The targets included the U.S. base at Bienhoa, the U.S. Embassy at Saigon, and Hue. Later, at Hue, about 3,000 bodies of people that had died from beatings, gunshots or being buried alive will be discovered.

February 24, 1968 - U.S. Marines supported by South Vietnamese, retake Hue. Also, army forces including the 82nd and 101st Airborne are heavily engaged during February and March in such actions as Operation Carentan I.

March 16, 1968 - My Lai Massacre (Vietnam).

March 31, 1968 - President Lyndon B. Johnson announces a cessation of U.S. bombing north of the 20th Parallel in North Vietnam.

April 2, 1968 - Operation Toan Thang, a mission to clear the area around Saigon of Communist forces commences; it terminates on May 31.

April 5, 1968 - The Marine garrison at Khesahn under siege since January 20th, prevails as the siege is lifted (Operation Pegasus).

April 23, 1968 - More college protestors stage a demonstration, this time at Columbia University in New York. These Left-wing demonstrations continue.

May 13, 1968 - U.S. and Communist North Vietnamese representatives hold the initial discussion on peace in Paris, France.

May 17 - May 22, 1968 - On May 17, the USS *Scorpion* acting on secret orders moves towards the Canary Islands, 1,500 miles off the east coast of Africa to track a group of Soviet Warships, including a nuclear sub. Initially, the *Scorpion* was en route to the States from a mission in the Mediterranean, but special orders arrive ordering it to change course. The *Scorpion* sinks off the Azores (cause is listed as mechanical malfunction. There are uncertain circumstances surrounding its disappearance on 22 May). The Soviets had knowledge of U.S. Navy codes (supplied by a spy, Warrant Officer John Walker). The crew of 99 is lost.

October 11-22, 1968 - The U.S. launches its first Apollo spacecraft (*Apollo* 7), manned by Walter M. Schirra, Don F. Eisele, and R. Walter Cunningham.

November 1, 1968 - U.S. bombing missions over N. Vietnam are suspended.
December 21, 1968 - *Apollo* 8 (first lunar orbit) manned by Frank Borman (2nd), James A. Lovell (3rd) William A. Anders is launched.
January 7, 1969 - U.S. college campuses continue to gather opposition to the ongoing war in Vietnam as students (deferred from serving) spread turmoil (riots) across the land. The unrest serves as propaganda for the Communists.
January 20, 1969 - Richard Nixon is inaugurated as 37th President of the U.S.
February 23-24, 1969 - The Communists launch attacks against more than one hundred cities, towns and military bases across South Vietnam.
March 3-13, 1969 - The U.S. launches *Apollo* 9 (third Apollo), manned by James A. McDivitt (2nd), David R. Scott (2nd) and Russell L. Schweickart.
May 18-26, 1969 - The U.S. launches its 4th Apollo spacecraft (Apollo.10), manned by Thomas Stafford (3rd), John W. Young (3rd) and Eugene A. Cernan.
June 8, 1969 - President Nixon meets with S. Vietnamese President Thieu at Midway Island. Nixon states that 25,000 troops will be withdrawn. By early 1972, about 100,000 (of 500,000) remain. The 1st units embark on 8 July.
July 16-24, 1969 - The U.S. launches its fifth Apollo spacecraft (*Apollo* 11), manned by Neil Armstrong (2nd), Michael Collins (2nd) and Edwin W. "Buzz" Aldrin. On the 20th, Neil Armstrong, commander of the *Apollo* II mission, becomes the first man on the moon. He remarks: "One small step for a man, one giant leap for mankind."Aldrin also walks on the moon.
November 14-24, 1969 - *Apollo* 12 (6th Apollo-2nd moon landing) is launched (Charles Conrad (3rd), Richard Gordon Jr. (2nd) and Alan L. Bean).
November 15, 1969 - War protesters gather in San Francisco & Washington.
April 11-17, 1970 - *Apollo* 13 (7th Apollo manned by James Lovell (4), Fred Haise and John Swigart is launched, but later aborted; the crew returns safely.
April 30-June 29, 1970 - Due to Communist actions in Laos and Cambodia, President Nixon states that the U.S. forces will retaliate.
January 31-February 9, 1971- *Apollo* 14 (8th Apollo) is launched, manned by Alan B. Shepard (2nd), Stuart A. Roosa and Edgar. Mitchell (3rd moon landing).
February 8, 1971 - South Vietnamese forces supported by U.S. artillery and planes enter Cambodia (Operation Lam Son 719) to sever the Ho Chi Minh Trail, the primary Communist supply route. The mission lasts 44 days.
May 1, 1971 - Quang Tri City is lost, but S. Vietnamese retake it on 16 May.
June 17, 1971 - The U.S. agrees (treaty) to return Okinawa to Japan (15 May 1972). Also, Secretary of State, Henry Kissinger initiates clandestine talks with the Communists regarding the war in Vietnam.
July 26-August 7, 1971 - *Apollo* 15 (ninth Apollo) is launched, manned by David Scott (3rd), James B. Irwin and Alfred M. Worden (fourth moon landing).The astronauts also use the Lunar Rover for the first time.
January 25, 1972 - The U.S. publicizes a proposal for an end to hostilities in Vietnam, including a total withdrawal of U.S. troops.
March 30, 1972 - South Vietnam is invaded by North Vietnam forces.
April 3, 1972 - The two U.S. carriers off Vietnam are greeted by a third, the USS *Kitty Hawk* and more follow. The North Vietnamese are taking advantage of the absence of many of the U.S. ground forces. By mid-April, retaliatory bombing missions are begun against targets such as Haiphong and Hanoi.
April 16-27, 1972 - *Apollo* 16 (tenth Apollo) is launched, manned by John Young (4th)Charles Duke Jr. and Thomas Mattingly II. (5th moon landing).
December 7-19, 1972 - *Apollo* 17 (eleventh Apollo) the first night-launch goes into space slightly after midnight, manned by Eugene Cernan (2nd), Ronald E. Evans and Harrison H. Schmitt. (6th and final Lunar landing).
August 12, 1972 - The final U.S. ground troops embark from Vietnam.
November 7, 1972 - Peace protesters against the Vietnam War occur in many cities and towns. One Hollywood celebrity, Jane Fonda, dubbed "Hanoi Jane," while in N. Vietnam with the enemy, actually posed on an artillery piece. The protestors apparently did little to help the candidacy of George McGovern, the

59

peace candidate. This day, he loses the election (landslide) to Richard Nixon.
December 18, 1972 - The U.S. reinitiates bombing missions over North Vietnam.
December 30, 1972 - The U.S. bombing missions in North Vietnam cease in accordance with a North Vietnamese agreement to come to peace terms.
January 15, 1973 - The U.S. halts its military operations against North Vietnam.
January 20, 1973 - Richard M. Nixon is inaugurated (2nd term) as President.
January 27, 1973 - In Paris, an agreement is signed ending the Vietnam War.
March 29, 1973 - The remaining U.S. forces (except a small Defense Detache Office), depart Vietnam. Although the U.S. has agreed to peace with North Vietnam, the South Vietnamese continue to struggle against the Communists.
April 5, 1973 - U.S. launches *Pioneer* II, the first successful fly-by of Saturn.
May 14, 1973 - The U.S. launches *Skylab* (1st unmanned U.S. space station).
May 25-June 22, 1973 - Skylab 1 is launched and its crew (Peter Conrad, Joseph Kerwin and Paul Weitz) boards the space station. (28 days).
July 28-September 25, 1973 - *Skylab* 3 is launched, manned by Alan Bean, Owen Garriott and Jack Lousma.
November 16, 1973 - February 8, 1974 - Skylab 4 is launched. Gerald Carr, Ed Gibson & William Pogue; the final crew to occupy space station (84 days).
August 9, 1974 - President Richard Nixon resigns (Watergate scandal) after it is known that he had knowledge of a political break-in at Democratic Headquarters. Vice President Gerald Ford assumes the office as 38th President.
September 8, 1974 - President Ford issues a pardon ("unconditional") to former President Richard Nixon who had resigned from office rather than face impeachment for his actions during the "Watergate Scandal."
April 30, 1975 - The Communists enter Saigon, while the few remaining Americans are being evacuated, along with as many refugees as can be handled. Television cameras capture the dramatic scenes of an American helicopter attempting to take off from a roof, while the Communists take control of the city. The footage is unable to depict the fact that U.S. combat forces have been absent from Vietnam since June 1972. The footage, frequently shown on television, gives an illusion that the U.S. had been vanquished, but the U.S. had not suffered a single defeat in a major battle during the conflict. Also, U.S. forces were often refused permission to return fire.
May 13-15, 1975 - During a mission to rescue a captured U.S. ship, the *Mayaguez*, an Air Force helicopter crashes (13th) en route to Utapao, Thailand. All 23 crewmen (security personnel)l are lost; the main mission occurs on 15 May. On the 15th, U.S. Marines storm the Mayaguez, but the crew is not there. Other Marines transported by Air Force helicopters land at Koh Tang Island (Cambodia) to rescue the crew which had been captured by the Cambodian Communists (Khmer Rouge) on 12 May, but the crew had again been moved. The crew, now aboard another vessel is rescued by the USS *Wilson*. One helicopter is hit by fire, costing the lives of 15 troops including 2 navy corpsmen and 2 airmen; 3 Marines, after expending all their ammunition, fail to make it back to the final helicopter before it departed; their fate is unknown.
July 15, 1975 - An assassination attempt against President Gerald Ford fails.
July 15-24, 1975 - The U.S. Apollo docks (July 17) with the Soviet Soyuz. This is the first international rendezvous and docking in space).
September 22, 1975 - A second attempt on the life of President Ford fails.

Post Vietnam Era

February 24, 1976 - The U.S. Senate votes affirmatively to accept the Marianas Islands in the South Pacific as a U.S. commonwealth
January 20, 1977 - Jimmy Carter is inaugurated as the 39th President of U.S.
September 7, 1977 - The Carter Administration signs a treaty with Panama, which will transfer control of the canal (linkage between the Atlantic and Pacific Oceans) from the U.S. to Panama on December 31, 1999. A second treaty is

signed guaranteeing permanent neutrality for the canal.

May 19-20, 1978 - U.S. Air Force planes (18) transport French and Belgian troops to Zaire where they parachute to rescue Europeans trapped by rebels.

January 16, 1979 - The pro-American Shah of Iran, Mohammed Reza Pahlavi leaves the country, but demonstrations by Moslem extremists continue.

January 21, 1979 - President Jimmy Carter pardons about 10,000 draft-dodgers igniting the ire of veterans, particularly those who fought in Vietnam.

March 7, 1979 - U.S. troops (advisors) embark for North Yemen. South Yemen, is backed by Cubans and Russians. A cease fire is called on 17 March.

October 1, 1979 - The Panama Canal Zone is eliminated. Panama assumes control of the area. The U.S. will control the canal until 31 December,1999.

November 4, 1979 - Iranian extremists seize the U.S. Embassy in Tehran and take nearly 100 captives including 65 Americans.

November 24, 1979 - The U.S. government reports that troops who served in the Vietnam War were exposed to a dangerous herbicide, "Agent Orange."

January 29, 1980 - Six Americans, concealed by the Canadian Embassy in Iran, escape. The CIA had disguised the Americans as a movie crew.

February 2, 1980 - The U.S. severs diplomatic ties with Iran due to seizure of the U.S. Embassy and Iran's assets in the U.S. are frozen.

April 25, 1980 - During a failed mission to retrieve U.S. captives in Iran, eight troops die when a plane and helicopter collide over the desert; 5 others are injured. Those killed: Richard L. Bakke, USAF; John Davis Harvey, USMC, George N. Holmes Jr., USMC; Dewey L. Johnson, USMC, Harold L. Lewis, USAF; Joel C. Mayo, USAF; Lynn Davis McIntosh USMC and Charles T. McMillan, USAF. A primary reason for the failure of the mission was malfunctioning equipment due to desert conditions.

July 27, 1980 - Mohammed Reza Pahlavi, the Shah of Iran (pro-American) succumbs. He had fled Iran for the U.S. where he received medical attention. Later he departed for Panama and afterwards Egypt. Iran under Ayatollah Ruholla Khomeini had unsuccessfully sought to have him brought back.

January 20, 1981 - Ronald Reagan is inaugurated as the 40th President of the U.S. Within minutes after Reagan takes his oath, Iran frees the 52 hostages.

March 30, 1981 - President Ronald Reagan is shot by an assassin, but he survives.

April 12-14, 1981 - The *Challenger* (first space shuttle) takes its initial flight.

August 19, 1981- Navy F14s are attacked by 2 Libyan planes (international waters), claimed as Libyan territory; the Libyan planes are downed.

November 12-14, 1981 - The space shuttle *Columbia* makes its second trip.

April 30, 1982 - President Ronald Reagan announces that the U.S. will support England in the dispute between Argentina and England (Falkland Islands).

September 29, 1982 - U.S. Marines again land in Beirut, Lebanon to help keep peace as part of a force composed also of Italian and French troops.

1983 - The U.S. Navy re-designates UDTs as Seal Teams and or Seal Delivery Vehicle Teams. All missions regarding hydrographic reconnaissance and underwater demolition operations will become SEAL operations.

April 18, 1983 - The American Embassy in Beirut, Lebanon sustains a deadly explosion (car bomb), thought to have been planted by Iranian extremists.

June 18-24, 1983 - The Space shuttle Challenger is launched. The crew includes Sally K. Ride, the initial woman astronaut to go into space.

August 30, 1983 - Americans (63) die when a South Korean jet carrying 269 people is downed by a Soviet fighter (claim that plane strayed into Soviet air space). The craft was trailed by the fighter for about two hours prior to the attack.

October 23, 1983 - Marines lose 237 killed and 80 wounded when a truck (with explosives) is detonated by terrorists at the Marine barracks in Beirut, Lebanon.

October 25, 1983 - "Operation Urgent Fury" - U.S. forces, including Marines, Army units and some troops from several Caribbean nations invade Granada at the request of neighboring states to rescue American college students and to prevent a Communist takeover. The operation ends successfully within several

days. One innovative soldier, unable to get air support uses a telephone credit card and calls the states to get help; air support arrives. The U.S. encountered resistance from the People's Revolutionary Army and Cuban armed forces. The commander, Hudson Austin (PRA) is seized by the 82nd A/B Division.
December 4, 1983 - Carrier-based planes attack Syrian antiaircraft positions to retaliate for firing at U.S. planes near Beirut. The U.S. loses two planes during the strike. One pilot is killed, the other is captured, and released (12/31/1983).
January 10, 1984 - The Reagan Administration reinitiates official diplomatic relations with the Vatican, after an interruption of more than 100 years.
February 21, 1984 - The U.S. Marine peacekeeping force initiates its withdrawal from Lebanon and completes the operation by 26 February.
August 30-September 5, 1984 - The space shuttle *Discovery* is launched.
August 9, 1985 - Arthur J. Walker (retired USN officer) is convicted of spying (part of spy organization led by his brother Warrant Officer John Walker). The group caused serious damage to the U.S. including the loss of U.S. Navy codes to the Russians. Consequently, the Russians were able to track U.S. ships.
October 3-7, 1985 - The space shuttle *Atlantis* is launched.
November 21, 1985 - Jonathan Pollard, accused of spying for Israel is arrested. He receives a life sentence. His wife receives a five-year sentence.
January 28, 1986 - The space shuttle *Challenger* explodes shortly after lift off. The crew is killed instantly and the tragedy is witnessed on live television. The crew: Michael J. Smith (pilot), Judy A Resnik, Ellison S. Onizuka, and Ronald E. McNair (Mission Specialists), Gregory B. Jarvis (Payload Specialist), Francis R. Scobee, Commander, and, Christa McAuliffe, a teacher from New Hampshire.
May 17, 1987 - The frigate USS *Stark* in the Persian Gulf is hit by an Iraqi missile. Thirty-seven crewmen are killed. Iraq says it was an accidental strike.
April 16, 1987 - The Naval Special Warfare Command is commissioned at the Naval Amphibious Base, Coronado, California.
February 17, 1988 - Lt. Colonel William R. (Rich) Higgins, USMC, is seized by Iranian terrorists in Lebanon while a U.S. senior advisor with the U.N. He is tortured and murdered (exact date of death unknown). He was promoted Colonel 3/1/1989. The world observed Higgins hanging by the neck on television about 2 years later. During December 1991, his body was dropped on a street in Beirut. He was declared dead on 6 July, 1990. The State Depart. handled the incident.
December 21, 1988 - Terrorists (Libyans) blow up a Pan Am Jet (Flight 107-259 people, including U.S. college students and military personnel heading home for Christmas) over Lockerbie, Scotland. Eleven others, on the ground are killed.
January 4, 1989 - U.S. fighters down 2 Libyan planes (Mediterranean Sea).
January 20, 1989 - George Herbert Bush is inaugurated as 41st President of U.S.
August 29, 1989 - U.S. spacecraft, Voyager II, passes Neptune (largest planet).
December 20, 1989 - U.S. forces invade Panama to oust Manuel Noriega. All resistance ends by 24 December. Noriega is brought back to the U.S. for trial after his surrender (Jan.20, 1990). He is convicted and sent to a U.S. prison.
August 2, 1990 - Iraq invades Kuwait. The U.S. and its allies retaliate.
January 17-February 27, 1991 (Gulf War) - The U.S. begins a massive air attack against Iraq. A ground invasion commences on 24 February. Iraq is overwhelmed and Kuwait is liberated within several days, as a cease fire is ordered on 27 February. Many nations join in this conflict against Saddam Hussein. While the enemy and the media await an amphibious landing, the Marines come in the back door, apparently reusing a trick from their invasion of Tinian in the Pacific during July 1944. Army and Marine Corps units bolstered by planes and armor, overwhelm the world's fourth largest army. The U.S. captures about 80,000 men. The U.S. loses less than 150 killed (combat), 147 non-combat and 467 wounded.
December 25, 1991 - The Soviet Union dissolves. In Moscow, a Russian republic is formed and President Mikhail Gorbachev, a Communist with an amicable smile, resigns. The fall of the Soviet Union occurs during the presidency of

George H. Bush, but pressure under the Reagan Administration (George H. Bush is Vice President) cracked the foundation of the Communist regime. Communists had ruled since the fall of the Czar (early part of the 20th Century-Bolshevik Revolution). It is an irony that the Bolsheviks who overthrew the Christian Czar (Nicholas II) and forced Christianity underground now observe Russia become a republic on Christmas Day, and soon after, they discover that Russia during the early part of the 21st Century includes God in its revised national anthem.

May 7-16, 1992 - The *Endeavor* (space shuttle)is launched.

December 9, 1992 - March 3, 1995 - A U.N.- U.S. force arrives in Somalia.

January 20, 1993 - Bill Clinton is inaugurated as 42nd President of the U.S. He becomes the 1st elected President to be impeached (acquitted by Senate) and the 2nd President to lose his law license. On the last full day of his 2nd term, Jan. 19, 2001, a plea bargain is reached with a Special Prosecutor; he agrees to a 5-year suspension of his law license (lying under oath in a deposition).

February 26, 1993 - Arab terrorists bomb the World Trade Center in New York City. Although it is thought that a foreign country was behind the incident, it is not proven; however, six suspects are arrested and convicted.

October 3, 1993 - During an assault to capture a warlord in Somalia, two helicopters crash. Two volunteers, Sergeants Gary Gordon and Randall Shughart receive the Medal of Honor posthumously for their actions to save wounded personnel. They expended all ammunition prior to being killed. Eighteen U.S. troops are killed by mobs. It is thought that Osama Bin Laden, a Saudi Moslem terrorist was instrumental in the terrorism.

Dec. 2-13, 1993- Space shuttle *Endeavor* repairs the Hubble Space Telescope.

February 21, 1994- Aldrich Ames (CIA agent) & his wife are arrested for spying.

April 14, 1994 - In Iraq, two U.S. planes operating within the no-fly zone mistake two U.S. Blackhawk helicopters (thought to be Russian-built Iraqi craft) as enemy aircraft; both are shot down with a loss of 26 U.S. troops.

July 11, 1994 - The Clinton administration announces that diplomatic relations with Vietnam were being reinitiated to the consternation of many veterans.

February 3-11, 1995 - Shuttle *Discovery* rendezvous with Russian space station.

March 31, 1995 - The U.S. hands responsibility for peacekeeping duty in Haiti to the United Nations. Slightly less than 2,500 U.S. troops remain in Haiti. These U.S. troops are often used for purposes other than military duties.

April 19, 1995 - The Federal Building in Oklahoma City, Oklahoma is blown up by an anti-government group. Two men, Timothy McVeigh and Terry Nichols are both convicted of the crime which included the deaths of 167 people including 19 children; 1 other dies during a rescue attempt. McVeigh is executed on 6/11/01.

June 8, 1995 - Marines rescue Captain Scott O'Grady, USAF, shot down (2nd) over Bosnia-Herzegovina (operation to oust the Slobodon Milosevik government).

June 27-July 7, 1995- The *Atlantis* shuttle links with Soviet space-station Mir.

December 1995 - A peace treaty is signed to cease the fighting in Boznia and Herzegovina. The Clinton administration commits peace keeping forces to the area. About 20,000 troops will be dispatched.

June 25, 1996 - A terrorist bomb explodes at a U.S. military complex (Khobar Towers) in Saudi Arabia; 19 troops die (Air Force).

August 31, 1996 - U.S. attacks Iraq's air defenses (retaliates for firing at planes).

January 23, 1997 - A former CIA agent, Harold Nicholson pleads guilty to the charge of spying against the U.S. for Russia.

July 4, 1997 - A U.S. spacecraft initiates its study of Mars.

August 7, 1998 - Terrorists' bombs explode at U.S. Embassies in Nairobi, Kenya and Dar es Salaam, Tanzania. The attack kills 202 Kenyans and 12 Americans in Nairobi and about 5,000 are injured. The high number of casualties in Nairobi resulted from the collapse of a building next to the embassy. The car bombing at about the same time in Dar es Salaam, Tanzania, kills eleven and wounds about 70. During October 2001, 4 terrorists receive life sentences.

December 16-19, 1998 - The Clinton Administration orders the bombing of targets in Iraq. Later it is discovered that the target suspected of manufacturing illegal arms was actually an aspirin factory. Clinton's impeachment occurs in the House (charges of perjury & obstructing justice) on 19 December. The House votes along party lines; the Senate later (Feb. 12, 1999) acquits him.

March 24, 1999 - Serbia comes under attack by NATO, allegedly to end Serbian atrocities against Albanians in Kosovo; however, the media reports about massive killings by the Serbs are never substantiated. Atrocities occurred on both sides.

October 12, 2000 - The USS *Cole* is attacked and severely damaged while refueling in Yemen at Aden harbor (seventeen killed and 39 wounded).

January 20, 2001 - Marc Rich (Reich), a billionaire fugitive (living in Sweden) from the U.S. for about 17 years (charges of trading with the enemy (Iran) while U.S. hostages were being held and for allegedly evading income taxes of about $50 million is pardoned by Bill Clinton during the final hours of his presidency. Rich had denounced his U.S. citizenship and holds Israeli and Spanish citizenship.

January 20, 2001 - George W. Bush is inaugurated 43rd President of the U.S.

February 16, 2001 - U.S. launches missiles against Baghdad, Iraq to eliminate facilities that received new anti-aircraft defenses that threaten U.S. planes.

April 1, 2001 - Two Chinese fighters intercept a U.S. reconnaissance plane in international waters off China. A Chinese plane accidentally strikes the U.S. plane damaging it and forcing it to land in Chinese territory. The crew is held and interrogated, but later released. The Bush administration refuses to apologize for the incident which clearly was the fault of the Chinese pilot.

May 16, 2001 - An FBI agent, Robert P. Hanssen is indicted on charges of spying for the Russians (more than 15 years). Some of the information passed to the Russians is thought to have caused the death of U.S. operatives in Russia. Hanssen agrees to cooperate with the government in exchange for a life sentence rather than the death penalty.

July 2001 - President Bush awards Congressional Gold Medals (not Medal of Honor) to 29 Navajo Indians (former Marines) for their creation of the Navajo Code (code) during WW II; only 4 of the original members remain alive.

September 11, 2001 - Muslim terrorists operating under Osama bin Laden hijack three commercial jets. Two of these crash into the World Towers skyscrapers in New York City and one crashes into the Pentagon in Virginia just outside Washington, D.C. One other plane en route to the West Coast is diverted towards Washington, but several male passengers attack the Muslim terrorists and thwart the hijackers causing a crash in Pennsylvania. All passengers and all nineteen Muslim terrorists are killed. However, more Muslim terrorists remain on the loose in the U.S. In addition, casualties on the ground skyrocket past three thousand. The deaths include many firemen and policemen who rushed into the buildings and were there when they collapsed. The figures available are: World Trade Center- 2,954; Pentagon- 189; American Air Lines Flight 11 and United Airlines Flight 175 (both hit World Towers), 92 and 65 respectively; American Airlines Flight 77 (Pentagon) 64 - included Barbara Olson, wife of the Solicitor General, Ted Olson; United Airlines Flight 93 (Western Pennsylvania) 44, included Todd Beamer who coined the phrase "Lets Roll," while talking to his wife on a cell phone as he and other passengers attacked the terrorists on the ill-fated plane.

September 2001 - President George W. Bush announces to the nation that the U.S. and its allies would eliminate terrorism in the world and that the attack against the U.S. by terrorists under Osama bin Laden(and whichever states support him) had declared war against the U.S. President Bush made it clear that the campaign to eliminate terrorists would be long-lasting. At the time, the Taliban are described by some (similarly to the Iraqi troops description) as fierce fighters who had defeated Russia (Soviet Union) and would destroy also the U.S. The Taliban initially threaten to teach Americans a lesson and later proclaim they will fight to the last man. They dare the U.S. to send in ground troops.

64

September 21, 2001 - A DOD employee, Ana B. Montes is arrested (charges of spying for Cuba. This follows arrest of 2 Cuban agents in Florida during August.
October 7, 2001 - The U.S., supported by Great Britain, launches an attack against the Taliban government of Afghanistan, which harbors Osama bin Laden. The strikes were carried out by U.S. Air Force, U.S. Naval forces and British naval forces. The air-attacks will continue and will be followed by ground forces. The Taliban under Mullah Mohammed Omar control about eighty percent of Afghanistan, opposed by the Northern Alliance and other Afghan tribes in southern Afghanistan. By mid-November, U.S. air power clears the path for opposition forces, leaving the Taliban with very little maneuverability and severe casualties. Kabul the capital is liberated.
October 23 - 2001 - A former USAF analyst, Brian P. Regan, is indicted on charges of spying.
November 13 2001 - Former President Clinton by direction of the U.S. Supreme Court is stricken from the role of attorneys permitted to practice at the Supreme Court. He recently requested to resign rather than argue disbarment or suspension.
November 13 2001 - Kabul, Afghanistan falls without a shot to the Northern Alliance. U.S. ground forces had been pinpointing enemy targets. Also, eight hostages including two female Americans (Dayna Curry and Heather Mercer) are taken from Kabul by the Taliban but they are rescued on 15 November.
October 19 2001 - Army Special Forces complete a raid into Afghanistan, the first large ground operation. Six troops are wounded. In related activity, two others are killed in Pakistan by a helicopter crash, not due to enemy action. Also, the troops leave the Taliban a photograph, the one exhibiting the New York firemen raising Old Glory at the site of the World Towers attack (Ground Zero).
October 20 2001 - Marines attached to the USS *Peleliu* reach Army Rangers after a helicopter crash in Pakistan. The chopper is recovered. Two Rangers, Kristofer Stonesifer and John J. Edmunds, are killed in the accident.
November 18 2001 - U.S. forces board a tanker to search for illegal cargo from Iraq. The vessel sinks in the Arabian Sea. Two U.S. Sailors, Petty Officer 3rd Class Benjamin Johnson and Petty Officer 1st Class Vincent Parker are lost.
November 25 2001 - U.S. Marines (attached to Task Force 58) establish "Camp Rhino" at an undisclosed airbase south of Kandahar.
November 26 2001 - Northern Alliance forces seize Kunduz, a Pashtun Taliban stronghold. Many Arabs, Chechens and Pakistanis are among the Taliban forces.
December 5 2001 - Three U.S. Soldiers, Sergeants Brian Cody, Jefferson Davis and Daniel Petithory are killed and six others wounded near Kandahar. These the first U.S. war casualties, occur due to a bomb that strikes too close to their front-line positions. In conjunction, a CIA officer, Mike Spann had been killed at Mazar-E-Sharif the previous week when POWs, still holding weapons, rioted.
December 5 2001 - Hamid Karzai is named interim leader of Afghanistan.
December 6 2001 - U.S. Naval forces continue to check vessels that might be transporting Al-Quada members to escape from Afghanistan.
December 12 2001 - Green Berets, attired in Afghanistan garb and complete with scrubby beards act as guides for U.S. Marines who enter Kabul to take control of the American embassy.
December 17 2001 - U.S. Marines (15th and 26th Marine Expeditionary Unit) who seized Kandahar International Airport of 14 December, this day raise two American Flags, the Stars and Stripes and the legendary Gadsden Rattlesnake flag. On 18 December, the Marines hoist the Stars and Stripes which flew over New York City after the terrorist attack. It is inscribed with the names of police and members of the armed forces killed during the attack on New York, the Pentagon in Virginia and the earlier attack against the USS Cole at Yemen where seventeen Sailors were killed in the explosion. In conjunction, three Marines were injured here by a mine on 16 December.

December 17 2001 - The U.S. reopens its embassy at Kabul (vacant since 1989). Its last ambassador, Adolph Dubs was killed (1979) when Afghan troops tried to rescue him from Muslim terrorists; it remained open, lacking an ambassador.

December 2001 - The war on terrorism, as described by President Bush continues and will for an undetermined time. The Taliban described as fearless fighters who would vanquish American troops felt the pernicious sting of U.S. air power and observed the skills of the U.S. Special Forces first hand. Following the fall of the last stronghold, Tora Bora, CIA officers, Special Forces and British Special Air Service troops search caves there for Al-Qaeda and Taliban leaders including Osama bin Laden. In conjunction, some small pockets of Taliban and Al-Qaeda fighters continue to resist at Tora Bora. During the offensive, the U.S. loses only one plane (mechanical difficulties), but the 4-man crew of the B-1, is rescued. Two sailors are lost at sea, after falling from their respective ships, but one is rescued. Sergeant Evander E. Andrews, USAF died on 10 October in a forklift accident. Several Marines are injured by a mine, several Soldiers are injured by a mine and In addition to the Marines in the region around Kandahar, the 10th Mountain Division is in Uzbekistan (former Soviet Union) and the 101st Airborne is in Pakistan. Also, the U.S. Third Army prepares to relocate to Kuwait.

December 2001 - In accordance with the objectives of the War on Terrorism, many countries have pledged to support the U.S., some with troops, others with intelligence. Great Britain has supplied planes and ground troops. Japan for the first time since World War II has sent several vessels to act as supply ships. The French have promised help, some troops arrive in Kabul. Turkey and Jordan have offered troops. In addition, some former Soviet Union countries and Russia are working closely with the U.S. giving intelligence and providing bases for U.S. troops and planes. Pakistan has provided bases and India is a cooperating partner. More than 100 countries are stating they are part of the coalition, but this is a U.S. action, not a UN action which eliminates UN interference and it prevents U.S. plans from being leaked to the enemy. President Bush has thanked various countries for their condolences and flowers. He also tells them that it is time to perform. He requests action, not words from those who claim to support the U.S.

December 20 2001 - President George W. Bush reports on Day 100 of the War on Terrorism. He reiterates, referring to the terrorists,"If you think you can hide, we'll come and find you and bring you to justice...we'll do much more to rid the world of terrorists and evil.

December - 2001 - In about 100 days, U.S. air-power and Special forces working with the opposition (Afghanistan ground troops) has shredded the Taliban and al-Qaeda. Initially, media critics and TV pundits proclaimed that the Taliban was fearless and would punish the U.S. as it had the Soviet Union (Russia) which had been bogged-down in Afghanistan for about ten years. General Tommy Franks, a Texan, the overall commander and Donald Rumsfeld, the Secretary of Defense, meanwhile, continued with their plans and silenced the critics.

December 24 2001 - U.S. Marines and Soldiers on the ground in Afghanistan and away from their families, improvise and decorate Christmas trees in honor of the Holy Day. Their counterparts, defending Saudi Arabia from Iraq, are forbidden from celebrating Christmas. Christianity is forbidden in Saudi Arabia.

March 1 2002 - The U.S. opens offensive against Taliban stronghold in eastern Afghanistan. Planes bombard the mountains followed by ground attack on the following day. On Saturday, 2 March, one Americans is killed during the fighting. During the third day of the operation helicopters come under enemy fire. During operation about seven U.S. troops are killed and more than thirty wounded. The offensive Operation Anaconda launched to eliminate resistance.

Notable Facts on the Flag and the Country

Pre-1775 -The American colonists displayed various flags to designate their respective colonies and included such items as pictures of anchors, beavers, pine trees and rattlesnakes. These flags often held mottoes such as: Appeal to Heaven, Don't Tread on Me, Hope and Liberty.

July 13, 1755 - French and Indian War - At the Battle of Great Meadows, the former site of Fort Necessity (Pennsylvania), George Washington, had been repeatedly struck, but not wounded. He later stated in a letter to his brother: "By the all-powerful dispensation of Providence, I have been protected beyond all human probability or expectation; for I had four bullets through my coat, and two horses shot under me, and escaped unhurt, although death was leveling my companions on every side of me." Doctor Craik, also at the battle, later relates that 15 years after the rout, an Indian Chief travels to the forks of the Kenhawa and Ohio Rivers in search of Washington. The Chief is of the belief that Washington has special protections. He claims that during the fighting he personally selected Washington as a target and with his rifle, fired at him no less than fifteen rounds and he had also instructed his braves to fire at Washington, but none could slay him. Continuing, the Chief states that he became convinced that "the Great Spirit protected the young hero" and he ceased firing at him. About one month after the battle, Reverend Samuel Davies, while speaking to a company of volunteers, stated: "I can not but hope Providence has hitherto preserved him in so signal a manner, for some importance to his country."

March 10, 1774- A New England Newspaper in Boston, the Massachusetts Spy, publishes a piece which is the first known public mention of the flag: "A ray of bright glory now beams from afar, Blest dawn of an empire to rise. The American now sparkles a star, Which shall shortly flame wide through the skies."

1774 - The Taunton flag appears (New England); the British Jack in the canton, combined with a color of solid red, with the words "Liberty and Union."

1775 - The colonists unfurl the Rattlesnake flag which displays a rattlesnake in a defensive posture prepared for attack in the middle of thirteen alternate red and white stripes inscribed with the words "Don't Tread on Me."

December 1775 - The Colonial fleet in the Delaware River which separates Pennsylvania from New Jersey hoists the Grand Union flag for the first time. This is the first Colonial flag that resembles the Stars and Stripes.

January 1776 - The Grand Union Flag (Congress' Colors) becomes the standard of the Continental Army.

March 17, 1776 - The British, encircled at Boston by U.S. troops and artillery, evacuate the city by sea. General George Washington takes the city without firing a shot. Ironically, unbeknownst to the British, every cannon lacks ammunition. Boston has two celebrations on this day, St. Patrick's Day and Evacuation Day.

1776 - Betsy Ross of Philadelphia makes the first American flag (legend).

June 28, 1776 - A British fleet attacks Charleston, South Carolina, defended by Colonel William Moultrie who flies the Moultrie flag (flying since 1775), which has a crescent on a blue field with the word Liberty stamped upon it in white.

July 4, 1776 - John Hancock, President of the Continental Congress, is the first to sign the Declaration of Independence. The other signatures (55) come later.

1776 -1777 - At this time, American vessels at sea were required to fly a national flag, or face disaster if intercepted by the English who considered armed vessels to be pirate vessels unless a national flag was flying. The American vessels often flew the flags of their respective colonies prior to the emergence of Stars and Stripes. Subsequently, the Second Continental Congress received the resolution (for the national flag) from the Maritime Committee. The resolution will be passed during 1777. The first Navy Stars and Stripes displayed the stars in a staggered formation (alternate lines of threes and twos (stars) on a blue field). The stars seem to form the x-shaped cross of St. Andrew and the cross of St. George.

January 3, 1777 - During the battle at Princeton, New Jersey, while the Americans are in retreat, George Washington races from the rear to rally the troops. As he reaches the point, the Yanks rally and prepare to fire, while the British also begin to fire. Washington, despite being directly in the middle of the crossfire is not hit. Washington had fought in the French and Indian War and led the army on the field during the Revolution and never received a wound.

June 14, 1777 - The Congressional Resolution: "Resolved that the flag of the United States be thirteen stripes, alternate red and white; that the union be thirteen stars, white in a blue field, representing a new constellation. The resolution does not specify the arrangement of the stars within the blue union; therefore, the designs varied between flags with some stars formed in a circle and others in rows, while other flags seemed to have the stars simply scattered about the union lacking any design or order. The description of the flag: "White for Purity and Innocence, Red for Hardiness and Valor and Blue for Vigilance, Perseverance and Justice," is legend not certain fact. Francis Hopkinson, a Congressman and signer of the Declaration of Independence is credited for designing the U.S. Flag, but according to records of Congress he was never compensated for his work. Some things never change. Congress fails to notify the Army of the law, nor does it provide funds. Consequently, army regiments must purchase the flags with their own funds.

August 3, 1777 - The story that the Stars and Stripes was first flown against an approaching enemy at Fort Schuyler (Stanwix), N.Y., is not fact, only legend.

September 18, 1777 - The Continental Congress abandons the Statehouse (later Independence Hall) and evacuates Philadelphia for Lancaster, Pennsylvania, the Bell, cast in England during 1753 for the Statehouse (Independence Hall) is transported to Allentown, Pennsylvania to prevent the British from acquiring it. The Bell, not yet known as the "Liberty Bell" is not taken for sentimental reasons, rather to prevent it from being melted down for British bullets. The Bell is concealed under the floorboards of the Zion Lutheran Church in Allentown.

May 8, 1779 - Congress authorizes the War Office seal; it becomes the primary design of the Army Flag: "A cannon in front of a drum with two drumsticks and below the cannon, three cannon balls. Also a mortar is on a trunion and below the mortar, two powder flasks. Also a Roman breastplate (center) over a jupon (leather jacket) and above the breastplate rises a plain sword with a pommel and guard supporting a Phrygin cap between an esponton (pike) and an organizational color on one side and a musket with fixed bayonet and the National color on the other side. Above is a rattlesnake; its mouth holds a scroll: "This we'll Defend."

September 23, 1779 - French ships supporting John Paul Jones offer little help in the fight against the *Serapis*. When the *Bonhomme Richard* is nearly out of action, the French vessel *Alliance* finally moves into the fight, but it intentionally fires at Jones' vessel and then returns to fire another broadside at the *Bonhomme Richard*. Despite the grueling beating Jones is taking and his disadvantage of having too many foreign crewmen, the few Yanks and Jones capture the *Serapis*, a 50-gun British warship. Following the victory, Jones moves into Holland en route to France from where he will depart for the U.S. to receive his new vessel, a double decker, promised by Congress; however, instead the ship is given to France. John Paul Jones lacks a vessel for the remainder of the war.

October 18, 1781 - General Washington chooses not to attend the surrender of the British at Yorktown, rather he delegates Colonel John Laurens whom the British embarrassed along with General Benjamin Lincoln earlier at Charleston,

South Carolina when the British demanded that the Americans march out with their colors cased and their drums forbidden to play a German or British march. Washington signs the surrender document and adds one item, "Done in the trenches of Yorktown," just before giving it to French representatives. At Yorktown, after the surrender of General Cornwallis at 1000 hours, 8,000 British troops march out, colors encased, with their band playing a tune, "The World Turned Upside Down."

June 20, 1782 - Congress approves a design (verbal) of the seal of the United States, ending a project that was initiated on July 4, 1776 by the Continental Congress. No seal of the design has ever been cut and a drawing of the seal was not provided until 1786. The seal, designed by William Barton, displays the American Bald Eagle holding a ribbon, with the words "E Pluribus Unum," in its mouth. Its talons clasp an olive branch to designate peace and a band of arrows to designate war on the left and right respectively. The opposite side of the seal contains an incomplete pyramid and an eye (of Providence) above the pyramid.

May 1, 1795 - The Stars and Stripes changes from 13 stars and 13 stripes to 15 stars and 15 stripes (addition of Vermont & Kentucky). The bill was signed by President Washington on 13 January, 1794, the 1st bill to receive his signature.

1795 - 1818 - On May 1, 1795, subsequent to the resolution by Congress regarding the addition of 2 stars and 2 stripes to the flag (for Vermont and Kentucky), the Stars and Stripes contained fifteen stars and fifteen stripes. The additional stripes seemed to create a problem when even more states might later join the Union. Captain Samuel Reid, USN, suggested that the flag be limited to thirteen stripes, signifying the original thirteen States and that only stars be added to the flag with the entrance of a new State. This suggestion, through the untiring efforts of Congressman Peter H. Wendover became law during 1818. The Senate passed the legislation on 31March. President James Monroe signed it (Establish Flag of the United States) into law on April 4, 1818. The stars are not assigned to a particular state, nor is there any fixed order for numbering the stars in the flag. No star is to be designated as representative of any particular state (states are collectively, not individually, represented by stars).

1798 - President John Adams signs a bill authorizing the Marine Corps Band. It debuts at the White House on 1 January, 1801 and performs at the inauguration of President Jefferson and at the inauguration of every succeeding President including the most recent inauguration, that of President George W. Bush during 2001. The Marine Corps Band ("President's Own") is the oldest active musical organization in the U.S. It was led for many years by John Philip Sousa.

December 29, 1812 - The USS *Constitution* defeats the HMS *Java* and earns the nickname, "*Old Ironsides.*" The *Constitution* remains on the rolls of the U.S. Navy as an active warship. It is manned by sailors wearing uniforms of the 1812 era. *Old Ironsides* is docked at Charlestown in Boston harbor.

August 19-25, 1814 - The British introduce a new mysterious weapon at Bladensburg, Maryland. It causes panic among the U.S. defenders when 2,600 British troops receive support from what seems to be rockets that zoom through the sky and explode. Most of the 6,000 troops (primarily green militia) retire towards Virginia. One battalion of Marines and a contingent of Sailors hold the line for about two hours, giving President and Mrs. Madison time to escape Washington. Madison actually witnesses the battle. The Marines and Sailors had not been fooled by the rockets; these bombs bursting in air had actually been fireworks. The British occupy Washington unopposed and they are driven out on the following day, but not by the army, rather a sudden storm.

September 12-14, 1814 - During the attack against Ft. McHenry (Baltimore), an attorney, Francis Scott Key, while aboard a British vessel negotiating the surrender of a prisoner, pens the Star Spangled Banner, apparently using the tune

of an old English song, "Anacreon in Heaven." The original manuscript remains obscure for about sixty years and sells for more than fifty thousand dollars. During 1931, by act of Congress it becomes the National Anthem. In conjunction, Key had persuaded the British to release the captive, Dr. William Beanes. Key was retained by the British navy overnight during the shelling of the fort (13th). The original Star Spangled Banner is preserved (Smithsonian Institute). The U.S. Flag flies 24-hours a day at the birthplace (marker stands there) of Key in Keymar, Maryland, Mount Olivet Cemetery at Key's grave site and also at Fort McHenry.
April 4, 1818 - Congress designates the U.S. Flag to remain 13-striped, with the addition of stars only for newly admitted states- "An Act To Establish the Flag of the United States: "Be it enacted, etc. that from and after the 4th Day of July next, the Flag of the United States be 13 horizontal stripes, alternate red and white; that the union have 20 stars, white in a blue field." "Be it further enacted that on the admission of every new state in the Union, one star be added to the union of the flag, and that such addition shall take effect on the Fourth of July next succeeding such admission."
March 17, 1824 - William Driver, an American sea captain receives a new flag as a gift from his mother and some friends and when it is hoisted to the mast on his ship he is questioned about what he thought about the new large flag (12 foot by 24 foot). He is said to have been in awe and responded: "God bless you. I'll call it Old Glory." The name stuck and later during the Civil War era, when the Confederates took Nashville, Tennessee (1860), it is said that much effort was put forth, to no avail, to get the flag. During 1862, the flag is brought out of hiding (the Union arrives); the original flag is in the Smithsonian Institute in Washington.
1864 - The plantation of Robert E. Lee and his wife Mary (great granddaughter of Martha Washington and daughter of George Washington Parke Custis), becomes Arlington National Cemetery. The Union occupied the ground opposite Washington D.C. on May 24, 1861. During 1921, an unknown U.S. soldier from World War I was entombed in Arlington. The inscription on the Tomb of the Unknown Soldier: "Here Rests In Honored Glory An American Soldier Known But To God." During 1932, the cemetery was opened to the public. During May 1958, two more unknown American troops were buried in the Tomb of the Unknown Soldier, one from World War II and the other from the Korean War. On 28 May, 1984), another unknown soldier (Vietnam War) was buried there. Because of DNA testing, the latter's identity was later discovered and identified as 1st Lt. Michael Blassie (St. Louis, Mo.), a pilot in the Air Force. The 3rd U.S. Infantry Regiment (Old Guard), the Army ceremonial unit since World War II, keeps a 24-hour vigil at the Tomb of the Unknown Soldier.
September 1862 - Stonewall's Jackson's Army enters Frederick, Maryland (pro-Union) and the troops encounter a 93-year old obstacle, a lady named Barbara Fritchie who refuses to take down Old Glory. She defies the Confederates despite a "supposed threat" to shoot her: "Fire at this old head then boys, it is not more venerable than your flag." Barbara Fritchie is unharmed as the troops pass.
October 28, 1886 - President Grover Cleveland accepts the Statue of Liberty from France (honors French alliance with the U.S. during American Revolution.
1892 - Francis Bellamy, a minister and Mason wrote the "Pledge of Allegiance" in honor of the 400th anniversary of the discovery of America by Columbus during 1492. Soon after it was penned, the pledge was being spread throughout the country in the schools. The original pledge: "I pledge allegiance to my flag and to the republic for which it stands, one nation indivisible with Liberty and Justice for all. During 1923, the words "my flag" were changed to "the flag of the United States of America." Later, President Eisenhower signs another modification, adding of the words "under God" into law during 1954. Bellamy persuaded President Benjamin Harrison to fly the flag at every school. Harrison, elected 100

years after Washington, is also responsible for the flag flying from every Federal Building. The pledge is recited for the 1st time on Columbus Day (1892) in schools across the nation and it is recognized by Congress during 1942.

March 18, 1896 - The Department of War issued an order to standardize the arrangement of the stars in the union of the flag. Although the flag laws had mandated white stars, the army had been using silver stars and after the Civil War it had used gold stars. The army utilized 5-pointed and 6-pointed stars in no particular formation. The order: "The field or union of the National Flag in use in the Army will on and after July 4, 1896, consist of forty-five stars in six rows, the first, third and fifth rows to have eight stars, and the second, fourth, and sixth rows, seven stars each, in a blue field." The order was signed by the Secretary of War, David S. Lamont. After this order, all army units carry an identical U.S. flag. The U.S. Army flag is white embroidered in blue, a replica of the official seal of the War Office. The words United States Army implanted in a scroll are located under the seal and below that, the year 1775 (Army established) is inscribed.

December 7, 1941 - The Japanese attack Pearl Harbor, Hawaii. The U.S. Flag flying over the harbor will fly over the capital on August 14, 1945 while the Japanese accept the "unconditional surrender" mandated by the U.S. The U.S. Flag flying over the capitol on 8 December, the date of declaring war against Japan and on 11 December, when war was declared against Germany and **Italy,** will be flown over the cities of Rome, Italy, Berlin, Germany and Tokyo, Japan.

April 3-9, 1942 - Fall of Bataan and the Bataan Death March - About 78,000 U.S. and Philippine troops under Gen. Ernest King surrender under a white flag, but about 2,000 escape to Corregidor. The Japanese march the POWs about 80 miles in torrid weather from Balanga to San Fernando and many of those who fall along the road are bayoneted and beaten; thousands die en route. Those who escape to Corregidor join General Wainwright; but it too falls. When General MacArthur returns, he visits Bataan. While at the spot where the Japanese ripped down Old Glory, MacArthur states: "I see the old flag staff still stands. Have your troops hoist the Colors to its peak and let no enemy ever haul them down."

February 23, 1945 - Marines and one Navy Corpsman raise the Stars and Stripes on Mt. Suribachi, Iwo Jima. At 1031, the cry goes out: "There goes the Flag!" The photograph of AP photographer, Joe Rosenthal captures the moment; however, the first flag-raising was already completed. The Marine Regiment, concerned it would lose its ceremonial flag sent up a larger replacement. The picture was of the second raising. Meanwhile, a Marine photographer Pvt. Robert Campbell (killed several days later) and Sgt. William Genaust also captured the identical scene, but the A.P. published its photo. The movie film that captured the moment was filmed by Genaust, and for decades it was shown on TV without credit to Genaust.

May 5, 1945 - The Holbrook-Patton flag - CCA, 11th Armored Division under General Willard Holbrook reaches the Danube opposite Linz, Austria. TF Wingard after taking Urfahr-Linz Industrial center at 1100, takes Linz at 1800. Linz offers to surrender, but Holbrook goes in first with only two troops and discovers white sheets flying from nearly every window. Soon after, Holbrook orders the Stars and Stripes hoisted. Later, upon the death of General George S. Patton, during December, 1945, a search is unleashed to find the Stars and Stripes that had penetrated to the furthermost eastern point. The flag that flew at Linz was retrieved and used on the casket of General Patton. Coincidentally, Joanne, the daughter of General Holbrook would later meet and marry the son of Patton, also named George S. Patton (later Major General). The original flag was later discovered with the documents that unveiled the unknown story of its travels. That same flag was used at the funeral of General Holbrook when he was buried at West Point (July 1986). It was also borrowed by the city of Linz for their 50-year celebration; it is now back at the Patton Museum (Ft. Knox).

71

August 3, 1949 - Congress passes a Joint Resolution establishing 14 June as Flag Day. President Truman signs it. "That the 14th of June of each year is hereby designated as Flag Day and the President of the U. S. is authorized and requested to issue annually a proclamation calling upon all officials of the Government to display the Flag of the U. S. on all Government buildings on such day as an anniversary of the adoption on June 14, 1777, by the Continental Congress of the U. S. of the Stars and Stripes as the official Flag of the U.S. of America."

1958 - Congress passes Public Law 529 designating May 1, as Loyalty Day. The Veterans of Foreign Wars have pushed this legislation for years. A similar bill failed in the Senate (1954), but another passed (1955) that merely designated May 1, as Loyalty Day, which coincides with the Communists' May Day.

1974 - The mayor of Cambridge, Massachusetts requests troops from General George S. Patton's command to reenact George Washington's commission ceremony. Patton offers Green Berets; the mayor refuses, but later agrees. At the ceremony, a hippie calls a Green Beret Sgt. Major (in formation) a "Baby Killer" and pushes a flower in his face. With Patton's permission, the soldier speaks just a few words. The hippie hurriedly vanishes; the ceremony continues uninterrupted.

Notable Quotes on Flag and Country

1774 - Thomas Jefferson: "The God who gave us life, gave us liberty at the same time."

March 23, 1775 - Patrick Henry - "...I know not what course others may take, but for me, give me liberty or give me death."

April 19, 1775 - John Parker, the American commander at Lexington: "Don't fire unless fired upon, but if they mean to have a war, then let it begin here."

June 1775 - American Colonel William Prescott at Bunker Hill: "Don't fire till you see the whites of their eyes." After the battle, General Nathaniel Greene states: "I wish I could sell them (British) another hill at the same price."

July 1775 - Thomas Paine "...From the east to the west blow the trumpet to arms! Through the land let the sound of it flee. Let the far and the near all unite with a cheer, in defence of our Liberty Tree."

January 9, 1776 - Thomas Paine: "Society in every state is a blessing, but government even in its best state, is but a necessary evil; in its worst state, an intolerable one."

1776 - John Hancock: "We must all hang together." Ben Franklin responds: "We must all hang together or most assuredly we shall each hang separately."

July 4, 1776 - John Hancock, after he made his conspicuous mark to sign the Declaration of Independence: "King George can read that without his glasses."

1776 - It is reported that George Washington, upon seeing the Stars and Stripes flown by the Continental Army for the first time, described it as: "We take the stars from heaven, the red from our mother country, separating it by white stripes, thus showing that we have separated from her, and the white stripes shall go down to posterity representing liberty." This is legend, rather than a proven fact.

September 22, 1776 - Captain Nathan Hale is hanged by the British as a spy. He states: "I regret that I have but one life to give for my country."

Spring 1777 - An English newspaper, after a visit by the USS *Lexington* to the Irish Sea, reports: "The coast of England has been insulted by the Yankees."

1777 - John Paul Jones: " That flag and I are twins, born in the same hour from the same womb of destiny. We cannot be parted in life or death. So long as we can float, we shall float together. If we must sink, we shall go down as one"; This is legend, rather than a proven fact.

August 16, 1777 - Battle of Bennington (Vermont) - General John Stark:"There my boys are your enemies, Redcoats & Tories. You must beat them or Molly

Stark is a widow tonight "

September 1780 - British Major Patrick Ferguson, commanding officer of Loyalists in the Carolinas sends an ultimatum to American Colonel Isaac Selby: "That if they (Americans) did not desist to the opposition to the British arms, he (Ferguson) would march his army over the mountains, hang their leaders, and lay their country to waste with fire and sword."

January 30, 1787 - Thomas Jefferson: "I hold that a little rebellion now and then is a good thing, and as necessary in the political world as storms in the physical."

January 8, 1790 - George Washington in his first annual address to Congress: "To be prepared for war is one of the most effectual means of preserving peace."

October 1797 - Charles Cotesworth Pinckney: "Millions for defence, but not one penny for tribute."

Dec. 1799 - Gen. Henry "Light Horse" Lee (Robert E. Lee's father) eulogizes George Washington: "First in war, first in peace, first in the hearts of his countrymen...He was second to none in the humble and endearing scenes of private life."

October 1780 - British Major Ferguson, upon hearing the patriot mountain men were approaching Gilbert Town, abandons it and moves to King's Mountain after issuing this message for his loyalist North Carolinians: "Run to camp to save themselves from the back-water men...A set of mongrels."

September 1800 - Thomas Jefferson: "I have sworn upon the altar of God, eternal hostility against every form of tyranny over the mind of man."

August 1, 1801 - During the hostilities with Tripoli, Lt. Andrew Sterett, USN aboard the *Intrepid* in a letter to Commodore Richard Dale: "Sir, I have the honor to inform you that...I fell in with a Tripopolitan ship of war called the *Tripoli*, as action commenced within pistol shot, which continued three hours incessantly. She then struck her colors, having 30 men killed and 30 wounded ...we have not a man wounded and we have sustained no material damage."

February 16, 1804 - Lt. Stephen Decatur, USN who led the raid to recapture the USS *Philadelphia* in Tripoli harbor: "My country right or wrong."

1807 - Thomas Jefferson: "When a man assumes a public trust, he should consider himself as public property."

August 19, 1812 - After the USS *Constitution* defeats the HMS *Guerriere* off Nova Scotia, British captain Dacres (had boasted he could "beat any U.S. warship in fifteen minutes of fighting," offers his sword to Captain Isaac Hull. He declines Dacres' sword and states: "But I'll trouble you sir, for that hat."

June 1, 1813 - Captain James Lawrence (mortally wounded), during the sea battle between the USS *Chesapeake* and the HMS *Shannon*: "Tell the men to fire faster and not to give up the ship. Fight her till she sinks." His words, "Don't give up the ship" become the motto of the U.S. Navy.

Summer 1813 - Major George Armistead in a letter to Sam Smith: "We sir, are ready at Fort McHenry to defend Baltimore against invading by the enemy, and it is my desire to have a flag so large, that the British will have no difficulty seeing it from a distance." Shortly thereafter, his request is fulfilled. Mrs. Mary Pickersgill of Baltimore and her daughter, Caroline Purdy create a huge Stars and Stripes that measures 42' long by 30' high with stripes of 2' each and stars that measure 2' from point-to-point. At the time, the flag consisted of 15 stars and 15 stripes. The extra stripes modify the color of the formation as the stripe immediately under the union is red. When the flag later returns to 13 stripes during 1818, a white stripe will again be immediately under the union.

September 1813 - Admiral Oliver H. Perry in a letter to General William Harrison after the Battle of Lake Erie: "We have met the enemy and they are ours."

Sept. 12, 1814 - British General Robert Ross (battle for Baltimore): "He would eat dinner tonight at Baltimore or in Hell." He did not dine in Baltimore.

September 25, 1814 - Captain Samuel Reid, aboard the privateer *Armstrong* rejects a British ultimatum to surrender (Azores) and responds: "Surrender Hell."

September 1814 - Reverend John Gruber: "May the Lord bless King George, convert him and take him to heaven as we want no more of him."

December 1814 - General Andrew Jackson when unformed in New Orleans of approaching British troops: "By the eternal, they shall not sleep on our soil."

1820 - Marine Commandant, Archibald Henderson: "Take care to be right, and then they are powerless."

February 1847 - General Zachary Taylor's response to a surrender demand by Santa Anna at Buena Vista: "Tell Santa Anna to go to hell. Put it in Spanish and send it back by this Dutchman."

June 1858 - Abraham Lincoln: "I believe this government cannot endure permanently, half slave and half free."

March 4, 1861 - Abraham Lincoln: "No state on its own mere action can get out of the Union, thus if war is to come, it will come over secession, not slavery."

April 1861 - General William T. Sherman: " I thought and may have said, the national crisis has been brought about by the politicians, and as it was upon us, they might fight it out."

April 1861 - Jefferson Davis: " We protest solemnly in the face of mankind, that we desire peace at any sacrifice, save that of honor and independence."

April 20, 1861 - Robert E. Lee: "Save in the defence of my native state (Virginia), I never desire again to draw my sword."

November 19, 1863 - President Abraham Lincoln while reading his Gettysburg Address: "The world will little note, nor long remember what we say here today."

March 1864 - President Lincoln after promoting U.S. Grant to Commander-in-Chief: "...As the country here intrusts you, so under God, it will sustain you."

July 1864 - General William T. Sherman on political promotions in the army: "If the rear be the post of honor, then we had better all change front on Washington."

August 5, 1864 - Commodore David Farragut at the battle of Mobile: "Damn the torpedoes. Full speed ahead." Farragut is also known for this quote: "I would see every man of you damned before I would raise my hand against that Flag."

Dec. 1864 -General John Dix's order (Treasury Department at New Orleans): "If anyone attempts to haul down the American flag, shoot him on the spot."

May 24, 1865 - General Sherman later remarks about his army on this day: "The column was compact and the glittering muskets looked like a solid mass of steel, moving with the regularity of a pendulum. The sight was simply magnificent. Sixty-five thousand men of the Army of the West, marched in precision, past the White House. The National Flag, our Stars and Stripes was flying from nearly every building in the capital during the parade."

1885 - A reporter, Richard H. Harris, reported on Marines landing in Panama City, Panama: "The Marines have landed and have the situation well in hand."

June 1918 - A U.S. Marine Officer responds to a French officer (after being told to retreat with the French as the Germans were approaching): "Retreat Hell, we just got here." The Germans afterwards, dub the Marines "Devil Dogs."

September 1918 - George S. Patton (later General), while in France: "...You must establish the fact that American tanks do not surrender."

May 1933 - President Franklin D. Roosevelt: "Let me assert that the only thing we (Americans) have to fear is fear itself."

July 27, 1941 - General Douglas MacArthur (Philippines): "...The soldier above all men is required to perform the highest act of religious teaching...sacrifice. In battle and in the face of danger and death, he discloses those Divine attributes which his Master gave when He created man in His own image. However horrible the incidents of war may be, the soldier who is called upon to offer and to give his life for his country is the noblest development of mankind."

April 1942 - A Japanese naval officer informs his captain: "Two of our beautiful carriers ahead sir." Captain: "They're beautiful, but they are not ours."

May 1942 - General Joseph Stilwell after departing Burma: " ...We (Americans) got run out of Burma and it is humiliating as Hell. I think we ought to find out what caused it and go back and take it..."What a hell of a way to fight a war! This is probably the first time in history that an American general has gone into combat without a single American combat soldier. How do you win a war without troops?"

August 1942 - Japanese radio after the U.S. loss of Guam and Guadalcanal invasion: "At this rate of advance, America won't recover its lost territory for perhaps two hundred years." A later broadcast: "We will sell you (Americans) land at 1,000 lives an acre. For such a price we will be willing to sell you one million square miles."

August 1942 - Marine Colonel Leroy Hunt prior to invasion of Guadalcanal: "Our country expects nothing but victory from us and it shall have just that. The word failure should not even be considered as a word in our vocabulary."

November 11, 1942 - General Patton in a letter to his wife (surrender of the Vichy French North Africa):"I had a guard of honor; no use kicking a man when he is down."

1942 - General MacArthur (Father of the Year for 1942) notes: "...A soldier destroys in order to build, a father only builds, never destroys. It is my hope that my son, when I am gone, will remember me not from the battle, but in the home, repeating with him our simple daily prayer, 'Our Father who art in Heaven...'"

March 13, 1943 - General George S. Patton's orders (regarding enemy) to the 1st Division in Tunisia: "Find them. Attack Them. Destroy them."

April 18, 1943 - Admiral Bill Halsey after hearing that Japanese Admiral Yamamoto's plane had been downed by the U.S. 339th Fighter Squadron: "I have in mind the nuns they caught on Guadalcanal and raped for 48 hours before cutting their throats; and the two Marines whom they vivesected; and the young girl on New Guinea whom they forced to watch her parents being beheaded, before her turn came; and the execution of Colonel Doolittle's pilots; and the Marine pilot in a parachute whose feet were cut off by the propellor of a Zeke (plane)."

June 1943 - General George S. Patton, speaking to the 45th Division: "All men are afraid in battle. The coward is the one who lets his fear overcome his duty."

June 13, 1943 - General Patton, informed by the King of England (visiting in North Africa) that General Alexander had said: "That the American soldiers would soon be the best soldiers in the world. Patton responds: "I do not like to disagree with General Alexander, but at present, the American soldiers are the best soldiers in the world and will take on any soldier of any country at any time."

July 1943 - A retrieved letter taken from a deceased German soldier (Sicily) and given to General Omar Bradley: "These astonishing Americans, they fight all day, attack all night and shoot all the time."

July 20, 1943 - General Omar Bradley's force takes Enna, Sicily, which had been bypassed by the British Eighth Army (Canadian troops). Colonel Benjamin Dickson quips to Bradley: "Not bad, not bad at all. It took the Saracens twenty years in their siege of Enna. Our boys did it in five hours." On the following day, British Broadcasting reports around the world that the British Eighth Army took Enna; however there were no British troops in the region.

August 10, 1943 - Germans are ordered to evacuate Sicily. General George Patton continues to advance to beat General Montgomery to Messina. The British press has been hard on the U.S. It has recently reported around the world that: "The going on the 7th Army front has been so easy that the troops were eating grapes and swimming while the (British) Eighth Army is fighting hard against German opposition." Also, Montgomery is unable to advance at Maletto.

November 20, 1943 - "The Japanese Commander, Admiral Shibasaki recently boasted about Tarawa-Makin: "The Americans couldn't take Betio with a million men in a million years." On this day, the Marines storm Tarawa and the Army invades Makin. By the 23rd, the Stars and Stripes prevails.

January 1944 - General (later President) Dwight D. Eisenhower regarding Operation Overlord-Normandy Invasion: "An aroused democracy is the most formidable fighting machine that can be devised."

January 1944 - An U.S. officer, Major Jordan (Lend-Lease) regarding Russian shipments out of U.S. without checks: "The Russians could have shipped the capitol dome to Moscow without us (U.S.) ever knowing what was in the boxes."

June 1944 - General George C. Marshall while in England at a conference: "You (English) have three Commanders in Chief; none of them will fight (Burma). We have one man (General Stilwell) who wants to fight and you want him taken out."

August 13, 1944 - General Eisenhower's order to the allied commands: "I request every airman to make it his direct responsibility that the enemy is blasted unceasingly by day and night and is denied safety either in fight or in flight. I request every sailor to make sure that no part of the hostile force can either escape or be reinforced by sea. I request of every soldier to go forward...Let no foot of ground once gained be relinquished nor a single German soldier escape through a line once established."

October 20, 1944 - Admiral William Halsey in a report to Admiral Chester Nimitz following a Japanese report about the sinking of all of Admiral Marc Mitscher's carriers: "All Third Fleet ships reported by Tokyo radio as sunk have been salvaged and are retiring in the direction of the enemy."

December 22, 1944 - General Anthony Clement McAuliffe's (101st Airborne) response to German ultimatum to surrender at Bastogne: "Nuts." The German siege is dissolved by Patton's 3rd Army the day after Christmas (26th).

March 24, 1945 - General George S. Patton to General Omar Bradley about crossing the Rhine River: "Brad, tell the world we're across...I want the world to know 3rd Army made it before Monty (General Montgomery) starts across."

April 15, 1945 - Captain Julian Becton, USS *Laffey* during a severe kamikaze attack (struck repeatedly and heavily damaged): "I'll never abandon ship as long as a gun will fire." She is still afloat at Patriots Point, near Charleston, S.C.

August 15, 1945 - Admiral William Halsey: "I hope that it (the world) will remember also that when hostilities ended, the capital of the Japanese Empire had just been bombed, strafed and rocketed by planes of the Third Fleet, and was about to be bombed, strafed and rocketed again (in-flight mission aborted at news). Last, I hope it will be remember that seven of the men on Strike Able 1, did not return." "I hope no nation ever dares challenge this record, but if it does, I hope the Third Fleet is there to defend it."

August 19, 1945 - A Japanese Lieutenant speaking to U.S. POWs in Manchuria: "By order of the Emperor (Hirohito), the war has been amicably terminated."

1945 - General Jonathan Wainwright, captured during the fall of the Philippines, and speaking subsequent to his captivity under the Japanese: "My men and I were the victims of shortsightedness at home and blind trust in the respectability of scheming aggressors. Terrible as was the ordeal of captivity, I often feel that we were spared, chiefly to warn against an infinitely more terrible fate. The price of unpreparedness for a World War III would be death to the millions of us and the disappearance from the earth of its greatest nation."

1945 - Father Joseph Morley, Catholic chaplain, 40th Division (subsequent to the close of hostilities while reflecting on his service as chaplain): "God, Liberty and Country are certainly worthy of defense."

Post World War II - Admiral William Halsey: "Peacetime security lies with the State Department, not the army and navy. It should be made to bear it in the open....Neither the army or navy ever started a war."

Post W. W. II - General Matthew Ridgway, Supreme Commander, Allied

Forces, Mediterranean: "During that particular tour of duty I had the unhappy responsibility of tearing down a great military establishment...The cry of bring the boys home was ringing from the U.S...and we were plunging headlong into the shameful demobilization of one of the greatest military organizations the world has ever seen. The magnificent U.S. Army that had done its full share in beating down the German, Italian and Japanese Armies to their knees."

April 15th 1947 - President Truman makes his views known concerning the emerging Communist arrogance of power. During a speech (Thomas Jefferson dinner): "We must take a positive stand. It is no longer enough merely to say we don't want war. We must act in time-ahead of time-to stamp out the smoldering beginnings of any conflict that may threaten to spread over the world..."

April 6, 1948 - President Harry S Truman regarding Germany: "The first year after the war, the British and Americans made every effort to make a joint control succeed. The Russians, however, with a good assist from the French, defeated these efforts."

July 1950 - General Walton Walker, while attempting to hold the Pusan line in Korea issues this order: "Stand and fight or die."

April 19, 1951-General Douglas MacArthur's Farewell Speech to Congress: "...The world has turned over many times since I took the oath on the plain at West Point, and the hopes and dreams have long since vanished, but I still remember the refrain of one of the most popular barracks' ballads of that day which proclaimed most proudly that old soldiers never die; they just fade away. And like the old soldier of that ballad, I now close my military career and just fade away, an old soldier who tried to do his duty as God gave him the light to see that duty. Good-by."

June 1963 President John F. Kennedy while speaking in Germany at the wall (constructed by the Communists) separating East and West Berlin: "Freedom has many difficulties and democracy is not perfect, but we have never had to put a wall up to keep our people in to prevent them from leaving us."

August 5, 1964 - President Lyndon B. Johnson addressing Congress "...Our policy in southeast Asia has been consistent and unchanged since 1954. I summarized it on June 2 in four simple propositions.-(1) America keeps her word. Here as elsewhere, we must and shall keep our committment.(2) The issue is the history of southeast Asia as a whole. A threat to any nation in that area is a threat to all and a threat to us. Our purpose is peace. (3) We have no military, political or territorial ambitions in the area. This is not just a jungle war, but a struggle for freedom on every front of human activity. (4) Our military and economic help to South Vietnam and Laos in particular has the purpose of helping these countries to repel aggression and strengthen their independence..."

January 1981 - President Ronald Reagan during his first Inaugural speech: "No arsenal or no weapon in the arsenals of the world is so formidable as the will and moral courage of free men and women."

1982 - President Ronald Reagan at the British Parliament: "It is the Soviet Union that runs against the tide of history...(It is) the march of freedom and democracy which will leave Marxism-Leninism on the ash heap of history, as it has left other tyrannies which stifle the freedom and muzzle the self-expression of the people."

June 6 1984 - President Ronald Reagan at Normandy France:"The men of Normandy had faith that what they were doing was right, faith that they fought for all humanity, faith that a just God would grant them mercy on this beachhead or the next. It was the deep knowledge–and pray God we have not lost it–that there is a profound moral difference between the use of force for liberation and the use of force for conquest."

September 25, 1987 - President Ronald Reagan: "How do you tell a Communist? Well, it's someone who reads Marx and Lenin. And how do you tell an anti-Communist? It's someone who understands Marx and Lenin."

1987 - President Reagan at the Berlin Wall in Germany: "Mr. Gorbachev, open this gate! Mr. Gorbachev, tear down this wall." The Berlin Wall began to come down on November 11, 1989 and on the following day, the Wall was opened at the Potsdamer Platz. Before Christmas (22nd), the Brandenberg Gate was opened.
January 1989 - President George Herbert Walker Bush (Inaugural Address): "...And my first act as President is a prayer. I ask you to bow your heads. Heavenly Father we bow our heads and ask You for Your love. Accept our thanks for the peace that yields this day and the shared faith that makes its continuance likely."
October 15, 1997 - President William Jefferson Blythe Clinton (University of Connecticut speech): - "...The road to tyranny, we must remember, begins with the destruction of the truth."
January 2001 - President George W. Bush (Inaugural Address) - "...The enemies of liberty and our country should make no mistake: America remains in the world by history and by choice, shaping a balance of power that favors freedom. We will defend our allies and our interests. We will show purpose without arrogance. We will meet aggression and bad faith with resolve and strength..." In conjunction, during September of this year, the President's words are tested by a terrorist attack.
September 20, 2001- Excerpt from President George W. Bush's Address to Congress regarding the terrorist attack against the U.S. that included the destruction of the World Trade Towers in New York and the Pentagon in Virginia as he declares war against terrorism around the world: "...And I will carry this. It is the police shield of a man named George Howard, who died at the World Trade Center trying to save others. It was given to me by his mom, Arlene, as a proud memorial to her son. This is my reminder of lives that ended, and a task that does not end. I will not forget this wound to our country, or those who inflicted it. I will not yield. I will not rest. I will not relent in waging this struggle for the freedom and security of the American people. The course of this conflict is not known, yet its outcome is certain. Freedom and fear, justice and cruelty, have always been at war, and we know that God is not neutral between them. Fellow citizens, we will meet violence with patient justice assured of the rightness of our cause, and confident of the victories to come. In all that lies before us, may God grant us wisdom, and may He watch over the United States of America.

Declaration of Independence

When in the Course of human events, it becomes necessary for one people to dissolve the political bands which have connected them with another, and to assume among the Powers of the earth, the separate and equal station to which the Laws of Nature and of Nature's God entitle them, a decent respect to the opinions of mankind requires that they should declare the causes which impel them to the separation.

We hold these truths to be self-evident, that all men are created equal, that they are endowed by their Creator with certain unalienable Rights, that among these are Life, Liberty, and the pursuit of Happiness. That to secure these rights, Governments are instituted among Men, deriving their just powers from the consent of the governed. That whenever any Form of Government becomes destructive of these ends, it is the Right of the People to alter or to abolish it, and to institute new Government, having its foundation on such principles and organizing its powers in such form, as to them shall seem most likely to effect their Safety and Happiness. Prudence, indeed, will dictate that Governments long established should not be changed for light and transient causes; and accordingly all experience hath shown that mankind are more disposed to suffer, while evils are sufferable, than to right themselves by abolishing the forms to which they are accustomed. But when a long train of abuses and usurpations pursuing invariably the same Object evinces a design to reduce them under absolute Despotism, it is their right, it is their duty, to throw off such Government, and to provide new Guards for their future security. Such has been the patient suffrance of these Colonies; and such is now the necessity which constrains them to alter their former Systems of Government. The history of the present King of Great Britain is a history of repeated injuries and usurpations, all having in direct object the establishment of an absolute Tyranny over these States. To prove this, let Facts be submitted to a candid world.

He has refused his Assent to Laws, the most wholesome and necessary for the public good.

He has forbidden his Governors to pass laws of immediate and pressing importance, unless suspended in their operation till his Assent should be obtained; and when so suspended, has utterly neglected to attend to them.

He has refused to pass other Laws for the accommodation of large districts of people, unless those people would relinquish the right of Representation in the Legislature, a right inestimable to them and formidable to tyrants only.

He has called together legislative bodies at places unusual, uncomfortable, and distant from the depository of their Public Records, for the sole purpose of fatiguing them into compliance with his measures.

He has dissolved Representative Houses repeatedly, for opposing with manly firmness his invasions on the rights of the people.

He has refused for a long time, after such dissolutions, to cause others to be elected; whereby the Legislative Powers, incapable of Annihilation, have returned to the People at large for their exercise; the State remaining in the meantime exposed to all the dangers of invasion from without, and convulsions within.

He has endeavored to prevent the population of these States; for that purpose obstructing the Laws for Naturalization of Foreigners; refusing to pass others to encourage their migration hither, and raising the conditions of new Appropriations of Lands.

He has obstructed the Administration of Justice, by refusing his Assent to Laws for establishing Judiciary Powers.

He has made Judges dependent on his Will alone, for the tenure of their offices, and the amount and payment of their salaries.

He has erected a multitude of New Offices, and sent hither swarms of Officers to harass our people, and eat out their substance.

He has kept among us, in times of peace, Standing Armies without the Consent of our legislatures.

He has affected to render the military independent of and superior to the Civil Power.

He has combined with others to subject us to a jurisdiction foreign to our constitution, and unacknowledged by our laws; giving his Assent to their acts of pretended legislation.

For quartering large bodies of armed troops among us:

For protecting them, by a mock Trial, from Punishment for any Murders which they should commit on the Inhabitants of these States:

For cutting off our Trade with all parts of the world:

For imposing taxes on us without our Consent:

For depriving us in many cases, of the benefits of Trial by Jury:

For transporting us beyond Seas to be tried for pretended offenses:

For abolishing the free System of English Laws in a neighboring Province, establishing therein an Arbitrary government, and enlarging its Boundaries so as to render it at once an example and fit instrument for introducing the same absolute rule into these Colonies:

For taking away our Charters, abolishing our most valuable Laws, and altering fundamentally, the Forms of our Governments:

For suspending our own Legislatures, and declaring themselves invested with Power to legislate for us in all cases whatsoever:

He has abdicated Government here, by declaring us out of his Protection and waging War against us.

He has plundered our seas, ravaged our Coasts, burnt our towns, and destroyed the lives of our people.

He is at this time transporting large armies of foreign mercenaries to complete the works of death, desolation and tyranny, already begun with circumstances of Cruelty & perfidy scarcely paralleled in the most barbarous ages, and totally unworthy the Head of a civilized nation.

He has constrained our fellow Citizen taken Captive on the high Seas to bear Arms against their Country, to become the executioners of their friends and Brethren, or to fall themselves by their Hands.

He has excited domestic insurrections amongst us, and has endeavored to bring on the inhabitants of our frontiers, the merciless Indian Savages, whose known rule of warfare, is an undistinguished destruction of all ages, sexes and conditions.

In every stage of these Oppressions We have Petitioned for Redress in the most humble terms: Our repeated Petitions have been answered only by repeated injury. A Prince, whose character is thus marked by every act which may define a Tyrant, is unfit to be the ruler of a free people.

Nor have We been wanting in attention to our British brethren. We have warned them from time to time of attempts by their legislature to extend an unwarrantable jurisdiction over us. We have reminded them of the circumstances of our emigration and settlement here. We have appealed to their native justice and magnanimity, and we have conjured them by the ties of our common kindred to disavow these usurpations, which would inevitably interrupt our connection and correspondence. They too have been deaf to the voice of justice and of consanguinity. We must, therefore, acquiesce in the necessity, which denounces our Separation, and hold them, as we hold the rest of mankind, Enemies in War, in Peace Friends.

We, therefore, the Representatives of the United States of America, in General Congress, assembled, appealing to the Supreme Judge of the world for the rectitude of our intentions, do, in the name, and by authority of the good People of these

Colonies, solemnly publish and declare, That these United Colonies are, and of Right ought to be Free and Independent States; that they are Absolved from all Allegiance to the British Crown, and that all political connection between them and the State of Great Britain, is and ought to be totally dissolved; and that as Free and Independent States, they have full power to levy War, conclude Peace, contract Alliances, establish Commerce, and to do all other Acts and Things which Independent States may of right do. And for the support of this Declaration, with a firm reliance on the Protection of Divine Providence, we mutually pledge to each other our Lives, our fortunes and our sacred Honor.

The Constitution

Preamble

We the People of the United States, in Order to form a more perfect Union, establish Justice, insure domestic Tranquility, provide for the common defence, promote the general Welfare, and secure the Blessings of Liberty to ourselves and our Posterity, do ordain and establish this Constitution for the United States of America.

Article I Section 1

All legislative Powers herein granted shall be vested in a Congress of the United States, which shall consist of a Senate and House of Representatives.

Section 2

The House of Representatives shall be composed of Members chosen every second Year by the People of the several States, and the Electors in each State shall have the Qualifications requisite for Electors of the most numerous Branch of the State Legislature.

No Person shall be a Representative who shall not have attained to the Age of twenty five Years, and been seven Years a Citizen of the United States, and who shall not, when elected, be an Inhabitant of that State in which he shall be chosen.

Representatives and direct Taxes shall be apportioned among the several States which may be included within this Union, according to their respective Numbers, which shall be determined by adding to the whole Number of free Persons, including those bound to Service for a Term of Years, and excluding Indians not taxed, three fifths of all other Persons. The actual Enumeration shall be made within three Years after the first Meeting of the Congress of the United States, and within every subsequent Term of ten Years, in such Manner as they shall by Law direct. The Number of Representatives shall not exceed one for every thirty Thousand, but each State shall have at Least one Representative; and until such enumeration shall be made, the State of New Hampshire shall be entitled to choose three, Massachusetts eight, Rhode-Island and Providence Plantations one, Connecticut five, New-York six, New Jersey four, Pennsylvania eight, Delaware one, Maryland six, Virginia ten, North Carolina five, South Carolina five, and Georgia three.

When vacancies happen in the Representation from any State, the Executive Authority thereof shall issue Writs of Election to fill such Vacancies.

The House of Representatives shall choose their speaker and other Officers; and shall have the sole Power of Impeachment.

Section 3

The Senate of the United States shall be composed of two Senators from each State, chosen by the Legislature thereof, for six Years; and each Senator shall have one Vote.

Immediately after they shall be assembled in Consequence of the first Election, they shall be divided as equally as may be into three Classes. The Seats of the Senators of the first Class shall be vacated at the Expiration of the second Year, of the second Class at the Expiration of the fourth Year, and of the third Class at the Expiration of the sixth Year, so that one third may be chosen every second Year; and if Vacancies happen by Resignation, or otherwise, during the Recess of the Legislature of any State, the Executive thereof may make temporary Appointments until the next Meeting of the Legislature, which shall then fill such Vacancies.

No Person shall be a Senator who shall not have attained to the Age of thirty Years, and been nine Years a citizen of the United States, and who shall not, when elected, be an Inhabitant of that State for which he shall be chosen.

The Vice President of the United States shall be President of the Senate, but shall have no Vote, unless they be equally divided.

The Senate shall choose their other Officers, and also a President pro tempore, in the Absence of the Vice President, or when he shall exercise the Office of President of the United States.

The Senate shall have the sole Power to try all Impeachments. When sitting for that Purpose, they shall be on Oath or Affirmation. When the President of the United States is tried, the Chief Justice shall preside: And no Person shall be convicted without the Concurrence of two thirds of the Members present.

Judgment in Cases of Impeachment shall not extend further than to removal from Office, and disqualification to hold and enjoy any Office of honor, Trust or Profit under the United States: but the Party convicted shall nevertheless be liable and subject to Indictment, Trial, Judgment and Punishment, according to law.

Section 4

The Times, Places, and Manner of holding Elections for Senators and Representatives, shall be prescribed in each State by the Legislature thereof; but the Congress may at any time by Law make or alter such Regulations, except as to the Places of choosing Senators.

The Congress shall assemble at least once in every Year, and such Meeting shall be on the first Monday in December, unless they shall by Law appoint a different Day.

Section 5

Each House shall be the Judge of the Elections, Returns, and Qualifications of its own Members, and a Majority of each shall constitute a Quorum to do Business; but a smaller Number may adjourn from day to day, and may be authorized to compel the Attendance of absent Members, in such Manner, and under such Penalties as each House may provide.

Each House may determine the Rules of its Proceedings, punish its Members for disorderly Behaviour, and, with the Concurrence of two thirds, expel a Member.

Each House shall keep a journal of its Proceedings, and from time to time publish the same, excepting such Parts as may in their Judgment require Secrecy; and the Yeas and Nays of the Members of either House on any question shall, at the Desire of one fifth of those Present, be entered on the journal.

Neither House, during the Session of Congress, shall, without the Consent of the other, adjourn for more than three days, nor to any other Place than that in which the two Houses shall be sitting.

Section 6
The Senators and Representatives shall receive a Compensation for their Services, to be ascertained by Law, and paid out of the Treasury of the United States. They shall in all Cases, except Treason, Felony and Breach of the Peace, be privileged from Arrest during their Attendance at the Session of their respective Houses, and in going to and returning from the same; and for any Speech or Debate in either House, they shall not be questioned in any other Place.

No Senator or Representative shall, during the Time for which he was elected, be appointed to any civil Office under the Authority of the United States, which shall have been created, or the Emoluments whereof shall have been increased during such time; and no Person holding any Office under the United States, shall be a Member of either House during his Continuance in Office.

Section 7
All Bills for raising Revenue shall originate in the House of Representatives; but the Senate may propose or concur with Amendments as on other Bills.

Every Bill which shall have passed the House of Representatives and the Senate, shall, before it become a Law, be presented to the President of the United States; If he approve he shall sign it, but if not he shall return it, with his Objections to that House in which it shall have originated, who shall enter the Objections at large on their Journal, and proceed to reconsider it. If after such Reconsideration two thirds of that House shall agree to pass the Bill, it shall be sent, together with the Objections, to the other House, by which it shall likewise be reconsidered, and if approved by two thirds of that House, it shall become a Law. But in all such Cases the Votes of both Houses shall be determined by Yeas and Nays, and the Names of the Persons voting for and against the Bill shall be entered on the Journal of each House respectively. If any Bill shall not be returned by the President within ten Days (Sundays excepted) after it shall have been presented to him, the Same shall be a Law, in like Manner as if he had signed it, unless the Congress by their Adjournment prevent its Return, in which Case it shall not be a Law.

Every Order, Resolution, or Vote to which the Concurrence of the Senate and House of Representatives may be necessary (except on a question of Adjournment) shall be presented to the President of the United States; and before the Same shall take Effect, shall be approved by him, or being disapproved by him, shall be repassed by two thirds of the Senate and House of Representatives, according to the Rules and Limitations prescribed in the Case of a Bill.

Section 8
The Congress shall have Power To lay and collect Taxes, Duties, Imposts and Excises, to pay the Debts and provide for the common Defence and general Welfare of the United States; but all Duties, Imposts and Excises shall be uniform throughout the United States;

To borrow Money on the Credit of the United States;

To regulate Commerce with foreign Nations, and among the several States, and with the Indian Tribes;

To establish an uniform Rule of Naturalization, and uniform Laws on the subject of Bankruptcies throughout the United States;

To coin Money, regulate the Value thereof, and of foreign Coin, and fix the Standard of Weights and Measures;

To provide for the Punishment of counterfeiting the securities and current Coin of the United States;

To establish Post Offices and post Roads;

To promote the Progress of Science and useful Arts, by securing for limited Times to Authors and Inventors the exclusive Right to their respective Writings and Discoveries;

To constitute Tribunals inferior to the supreme Court;

To define and punish Piracies and Felonies committed on the high Seas, and Offences against the Law of Nations;

To declare War, grant Letters of Marque and Reprisal, and make Rules concerning Captures on Land and Water;

To raise and support Armies, but no Appropriation of Money to that Use shall be for a longer Term than two Years;

To provide and maintain a Navy;

To make Rules for the Government and Regulation of the land and naval Forces;

To provide for calling forth the Militia to execute the Laws of the Union, suppress Insurrections and repel Invasions;

To provide for organizing, arming, and disciplining, the Militia, and for governing such Part of them as may be employed in the Service of the United States, reserving to the States respectively, the Appointment of the Officers, and the Authority of training the Militia according to the discipline prescribed by Congress;

To exercise exclusive Legislation in all Cases whatsoever, over such District (not exceeding ten Miles square) as may, by Cession of particular States, and the Acceptance of Congress, become the Seat of the Government of the United States, and to exercise like Authority over all Places purchased by the Consent of the Legislature of the State in which the Same shall be for the Erection of Forts, Magazines, Arsenals, dock-Yards, and other needful Buildings;——And

To make all Laws which shall be necessary and proper for carrying into Execution the foregoing Powers, and all other Powers vested by this Constitution in the Government of the United States, or in any Department or Officer thereof.

Section 9

The Migration of Importation of such Persons as any of the States now existing shall think proper to admit, shall not be prohibited by the Congress prior to the Year one thousand eight hundred and eight, but a Tax or duty may be imposed on such Importation, not exceeding ten dollars for each Person.

The Privilege of the Writ of Habeas Corpus shall not be suspended, unless when in Cases of Rebellion or Invasion the public Safety may require it.

No Bill of Attainder or ex post facto Law shall be passed.

No Capitation, or other direct, Tax shall be laid, unless in Proportion to the Census or Enumeration herein before directed to be taken.

No Tax or Duty shall be laid on Articles exported from any State.

No preference shall be given by any Regulation of Commerce or Revenue to the Ports of one State over those of another: nor shall Vessels bound to, or from, one

State, be obliged to enter, clear, or pay Duties in another.

No money shall be drawn from the Treasury, but in Consequence of Appropriations made by Law; and a regular Statement and Account of the Receipts and Expenditures of all public Money shall be published from time to time.

No Title of Nobility shall be granted by the United States: And no Person holding any Office of Profit or Trust under them, shall, without the Consent of the Congress, accept of any present, Emolument, Office, or Title, of any kind whatever, from any King, Prince, or foreign State.

Section 10

No State shall enter into any Treaty, Alliance, or Confederation; grant Letters of Marque and Reprisal; coin Money; emits Bills of Credit; make any Thing but gold and silver Coin a Tender in Payment of Debts; pass any Bill of Attainder, ex post facto Law, or Law impairing the Obligation of Contracts, or grant any Title of Nobility.

No State shall, without the Consent of the Congress, lay any Imposts or Duties on Imports or Exports, except what may be absolutely necessary for executing it's inspection Laws: and the net Produce of all Duties and Imposts, laid by any State on Imports or Exports, shall be for the Use of the Treasury of the United States; and all such Laws shall be subject to the Revision and Control of the Congress.

No State shall, without the Consent of the Congress, lay any Duty of Tonnage, keep Troops, or Ships of War in time of Peace, enter into any Agreement or Compact with another State, or with a foreign Power, or engage in War, unless actually invaded, or in such imminent Danger as will not admit of delay.

Article II   Section 1

The executive Power shall be vested in a President of the United States of America. He shall hold his Office during the Term of four Years, and, together with the Vice President, chosen for the same term, be elected, as follows

Each State shall appoint, in such Manner as the Legislature thereof may direct, a Number of Electors, equal to the whole Number of Senators and Representatives to which the State may be entitled in the Congress: but no Senator or Representative, or Person holding an Office of Trust or Profit under the United States, shall be appointed an Elector.

The Electors shall meet in their respective States, and vote by Ballot for two Persons, of whom one at least shall not be an Inhabitant of the same State with themselves. And they shall make a List of all the Persons voted for, and of the Number of Votes for each; which List they shall sign and certify, and transmit sealed to the Seat of the Government of the United States, directed to the President of the Senate. The President of the Senate shall, in the Presence of the Senate and House of Representatives, open all the Certificates, and the Votes shall then be counted. The Person having the greatest Number of Votes shall be the President, if such Number be a majority of the whole Number of Electors appointed; and if there be no more than one who have such Majority, and have an equal Number of Votes, then the House of Representatives shall immediately choose by Ballot one of them for President: and if no Person have a Majority, then from the five highest on the List the said House shall in like Manner choose the President. But in choosing the President, the Votes shall be taken by the states, the Representation from each State having one Vote; A quorum for this Purpose shall consist of a Member or Members from two thirds of the States, and a Majority of all the States shall be necessary to a Choice. In every Case, after the Choice of the President, the Person having the greatest Number of Votes of the Electors shall be the Vice President. But if there should remain two or more who have equal Votes, the Senate shall choose from them by Ballot the Vice President.

The Congress may determine the Time of choosing the Electors, and the Day on which they shall give their Votes; which Day shall be the same throughout the United States No Person except a natural born Citizen, or a Citizen of the United States, at the time of the Adoption of this Constitution, shall be eligible to the Office of President; neither shall any Person be eligible to that Office who shall not have attained to the Age of thirty five Years, and been fourteen Years a Resident within the United States.

In Case of the Removal of the President from Office, or of his Death, Resignation, or Inability to discharge the Powers and Duties of the said Office, the Same shall devolve on the Vice President, and the Congress may by Law provide for the Case of Removal, Death, Resignation or Inability, both of the President and Vice President, declaring what Officer shall then act as President, and such Officer shall act accordingly, until the Disability be removed, or a President shall be elected.

The President shall, at stated Times, receive for his Services, a Compensation, which shall neither be increased nor diminished during the Period for which he shall have been elected, and he shall not receive within that Period any other Emolument from the United States, or any of them.

Before he enter on the Execution of his Office, he shall take the following Oath or Affirmation:—— "I do solemnly swear (or affirm) that I will faithfully execute the Office of President of the United States, and will to the best of my Ability, preserve, protect and defend the Constitution of the United States."

Section 2

The President shall be Commander in Chief of the Army and Navy of the United States, and of the Militia of the several States, when called into the actual Service of the United States; he may require the Opinion, in writing, of the principal Officer in each of the executive Departments, upon any Subject relating to the Duties of their respective Offices, and he shall have Power to grant Reprieves and Pardons for Offences against the United States, except in Cases of Impeachment.

He shall have Power, by and with the Advice and Consent of the Senate, to make Treaties, provided two thirds of the Senators present concur; and he shall nominate, and by and with the Advice and Consent of the Senate, shall appoint Ambassadors, other public Ministers and Consuls, Judges of the supreme Court, and all other Officers of the United States, whose Appointments are not herein otherwise provided for, and which shall be established by Law: but the Congress may by Law vest the Appointment of such inferior Officers, as they think proper, in the President alone, in the Courts of Law, or in the Heads of Departments.

The President shall have Power to fill up all Vacancies that may happen during the Recess of the Senate, by granting Commissions which shall expire at the End of their next Session.

Section 3

He shall from time to time give to the Congress Information of the State of the Union, and recommend to their Consideration such Measures as he shall judge necessary and expedient; he may, on extraordinary Occasions, convene both Houses, or either of them, and in Case of Disagreement between them, with Respect to the Time of Adjournment, he may adjourn them to such Time as he shall think proper; he shall receive Ambassadors and other public Ministers; he shall take Care that the Laws be faithfully executed, and shall Commission all the Officers of the United States.

Section 4

The President, Vice President, and all civil Officers of the United States, shall be removed from Office on Impeachment for, and Conviction of, Treason, Bribery, or other High Crimes and Misdemeanors.

Article III Section 1

The judicial Power of the United States, shall be vested in one supreme Court, and in such inferior Courts as the Congress may from time to time ordain and establish. The Judges, both of the supreme and inferior Courts, shall hold their Offices during good Behaviour, and shall, at stated Times, receive for their Services, a Compensation, which shall not be diminished during their Continuance in Office.

Section 2

The judicial Power shall extend to all Cases, in Law and Equity, arising under this Constitution, the Laws of the United States, and Treaties made, or which shall be made, under their Authority;——to all Cases affecting Ambassadors, other public Ministers and Consuls;——to all Cases of admiralty and maritime Jurisdiction;——to Controversies to which the United States shall be a Party;——to Controversies between two or more States; between a State and Citizens of another state;——between Citizens of different States;——between Citizens of the same State claiming Lands under Grants of different States, and between a State, or the Citizens thereof, and foreign States, Citizens or Subjects. In all Cases affecting Ambassadors, other public Ministers and Consuls, and those in which a State shall be Party, the supreme Court shall have original Jurisdiction. In all the other Cases before mentioned, the supreme Court shall have appellate Jurisdiction, both as to Law and Fact, with such Exceptions, and under such Regulations as the Congress shall make.

The Trial of all Crimes, except in Cases of Impeachment, shall be by Jury; and such Trial shall be held in the State where the said Crimes shall have been committed; but when not committed within any State, the Trial shall be at such Place or Places as the Congress may by Law have directed.

Section 3

Treason against the United States, shall consist only in levying War against them, or in adhering to their Enemies, giving them Aid and Comfort. No Person shall be convicted of Treason unless on the Testimony of two Witnesses to the same overt Act, or on Confession in open Court.

The Congress shall have Power to declare the Punishment of Treason, but no Attainder of Treason shall work Corruption of Blood, or Forfeiture except during the Life of the Person attainted.

Article IV   Section 1
Full Faith and Credit shall be given in each State to the public Acts, Records, and judicial Proceedings of every other State. And the Congress may be general Laws prescribe the Manner in which such Acts, Records and Proceedings shall be proved, and the Effect thereof.
Section 2
The Citizens of each State shall be entitled to all Privileges and Immunities of Citizens in the several States.

A Person charged in any State with Treason, Felony, or other Crime, who shall flee from Justice, and be found in another State, shall on Demand of the executive Authority of the State from which he fled, be delivered up, to be removed to the State having Jurisdiction of the Crime.

No Person held to Service or Labour in one State, under the Laws thereof, escaping into another, shall, in Consequence of any Law or Regulation therein, be discharged from such Service or Labour, but shall be delivered up on Claim of the Party to whom such Service or Labour may be due.
Section 3
New States may be admitted by the Congress into this Union; but no new State shall be formed or erected within the Jurisdiction of any other State; nor any State be formed by the Junction of two or more States, or Parts of States, without the Consent of the Legislatures of the States concerned as well as of the Congress.

The Congress shall have Power to dispose of and make all needful Rules and Regulations respecting the Territory or other Property belonging to the United States; and nothing in this Constitution shall be so construed as to Prejudice any Claims of the United States, or of any particular State.
Section 4
The United States shall guarantee to every State in this Union a Republican Form of Government, and shall protect each of them against Invasion; and on Application of the Legislature, or of the Executive (when the Legislature cannot be convened) against domestic Violence.
Article V
The Congress, whenever two thirds of both Houses shall deem it necessary, shall propose Amendments to this Constitution, or, on the Application of the Legislatures of two thirds of the several States, shall call a Convention for proposing Amendments, which, in either Case, shall be valid to all Intents and Purposes, as Part of this Constitution, when ratified by the Legislatures of three fourths of the several States, or by Conventions in three fourths thereof, as the one or the other Mode of Ratification may be proposed by the Congress; Provided that no Amendment which may be made prior to the Year One Thousand eight hundred and eight shall in any Manner affect the first and fourth Clauses in the Ninth Section of the first Article; and that no State, without its Consent, shall be deprived of its equal Suffrage in the Senate.
Article VI
All Debts contracted and Engagements entered into, before the Adoption of this Constitution, shall be as valid against the United States under this Constitution, as under the Confederation.

This Constitution, and the Laws of the United States which shall be made in

Pursuance thereof; and all Treaties made, or which shall be made, under the Authority of the United States, shall be the supreme Law of the Land; and the Judges in every State shall be bound thereby, any Thing in the Constitution or Laws of any State to the Contrary notwithstanding.

The Senators and Representatives before mentioned, and the Members of the several State Legislatures, and all executive and judicial Officers, both of the United States and of the several States, shall be bound by Oath or Affirmation, to support this Constitution; but no religious Test shall ever be required as a Qualification to any Office or public Trust under the United States.

Article VII

The Ratification of the Conventions of nine States, shall be sufficient for the Establishment of this Constitution between the States so ratifying the Same.

DONE in Convention by the Unanimous Consent of the States present the Seventeenth Day of September in the Year of our Lord one thousand seven hundred and Eighty seven and of the Independence of the United States of America the Twelfth IN WITNESS whereof We have hereunto subscribed our Names.

Amendments to the Constitution
(First Ten Amendments - Bill of Rights)

On December 15th, 1791, Congress Ratifies The First Ten Amendments To The Constitution. These Become Known As The Bill of Rights.

Amendment 1

Congress shall make no law respecting an establishment of religion, or prohibiting the free exercise thereof; or abridging the freedom of speech, or of the press, or the right of the people peaceably to assemble, and to petition the Government for a redress of grievances.

Amendment 2

A well regulated Militia, being necessary to the security of a free State, the right of the people to keep and bear Arms, shall not be infringed.

Amendment 3

N o Soldier shall, in time of peace be quartered in any house, without the consent of the Owner, nor in time of war, but in a manner to be prescribed by law.

Amendment 4

The right of the people to be secure in their persons, houses, papers, and effects, against unreasonable searches and seizures, shall not be violated, and no Warrants shall issue, but upon probable cause, supported by Oath or affirmation, and particularly describing the place to be searched, and the persons or things to be seized.

Amendment 5

No person shall be held to answer for a capital, or otherwise infamous crime, unless on a presentment or indictment of a Grand Jury, except in cases arising in the land or naval forces, or in the Militia, when in actual service in time of War or public danger; nor shall any person be subject for the same offence to be twice put in jeopardy of life or limb; nor shall be compelled in any criminal case to be a witness against himself, nor be deprived of life, liberty, or property, without due process of law; nor shall private property be taken for public use, without just compensation.

Amendment 6
In all criminal prosecutions, the accused shall enjoy the right to a speedy and public trial, by an impartial jury of the State and district wherein the crime shall have been committed, which district shall have been previously ascertained by law, and to be informed of the nature and cause of the accusation; to be confronted with the witnesses against him; to have compulsory process for obtaining witnesses in his favor, and to have the Assistance of Counsel for his defence.

Amendment 7
In Suits at common law, where the value in controversy shall exceed twenty dollars, the right of trial by jury shall be preserved, and no fact tried by a jury, shall be otherwise re-examined in any Court of the United States, than according to the rules of the common law.

Amendment 8
Excessive bail shall not be required, nor excessive fines imposed, nor cruel and unusual punishments inflicted.

Amendment 9
The enumeration in the Constitution, of certain rights, shall not be construed to deny or disparage others retained by the people.

Amendment 10
The powers not delegated to the United States by the Constitution, nor prohibited by it to the States, are reserved to the States respectively, or to the people.

Amendment 11 (Congress Ratifies on February 7th, 1795)
The Judicial power of the United States shall not be construed to extend to any suit in law or equity, commenced or prosecuted against one of the United States by Citizens of another State, or by Citizens or Subjects of any Foreign State.

Amendment 12 (Congress Ratifies on July 27th, 1804)
The Electors shall meet in their respective States and vote by ballot for President and Vice President, one of whom, at least, shall not be an inhabitant of the same State with themselves; they shall name in their ballots the person voted for as President, and in distinct ballots the person voted for as Vice President, and they shall make distinct lists of all persons voted for as President, and of all persons voted for as Vice President, and of the number of votes for each, which lists they shall sign and certify, and transmit sealed to the seat of the government of the United States, directed to the President of the Senate;——The President of the Senate shall, in the presence of the Senate and House of Representatives, open all the certificates and the votes shall then be counted;——The person having the greatest number of votes for President, shall be the President, if such number be a majority of the whole number of Electors appointed; and if no person have such majority, then from the persons having the highest numbers not exceeding three on the list of those voted for as President, the House of Representatives shall choose immediately, by ballot, the President. But in choosing the President, the votes shall be taken by states, the representation from each state having one vote; a quorum for this purpose shall consist of a member or members from two-thirds of the states, and a majority of all the states shall be necessary to a choice. And if the House of Representatives shall not choose a President whenever the right of choice shall devolve upon them, before the fourth day of March next following, then the Vice President shall act as President, as in the case of the death or other constitutional

disability of the President.——The person having the greatest number of votes as Vice President, shall be the Vice President, if such number be a majority of the whole number of Electors appointed, and if no person have a majority, then from the two highest numbers on the list, the Senate shall choose the Vice President; a quorum for the purpose shall consist of two-thirds of the whole number of Senators, and a majority of the whole number shall be necessary to a choice. But no person constitutionally ineligible to the office of President shall be eligible to that of Vice President of the United States.

Amendment 13 (Congress Ratifies on December 6th, 1865)
Section 1
Neither Slavery, nor involuntary servitude, except as a punishment for crime whereof the party shall have been duly convicted, shall exist within the United States, or any place subject to their jurisdiction.
Section 2
Congress shall have power to enforce this article by appropriate legislation.

Amendment 14 (Congress Ratifies on July 9th, 1868)
Section 1
All persons born or naturalized in the United States, and subject to the jurisdiction thereof, are citizens of the United States and of the State wherein they reside. No State shall make or enforce any law which shall abridge the privileges or immunities of citizens of the United States; nor shall any State deprive any person of life, liberty, or property, without due process of law; nor deny to any person within its jurisdiction the equal protection of the laws.
Section 2
Representatives shall be apportioned among the several States according to their respective numbers, counting the whole number of persons in each State, excluding Indians not taxed. But when the right to vote at any election for the choice of electors for President and Vice President of the United States, Representatives in Congress, the Executive and Judicial officers of a State, or the members of the Legislature thereof, is denied to any of the male inhabitants of such State, being twenty-one years of age, and citizens of the United States, or in any way abridged, except for participation in rebellion, or other crime, the basis of representation therein shall be reduced in the proportion which the number of such male citizens shall bear to the whole number of male citizens twenty-one years of age in such State.
Section 3
No person shall be a Senator or Representative in Congress, or elector of President and Vice President, or hold any office, civil or military, under the United States, or under any State, who, having previously taken an oath, as a member of Congress, or as an officer of the United States, or as a member of any State legislature, or as an executive or judicial officer of any State, to support the Constitution of the United States, shall have engaged in insurrection or rebellion against the same, or given aid or comfort to the enemies thereof. But Congress may by a vote of two-thirds of each House, remove such disability.
Section 4
The validity of the public debt of the United States, authorized by law, including debts incurred for payment of pensions and bounties for services in suppressing

insurrection or rebellion, shall not be questioned. But neither the United States nor any State shall assume or pay any debt or obligation incurred in aid of insurrection or rebellion against the United States, or any claim for the loss or emancipation of any slave; but all such debts, obligations and claims shall be held illegal and void.

Section 5
The Congress shall have power to enforce, by appropriate legislation, the provision of this article.

Amendment 15 (Congress Ratifies on February 3rd, 1870)
Section 1
The right of citizens of the United States to vote shall not be denied or abridged by the United States or by any State on account of race, color or previous condition of servitude.

Section 2
The Congress shall have power to enforce this article by appropriate legislation.

Amendment 16 (Congress Ratifies on February 3rd, 1913)
The Congress shall have power to lay and collect taxes on incomes, from whatever source derived, without apportionment among the several States, and without regard to any census or enumeration.

Amendment 17 (Congress Ratifies on April 8th, 1913)
The Senate of the United States shall be composed of two Senators from each State, elected by the people thereof for six years; and each Senator shall have one vote. The electors in each State shall have the qualifications requisite for electors of the most numerous branch of the State legislatures.

When vacancies happen in the representation of any State in the Senate, the executive authority of such State shall issue writs of election to fill such vacancies: Provided, That the legislature of any State may empower the executive thereof to make temporary appointments until the people fill the vacancies by election as the legislature may direct.

This amendment shall not be so construed as to affect the election or term of any Senator chosen before it becomes valid as part of the Constitution.

Amendment 18 (Congress Ratifies on January 16th, 1919)
Section 1
After one year from the ratification of this article the manufacture, sale, or transportation of intoxicating liquors within, the importation thereof into, or the exportation thereof from the United States and all territory subject to the jurisdiction thereof for beverage purposes is hereby prohibited.

Section 2
The Congress and the several States shall have concurrent power to enforce this article by appropriate legislation.

Section 3
This article shall be inoperative unless it shall have been ratified as an amendment to the Constitution by the legislatures of the several States, as provided in the Constitution, within seven years from the date of the submission hereof to the States by the Congress.

Amendment 19 (Congress Ratifies on Aug. 18, 1920)
The right of citizens of the United States to vote shall not be denied or abridged by the United States or by any State on account of sex.
Congress shall have power to enforce this article by appropriate legislation.

Amendment 20 (Congress Ratifies on Jan. 23, 1933)
Section 1
The terms of the President and Vice President shall end at noon on the 20th day of January, and the terms of Senators and Representatives at noon on the third day of January, of the years in which such terms would have ended if this article had not been ratified; and the terms of their successors shall then begin.
Section 2
The Congress shall assemble at least once in every year, and such meeting shall begin at noon on the third day of January, unless they shall by law appoint a different day.
Section 3
If, at the time fixed for the beginning of the term of the President, the President elect shall have died, the Vice President elect shall become President. If a President shall not have been chosen before the time fixed for the beginning of his term, or if the President elect shall have failed to qualify, then the Vice President elect shall act as President until a President shall have qualified; and the Congress may by law provide for the case wherein neither a President elect nor a Vice President elect shall have qualified, declaring who shall then act as President, or the manner in which one who is to act shall be selected, and such person shall act accordingly until a President or Vice President shall have qualified.
Section 4
The Congress may by law provide for the case of the death of any of the persons from whom the House of Representatives may choose a President whenever the right of choice shall have devolved upon them, and for the case of the death of any of the persons from whom the Senate may choose a Vice President whenever the right of choice shall have devolved upon them.
Section 5
Sections 1 and 2 shall take effect on the 15th day of October following the ratification of this article.
Section 6
This article shall be inoperative unless it shall have been ratified as an amendment to the Constitution by the legislatures of three-fourths of the several States within seven years from the date of its submission.
Amendment 21 (Congress Ratifies December 5th, 1933)
Section 1
The eighteenth article of amendment to the Constitution of the United States is hereby repealed.
Section 2
The transportation or importation into any State, Territory, or possession of the United States for delivery or use therein of intoxicating liquors, in violation of the laws thereof, is hereby prohibited.
Section 3
This article shall be inoperative unless it shall have been ratified as an amendment to the Constitution by conventions in the several States, as provided in the Constitution, within seven years from the date of the submission hereof to the States by the Congress. **Amendment 22 (Congress Ratifies February 27th, 1951)**

Section 1

No person shall be elected to the office of the President more than twice, and no person who has held the office of President, or acted as President, for more than two years of a term to which some other person was elected President shall be elected to the office of the President more than once. But this Article shall not apply to any person holding the office of President when this Article was proposed by the Congress, and shall not prevent any person who may be holding the office of President, or acting as President, during the term within which this Article becomes operative from holding the office of President or acting as President during the remainder of such term.

Section 2

This article shall be inoperative unless it shall have been ratified as an amendment to the Constitution by the legislatures of three-fourths of the several States within seven years from the date of its submission to the States by the Congress.

Amendment 23 (Congress Ratifies on March 29, 1961)

Section 1

The District constituting the seat of Government of the United States shall appoint in such manner as the Congress may direct:
A number of electors of President and Vice President equal to the whole number of Senators and Representatives in Congress to which the District would be entitled if it were a State, but in no event more than the least populous State; they shall be in addition to those appointed by the States, but they shall be considered, for the purposes of the election of President and Vice President, to be electors appointed by a State; and they shall meet in the District and perform such duties as provided by the twelfth article of amendment.

Section 2

The Congress shall have power to enforce this article by appropriate legislation.

Amendment 24 (Congress Ratifies on January 23rd, 1964)

Section 1

The right of citizens of the United States to vote in any primary or other election for President or Vice President, for electors for President or Vice President, or for Senator or Representative in Congress, shall not be denied or abridged by the United States or any State by reason of failure to pay any poll tax or other tax.

Section 2

The Congress shall have power to enforce this article by appropriate legislation.

Amendment 25 (Congress Ratifies February 10th, 1967)

Section 1

In case of the removal of the President from office or of his death or resignation, the Vice President shall become President.

Section 2

Whenever there is a vacancy in the office of the Vice President, the President shall nominate a Vice President who shall take office upon confirmation by a majority vote of both Houses of Congress.

Section 3

Whenever the President transmits to the President pro tempore of the Senate and the Speaker of the House of Representatives his written declaration that he is unable to discharge the powers and duties of his office, and until he transmits to them a written declaration to the contrary, such powers and duties shall be discharged by the Vice President as Acting President.

Section 4

Whenever the Vice President and a majority of either the principal officers of the executive departments or of such other body as Congress may by law provide, transmit to the President pro tempore of the Senate and the Speaker of the House of Representatives their written declaration that the President is unable to discharge the powers and duties of his office, the Vice President shall immediately assume the powers and duties of the office as Acting President.

Thereafter, when the President transmits to the President pro tempore of the Senate and the Speaker of the House of Representatives his written declaration that no inability exists, he shall resume the powers and duties of his office unless the Vice President and a majority of either the principal officers of the executive department or of such other body as Congress may by law provide, transmit within four days to the President pro tempore of the Senate and the Speaker of the House of Representatives their written declaration that the President is unable to discharge the powers and duties of his office. Thereupon Congress shall decide the issue, assembling within forty-eight hours for that purpose if not in session. If the Congress, within twenty-one days after receipt of the latter written declaration, or, if Congress is not in session, within twenty-one days after Congress is required to assemble, determines by two-thirds vote of both Houses that the President is unable to discharge the powers and duties of his office, the Vice President shall continue to discharge the same as Acting President; otherwise, the President shall resume the powers and duties of his office.

Amendment 26 (Congress Ratifies on July 1st, 1971)

Section 1

The right of citizens of the United States, who are 18 years of age or older, to vote shall not be denied or abridged by the United States or by any State on account of age.

Section 2

The Congress shall have power to enforce this article by appropriate legislation.

Amendment 27 (Congress Ratifies May 7th, 1992)

No law, varying the compensation for the services of the Senators and Representatives, shall take effect until an election of Representatives shall have intervened.

General Douglas MacArthur:
"Duty, Honor, Country."

Signers of the Declaration of Independence - and of the Constitution:

1.) John Adams (MA).
2.) Samuel Adams (MA)
3.) Josiah Bartlett (NH)
4.) Carter Braxton (VA)
5.) Charles Carroll (of Carrollton) (MD)
6.) Samuel Chase(MD)
7.) Abraham Clark (NJ)
8.) George Clymer (PA)
9.) William Ellery (RI)
10.) William Floyd (NY)
11.) Benjamin Franklin (PA)
12.)Elbridge Gerry (MA)
13.)Button Gwinnett (GA)
14.) Lyman Hall (GA)
15.) John Hancock (MA)
16.) Benjamin Harrison (VA)
17.) John Hart (NJ)
18.) Joseph Hewes (NC)
19.) Thomas Heyward, Jr. (SC)
20.) William Hooper (NC)
21.) Stephen Hopkins (RI)
22.) Francis Hopkinson (NJ)
23.) Samuel Huntington (CT)
24.) Thomas Jefferson (VA)
25.)Francis Lightfoot Lee (VA)
26.) Richard Henry Lee (VA)
27.) Francis Lewis (NY)
28.) Philip Livingston (NY)
29.) Thomas Lynch, Jr. (SC)
30.) Thomas McKean (DE)
31.) Arthur Middleton (SC)
32.) Lewis Morris (NY)
33.) Robert Morris (PA)
34.) John Morton (PA)
35.) Thomas Nelson, Jr. (VA)
36.) William Paca (MD)

37.) Robert T. Paine MA
38.) John Penn (NC)
39.) George Read (DE)
40.)Caesar Rodney (DE)
41.)George Ross (PA)
42.)Benjamin Rush (PA)
43.)Edward Rutledge (SC)
44.) Roger Sherman(CT)
45.)James Smith (PA)
46.) Richard Stockton (NJ)
47.) Thomas Stone (MD)
48.) George Taylor (PA)
49.) Matthew Thornton (NH)
50.)George Walton (GA)
51.) William Whipple (NH)
52.)William Williams (CT)
53.) James Wilson (PA)
54.) John Witherspoon (NJ)
55.) Oliver Wolcott (CT)
56.) George Wythe (VA)

Constitution In Convention September 17, 1787
The men who signed as state representatives to establish the U.S. Constitution:

George Washington President. and deputy from Virginia
John Langdon (NH)
Nicholas Gilman (NH)
Nathaniel Gorham (MA)
Rufus King (MA)
William S. Johnson (CT)
Roger Sherman (CT)
Oliver Ellsworth (CT)
Alexander Hamilton (NY)
William Livingston (NJ)
David Brearley (NJ)
Jonathan Dayton (NJ)

William Paterson (NJ)
Benjamin Franklin (PA)
Thomas Mifflin (PA)
Robert Morris (PA)
George Clymer (PA)
Thomas Fittz Simons (PA)
Jared Ingersol (PA)
James Wilson (PA)
Gouverneur Morris (PA)
George Read (Del.)
Gunning Bedford, Jr. (Del.)
John Dickinson (Del.)
Richard Bassett (Del.)
Jaco Broom (Del.)
James McHenry (Md.)
Dan of St. Thomas Jenifer (Md.)
Daniel Carroll (Md.)
John Blair (Va.)
James Madison Jr. (Va.)
William Blount (NC)
Richard Dobbs Spaight (NC)
Hugh Williamson (NC)
John Rutledge (SC)
Charles Cotesworth Pinckney (SC)
Charles Pinckney (SC)
Pierce Butler (SC)
William Few (Ga.)
Abraham Baldwin (Ga.)

Attest: William Jackson Secretary
Note: Rhode Island does not send a representative to the Constitutional Convention.

Lincoln's Gettysburg Address

FOURSCORE and seven years ago our fathers brought forth on this continent a new nation conceived in liberty and dedicated to the proposition that all men are created equal. Now we are engaged in a great civil war testing whether that nation, or any nation so conceived and so dedicated, can long endure. We are met on a great battlefield of that war. We have come to dedicate a portion of that field as a final resting-place for those who here gave their lives that that nation might live. It is altogether fitting and proper that we should do this. But, in a larger sense, we cannot dedicate-we can not consecrate-we cannot hallow-this ground. The brave men, living and dead, who struggled here have consecrated it far above our poor power to add or detract. The world will little note nor long remember what we say here, but it can never forget what they did here. It is for us the living rather to be dedicated here to the unfinished work which they who fought here have thus far so nobly advanced. It is rather for us to be here dedicated to the great task remaining before us–that from these honored dead we take increased devotion to that cause for which they gave the last full measure of devotion–that we here highly resolve that these dead shall not have died in vain-that this nation under God shall have a new birth of freedom-and that government of the people, by the people, for the people shall not perish from the earth.

(November 19, 1863 - Gettysburg National Cemetery)

Mayflower Compact

In the name of God, Amen. We, whose names are underwritten, the Loyal Subjects of our dread Sovereign Lord, King James, by the Grace of God, of Great Britain, France and Ireland, King, Defender of the Faith, &c.

Having undertaken for the Glory of God, and Advancement of the Christian Faith, and the Honour of our King and Country, a voyage to plant the first colony in the northern part of Virginia; do by these Presents, solemnly and mutually in the Presence of God and one of another, covenant and combine ourselves together in a civil Body Politic, for our better Ordering and Preservation and Furtherance of the Ends aforesaid; And by Virtue hereof to enact, constitute, and frame, such just and equal Laws, Ordinances, Acts, Constitutions and Offices, from time to time, as shall be thought most meet and convenient for the General good of the Colony; unto which we promise all due Submission and Obedience.

In Witness whereof we have hereunto subscribed our names at Cape Cod the eleventh of November, in the reign of our Sovereign Lord, King James of England, France and Ireland, the eighteenth, and of Scotland the fifty-fourth Anno Domini (Year of Our Lord) 1620.

Presidents of The United States of America.

1.) George Washington (Virginia) April 30th 1789-March 4th 1797. Married to Martha Dandridge Custis Washington.

2.) John Adams (Massachusetts) March 4th 1797-March 4th 1801. Married to Abigail Smith Adams.

3.) Thomas Jefferson (Virginia) March 4th 1801-March 4th 1809. Married to Martha Wayles Skelton Jefferson.

4.) James Madison (Virginia) March 4th 1809-March 4th 1817. Married to Dorothea "Dolley" Payne Todd Madison.

5.) James Monroe (Virginia) March 4th 1817-March 4th 1825. Married to Elizabeth Kortright Monroe.

6.) John Quincy Adams (Massachusetts) March 4th 1825-March 4th 1829. Married to Louise Catherine Johnson Adams.

7.) Andrew Jackson (Tennessee) March 4th 1829-March 4th 1837. Rachel Donelson Robards Jackson.

8.) Martin Van Buren (New York) March 4th 1837-March 4th 1841. Married to Hannah Hoes Van Buren.

9.) William Henry Harrison (Ohio) March 4th 1841-April 4th 1841(1 month). Married to Anna Symmes Harrison President Harrison succumbs to pneumonia and is replaced by his Vice President John Tyler.

10.) John Tyler (Virginia) April 4th 1841-March 4th 1845. President Tyler takes the oath of Office on the 6th of April. Married to Leticia Christian Tyler.

11.) James Knox Polk (Tennessee) March 4th 1845-March 4th 1849). Married to Sarah Childress Polk.

12.) Zachary Taylor (Louisiana) March 4th 1849-July 9th 1850. Married to Margaret Smith Taylor. (President Taylor dies of natural causes). Vice President Millard Fillmore assumes the office and finishes the term (**13**[th] **President**).

14.) Franklin Pierce (New Hampshire) March 4th 1853-March 4th 1857. Married to Jane Means Appleton Pierce.

15.) James Buchanan (Pennsylvania) March 4th 1857-March 4th 1861. President Buchanan does not marry.

16.) Abraham Lincoln (Illinois) March 4th 1861-April 14-15 1865. Married to Mary Todd Lincoln. President Lincoln is assassinated during the evening of the 14th and succumbs on the 15th. Vice President Andrew Johnson assumes the office.

17.) Andrew Johnson (Tennessee) April 15 1865-March 4th 1869. Married to Eliza McCardle Johnson.

18.) Ulysses Simpson Grant (Illinois) March 4th 1869-March 4th 1877. Married to Julia Dent Grant.

19.) Rutherford Birchard Hayes (Ohio) March 4th 1877-March 4th 1881. Married to Lucy Ware Webb Hayes.

20.) James Abram Garfield (Ohio) March 4th 1881- September 19th 1881 (shot July 2, dies later at home) Vice President Chester A. Arthur assumes the office Garfield married Lucretia Rudolf Garfield.

21.) Chester Alan Arthur (Vermont) Sept. 20th 1881-March 4th 1885. Married Ellen Lewis Herndon Arthur.

22.) Grover Cleveland (New Jersey) March 4th 1885-March 4th - 1889. Married to Frances Folsom Cleveland.

23.) Benjamin Harrison (Ohio) March 4th 1889-March 4th 1893. Married to Caroline Lavinia Scott Harrison who dies during 1892. President Harrison marries for the second time, Mary Scott Lord Dimmick Harrison.

24.) Grover Cleveland (New Jersey) March 4th 1893-March 4th 1897.

Presidents continued

25.) William McKinley (Ohio) March 4th 1897-September 14th 1901. President McKinley dies from wounds suffered when an assassin's bullet struck him on September 6th 1901. Vice President Theodore Roosevelt assumes the Presidency. President McKinley married Ida Saxton.

26.) Theodore Roosevelt (New York) September 14th 1901-March 4th 1909. Married Alice Hathaway Lee Roosevelt who dies during 1884. President Roosevelt marries for a second time; Edith Kermit Carow Roosevelt

27.) William Howard Taft (Ohio) March 4th 1909-March 4th 1913. Married Helen Heron Taft.

28.) Woodrow Wilson (Virginia) March 4th 1913-March 4th 1921. Married Ellen Louis Axson Wilson.

29.) Warren Gamaliel Harding (Ohio) March 4th 1921-August 2nd 1923 (dies in office). Married Florence King DeWolfe Harding. Vice President Calvin Coolidge assumes the Presidency and takes the oath the following day.

30.) Calvin Coolidge (Vermont) August 3rd 192:3-March 4th 1929. Married Grace Anna Goodhue Coolidge.

31.) Herbert Hoover (Iowa) March 4th 1929-March 4th 1933. Married Lou Henry Hoover.

32.) Franklin Delano Roosevelt (New York) March 4th 1933-April 12th 1945 dies in office. Married Anna Eleanor Roosevelt Roosevelt. Vice President Harry Truman assumes the Presidency.

33.) Harry S Truman (Missouri) April 20th 1945-January 20th 1953. Married Bess Wallace Truman.

34.) Dwight David Eisenhower (Texas) January 20th 1953-January 20th 1961. Married Mamie Geneva Doud Eisenhower.

35.) John Fitzgerald Kennedy (Massachusetts) Jan.20,1961- Nov. 22, 1963.

Married Jacqueline Lee Bouvier Kennedy. President Kennedy is assassinated. Vice President Lyndon Baines Johnson assumes the Presidency.

36.) Lyndon Baines Johnson (Texas) Nov. 22nd 1963-January 20th 1969. Married Claudia "Lady Bird" Alta Taylor Johnson.

37.) Richard Nixon (California) January 20th 1969 - August 9th 1974. Married to Thelma Catherine Patricia Ryan Nixon. President Nixon resigns from office on August 9th 1974. Vice President Gerald R. Ford, who had replaced Vice President Spiro Agnew during October of 1973, assumes the Presidency and will nominate Nelson Rockefeller for the Vice Presidency (25th Amendment to Constitution).

38.) Gerald R. Ford (Nebraska) August 9th 1974-January 20th 1977. Married Elizabeth "Betty" Bloomer Warren Ford. President Ford is the first non-elected President. President Ford is also the first non-elected Vice President chosen under the guidelines of the 25th Amendment.

39.) Jimmy (James Earl) Carter (Georgia) January 20th 1977-January 20th 1981. Married Rosalyn Smith Carter.

40.) Ronald Reagan (Illinois) January 20th 1981-(Second term ends January 20th 1989). President Reagan married Anne Frances "Nancy" Robbins Davis Reagan. President Reagan had been married previously to Jane Wyman.

41.) George Herbert Walker Bush (Texas) January 20, 1989-January 20, 1993. Married Barbara Pierce Bush.

42.) William Jefferson Blythe Clinton (Arkansas) January 20, 1993-January 20, 2001 Married Hillary Rodham Clinton.

43.) George W. Bush (Texas) Inaugurated January 20, 2001. Married Laura Welch Bush.

Vice Presidents of the United States

1.) John Adams (Massachusetts) April 1789-March 1797. (Served under President Washington).

2.) Thomas Jefferson (Virginia) March 1797-March 1801. (Served under President John Adams).

3.) Aaron Burr (New York) March 1801-March 1805. (Served under President Jefferson).

4.) George Clinton (New York) March 1805-April 20th 1812 (dies in office). (Served under Presidents Jefferson and Madison).

5.) Elbridge Gerry (Massachusetts) March 4th 1813-Nov. 23rd 1814. (Served under President Madison).

6.) Daniel D. Tompkins (New York) March 4th 1817-March 4th 1825. (Served under President Monroe).

7.) John C. Calhoun (New York) Mar.4th 1825-Mar. 4th 1832. (Resigns to take a position in the U.S. Senate) (Served under Pres. John Q. Adams & Andrew Jackson).

8.) Martin Van Buren (New York) March 4th 1833-March 4th 1837. (Served under President Jackson).

9.) Richard M. Johnson (Kentucky) Mar. 4, 1837-Mar. 4, 1841. (Served under President Van Buren).

10.) John Tyler (Virginia) March 4th 1841-April 4th 1841. Becomes President after the death of President Harrison and the Vice Presidency remains vacant.

11.) George M. Dallas (Pennsylvania) March 4th 1845-March 4th 1849. (Served under President Polk).

12.) Millard Fillmore (New York) March 4th 1849 - July 9th 1850. (Becomes President after the death of President Taylor). The Vice Presidency remains vacant.

13.) William R. King (North Carolina) King is elected with President Pierce but dies during April, 1853 leaving the Vice Presidency vacant until Mar. 1857.

14.) John C. Breckinridge (Kentucky) March 4th 1857-March 4th 1861. Breckinridge becomes a Confederate General during the Civil War. (under President Buchanan).

15.) Hannibal Hamlin (Maine) March 4th 1861-March 4th 1865. (Served under President Lincoln).

16.) Andrew Johnson (Tennessee) March 4th 1865-April 15th 1865. (Becomes President after the assassination of President Lincoln

17.) Schuyler Colfax (Indiana) March 4th 1869-March 4th 1873. Served under President U.S. Grant).

18.) Henry Wilson (Massachusetts) Mar.4, 1873-Nov. 22 1875. Dies in office (under President Grant).

19.) William A. Wheeler (New York) Mar. 4, 1877-Mar. 4, 1881. (Served under President Hayes).

20.) Chester A. Arthur (New York) March 4th 1881 September 20th 1881. Becomes President after the death of President Garfield.

21.) Thomas A. Hendricks (Indiana) March 4th 1885-November 25th 1885. Dies in office (Served under President Cleveland).

22.) Levi P. Morton (New York) March 4th 1889-March 4th 1893. (Served under President Harrison).

23.) Adlai E. Stephenson (Illinois) March 4th 1893-March 4th 1897. (Served under President Cleveland).

24.) Garret A. Hobart (New Jersey) March 4th 1897-November 21st 1899. Dies in office (Served under President McKinley).

25.) Theodore Roosevelt (New York) March 4th 190l-September 14th 1901. Becomes President upon death of President McKinley.

26.) Charles W. Fairbanks (Indiana) Mar. 4, 1905-Mar. 4, 1909. (under President Theodore Roosevelt).

27.) James S. Sherman (New York) March 4th 1909-October 30th 1912. Dies in office (Served under President Taft).

28.) Thomas R. Marshall (Indiana) March 4th 1913-March 4th 1921. (Served under President Wilson).

Vice Presidents
continued:

29.) Calvin Coolidge (Massachusetts) March 13th 1921-August 2nd 1923. Becomes President after the death of President Harding

30.) Charles G. Dawes (Illinois) March 4th 1925-March 4th 1929. (Served under President Coolidge).

31.) Charles Curtis March 4th 1929-March 4th 1933. (Served under President Hoover).

32.) John Nance Garner (Texas) March 4th 1933-January 20th 1937. Reelected with President Roosevelt during 1936 and inaugurated on January 20th 1937, becoming first Vice President inaugurated at a time other than March (Due to 20th Amendment to Constitution). Garner serves full second term.

33.) Henry Agard Wallace (Iowa) January 20th 1941-January 20th 1945. (Served under President F.D. Roosevelt).

34.) Harry S Truman (Missouri) January 20th 1945-April 12th 1945. Becomes President upon death of President Franklin D. Roosevelt.

35.) Alben W. Barkley (Kentucky) January 20th 1949-January 20th 1953. (Served under President Truman).

36.) Richard M. Nixon (California) January 20th 1953-1961. (Served under President Eisenhower).

37.) Lyndon B. Johnson (Texas) January 20th 1961-November 22nd 1963. Becomes President after the death of President John F Kennedy.

38.) Hubert H. Humphrey (Minnesota) January 20th 1965-January 20th 1969. (Served under President Johnson).

39.) Spiro T. Agnew (Maryland) January 20th 1969-November 10th 1973. (Resigns after pleading no contest on tax evasion charges) (Served under President Nixon).

40.) Gerald R. Ford (Michigan) Nominated by President Nixon on October 12th 1973 to fill the unexpired term of Spiro Agnew. Gerald Ford is confirmed by Congress and sworn in on the 6th of December 1973 (Authorized by 25th Amendment to the Constitution which spells out process of nominating Vice President for fulfilling unexpired term). Vice President Ford assumes the Presidency after the resignation of President Nixon on Aug.9, 1974).

41.) Nelson Rockefeller (Maine) President Ford nominates Rockefeller on August 20th 1974. He is confirmed by Congress on December 19th 1974 and takes the oath of office on the Same day.

42.) Walter Mondale (Minnesota) January 4th 1977-January 4th 1981. (Serves under President Carter).

43.) George Bush (Texas) January 20th 1981-January 20th 1985. Reelected with President Reagan in 1984. Vice President Bush's term expires on January 20th 1989.

44.) Danforth Quayle (Indiana) January 1989 - January 20 1993. Serves under President George H. Bush.

45.) Al Gore - (Tennessee) January 20 1993 - January 20, 2001. Serves under President Bill Clinton.

46.) Dick Cheney - (Arizona) Sworn in on January 20, 2001. Serves under President George W. Bush.

The American Flag

They call her by many names, and speak of whence she came, but
surely by any name, its certain she's one and the same.
Way back, so very long ago, when England was our foe, she
emerged to flutter in the breeze, the colonists made it so.

At first, when she arrived, around 1775, she wore several borrowed
designs, although King George's was merrily declined.
With faith in the Divine, and a strong patriot's spine, the colonists
did opine, while they worked on the grand design.

Some used trees of pine, or an anchor under stars, but others
thought it to be Liberty's wake, on the flag appeared a rattlesnake.
April came and shots were fired, than the call went out, followed
by shouts, its now or never, for Liberty, we'll fight forever.

The King was bold and quick to scold, but surely the colonists
refused to fold. Instead they appealed to Heaven as it is told.
The banners waved, for freedom's cry, Liberty, Don't Tread on Me.
The call was heard across the sea, America will be free.

By God, proclaim that we are free, our banners wave across the land
and on the sea, the flag of those who cherish liberty.
Time was quick and by '76, the British were humming, the Yanks
were drumming, each a different tune, a battle very soon.

One day in January, it was to be, the Colors were struck as the flag
of the Free and it was tagged to be, our Grand Union Flag.
They also called her "Congress' Colors," and by either name, she
prepared for fame, with thirteen stripes of red and white.

The stripes were dressed with the crosses of Saints Andrew and
George, up in the corner caressed in blue, as she so proudly flew.
By July it was clear, as the Fourth was so near, that the time had arrived
to rise up with pride, ring the Bell, show no fear.

The Declaration was made, the Flag unfurled, with God's blessings
just right, soon after came the birth of the Stars and Stripes.
On June 14th, 1777, it was an extraordinary day, oh yes they did say,
for the Stars and the Stripes, God's timing was exactly right.

102

The American Flag continued:

The sabers would clash, the cannon would fire, while Infantry and
long muskets would compel the British to quickly retire.
At the end of the battle, the end of the day, the British at Yorktown
had faltered, to make way for our Republic, the U.S.A.

The names they vary for that noble flag, but in all her glory, when
you hear her story, its clear she's the emblem of Liberty.
They call her Old Glory, the Star Spangled Banner, the Grand Ole Flag
and the Red White and Blue, with all of these true.

For Honor and Freedom, across this blessed land, she does stand,
whether off in a foreign land or out at sea, she's always grand.
Our Grand Ole Flag, forever free, while under God for Liberty,
always on scene to guard the free from all forms of tyranny.

She's our Star Spangled Banner, the banner we love, her Stars and
Stripes,
so bold and so bright, under God's precious light.
Other storms will come out of the night, but our gallant flag
will stand up to the fight, blessed by God to do what is right.

Americans pledge allegiance to their flag and republic, "...One Nation
under God, indivisible with Liberty and Justice for all."

So stand and cheer for the Red White and Blue, she's God's gift to you,
the Eternal Flag of the United States of America.

Written by Bud Hannings (Seniram Publishing) December 24, 2000

Illustrations By Fred Loeffler, Glenside. Pennsylvania.

History of the Medal of Honor

The President may award and present in the name of Congress, a Medal of Honor of appropriate design, with ribbons and appurtenances, to a person who, while a member of the armed forces, distinguished himself conspicuously by gallantry & intrepidity at the risk of his life above and beyond the call of duty.

1. while engaged in an action against an enemy of the United States;

2. while engaged in military operations involving conflict with an opposing foreign force; or

3. while serving with friendly foreign forces engaged in an armed conflict against an opposing armed force in which the United States is not a belligerent party.

During the Civil War, the Union pondered the need of a Decoration for individual valor and gallantry exhibited by individuals on behalf of their country. There was a tremendous need for such an award as a vehicle to inspire the troops to attain recognition for heroism in the face of the realities of war. The need for this Medal of Honor had not been conceived as a brand new idea. General George Washington had shown his personal desire for such an award for Valor when he initiated the "Purple Heart" during August of 1782 as an incentive for Individual Gallantry.

The "Purple Heart," a forerunner of the Medal of Honor had been established for recognition of bravery but records from the Revolutionary War Period show that only three men received the award. Congress had earlier authorized a special medal for the actions of three men who had been involved with the capture of Major John Andre, the co-conspirator of Benedict Arnold during the ill-fated attempt of the British to capture West Point (captured September 23rd 1780). This medal referred to as the Andre Medal is the first medal awarded to individuals by the United States for Gallantry.

The "Purple Heart" never becomes the ultimate accolade of American Valor and in fact simply falls by the wayside. Americans will continue to defend their liberty after the Revolution and participate in conflicts with France during the latter part of the 1700s and again with England during the early part of the 1800s but there is no personal decoration for bravery exemplified by the individual American Soldier, Sailor or Marine. Finally, during the conflict with Mexico towards the latter part of the 1840s, the Congress of the United States authorizes a "Certificate of Merit" which is signed by President James Polk. This award is specifically designed to inspire the soldiers who had exhibited personal Gallantry, but in essence it is a certificate and not worn on one's uniform; thus the American troops are still without a conspicuous decoration for bravery.

After the close of hostilities with Mexico, the "Certificate of Merit" follows the course of the "Purple Heart" and retires to oblivion. The approaching temporary collapse of the United States which occurs during the Civil War will once again emphasize the need for an Individual Decoration for recognition of personal gallantry above and beyond the call of duty, necessitated by the dismal positioning of the Union during the early days of the conflict. There was a great need for inspiration and a greater need for heroes during those somber days of the nation. The Medal was intended to be the ray of sunshine to motivate the disillusioned Union troops who were not faring too well during mid-1861.

History of the Medal of Honor (continued)

The Medal nears reality on December 9th 1861 when Legislation (Senate Bill No.82) is introduced "To further promote the efficiency of the Navy." The Army had not been as quick in determining the necessity of the award and would not see similar Legislation until February 12th 1862, when Senator Wilson of Massachusetts introduces a bill authorizing the President "To distribute Medals to Privates in the Army of the United States who distinguish themselves in battle." Commissioned Officers were exempt as it was thought that promotions would suffice for officers. The Legislation would be passed on May 13th 1862. During May of 1862 (19th) Senator Wilson's Resolution prompts the sum of $10,000.00 to be appropriated for the purpose of striking 2,000 Army Medals of Honor to be awarded to non-commissioned Officers and Privates (Approved July 12th, 1862).

On March 3rd 1863, Congress enacts legislation that makes the Medal of Honor a permanent award and also reverses itself (Congress) by the inclusion of both enlisted men and officers. No Medals had been presented to any individual prior to this date, although Medals would subsequently be awarded for "Deeds of Gallantry" which had occurred prior to March 3rd 1863. During the infancy stages of the distinguished Medal of Honor, presently the most prestigious award for Valor and Gallantry, there were some inconsistencies. Some recipients (911) would be stricken from the rolls during February of 1917, by the Army Medal of Honor Board (Upon authority granted by the Army Reorganization Act of June 3rd 1916. The Board determined that these individuals had not "Performed acts of sufficient merit to earn the award." One of these recipients, Doctor Mary Walker (Civil War Surgeon and civilian) would have her award restored on June 10th 1977 by the approval of Army Secretary Clifford L. Alexander Jr.

Total Medal of Honor Awards by Campaigns.: Civil War - (1861-1865): Army; 1,195, Navy; 308, Marine Corps; 17. Indian Campaigns - (1861-1898): Army; 428. Korean Campaign - (1871): Army; 0, Navy; 9, Marine Corps; 6. Spanish American War - (1898): Army; 30, Navy; 64, Marine Corps; 15. Philippines Samoa (1899-1913): Army; 70, Navy; 12. Marine Corps; 9. Boxer Rebellion - (1900): Army; 4, Navy; 22, Marine Corps; 33. Philippine Outlaws Campaign - (1911): Army; 0, Navy; 5. Marine Corps; 5. Mexican Campaign (Vera Cruz) -(1911):Army; 0, Navy; 46, Marine Corps; 9. Haitian Campaign - (1915): Army; 0, Navy; 0, Marine Corps 6. Dominican Republic Campaign - (1916): Army; 0, Navy; 0, Marine Corps; 3. World War 1 - (1917-1918): Army; 96, Navy; 21, Marine Corps; 7, Air Force: *4 (Air Force is part of Army from 1907 until September 18th 1947.) Also, 32 medals awarded posthumously. Medals of Honor Awarded by Interim Period. (1866-1870): Army; 0, Navy; 9, Marine Corps; 0. (1871-1898): Army; 0, Navy; 99, Marine Corps; 2. (1901-1910): Army; 0, Navy; 46, Marine Corps; 2. (1915-1916): Army; 0, Navy; 8, Marine Corps; 0. World War II - Army 301, Navy 57, Marines 81, Coast Guard 1 (250 posthumous). Korean War Army 78; Navy 7, Marines 57 (93 posthumous)- Vietnam; Army 155, Navy 15, Marines 57 (150 posthumous). Somalia Army 2 (both posthumous). In addition, on January 13, 1997, seven African-Americans of the identical platoon (WW II) are awarded the Medal of Honor and of these, five are posthumous. Also, during 2000 A.D., twenty-two Japanese Americans who served during World War II (members of the 100th Infantry Battalion or 442nd RCT) the Medal of Honor simultaneously for their service during the war. Also, Anthony Casamento, Company D, 1st Battalion, 5th Marines receives the Medal of Honor for his heroism on Guadalcanal during 1942.

The proper Definitions for the Flag of The United States.

The Flag of the United States of America referred to as the National Flag is also known as the National Ensign, National Color and National Standard. The term National Flag" is applicable regardless of size or manner of display, but the other terms have certain well-defined usages of long standing within the Armed Services.

1.) "National Ensign" is used by the Navy in a general manner, although it actually indicates the National Flag flown by airships, ships and boats.

The U.S. Navy in addition to displaying Old Glory on its vessels and stations from 8:00 a.m. to sunset, also flies the Flag outside those periods on special occasions:

a.) Ships entering port at night should hoist the Ensign at daylight for a short period to enable port authorities and other vessels to determine her nationality. It is customary for other ships to show their colors in return.

b). Upon anchoring or getting underway in sufficient light to be seen, the National Ensign should be displayed at the gaff.

c.) Under no circumstances shall an action be commenced or battle fought without display of the National Ensign (chapter V,1920 Navy Regulations).

d.) Custom dictates that when underway, the normal point of display (of the Flag) is at the gaff, while the flagstaff is the point of display at anchor. Prior to 8:00 a.m. or after sunset, the Flag should be hoisted at the gaff.

e.) The U.S. Navy never dips her Colors except to return the compliment. When a vessel registered by a nation formally recognized by the U.S., dips (salutes with colors) her flag, the U.S. Navy must return the dip. Upon reaching shore, only battalion or regimental colors should he dipped in rendering or acknowledging a salute.

2.) "National Color" pertains to Flags carried by dismounted units of the landing force and is stubbier than the National Ensign.

3.) "National Standard" is carried by mounted, mechanized and motorized units. The display of our National Flag is governed by law to insure that it will be treated with the respect due the Flag of a great nation. Public Law 829 enacted by the 77th Congress sets forth rules for the display and care of the Stars and Stripes and prescribes penalties for violations.

When reciting the pledge of Allegiance. you should stand at attention with your hand over your heart. Military personnel should salute.

The Pledge of Allegiance:

"I pledge allegiance to the flag of the United States of America, and to the republic for which it stands, one nation under God, indivisible with Liberty and Justice for all."

Signs of Respect for Our Flag.

The Stars and Stripes should be flown daily from Sunrise to Sunset in good weather from Public Buildings, Schools, Permanent Staffs in the open and near Polling Places on Election Days. The Flag may be flown at night on Special Patriotic Occasions.

The Stars and Stripes should always be flown on National and State Holidays and on those occasions proclaimed by the President. On Memorial Day, the Flag should be half staffed until noon.

The Flag should he raised briskly and lowered ceremoniously. It should never be dipped to any person or thing nor should it ever be displayed with the Union down except as a Signal of Distress.

The Flag should never be allowed to touch anything beneath it, nor should it ever be carried flat or horizontally always aloft and free. It should never be used as drapery or decoration, for carrying anything, or stored in such a manner that it will be damaged or soiled.

The Stars and Stripes should never be used for advertising purposes in any manner whatsoever, nor should any picture, drawing, insignia or other decoration he placed upon or attached to the Flag, its staff or halyard. The Flag should not be embroidered on personal items nor printed on anything designed for temporary use and then discarded. When the Flag is so worn or soiled that it is no longer suitable for display, it should be destroyed in a dignified manner, preferably by burning.

The Flag should never be used as a costume or athletic uniform; but a flag patch may be affixed to the uniform of military personnel, firemen, policemen & members of patriotic organizations.

"The Flag represents a living country and is itself considered a living thing. Therefore the lapel flag pin, being a replica, should be worn on the left lapel near the heart."

The flag should be displayed on all days, especially on:

1.) New Year's Day January 1st.
2.) Martin Luther King's Birthday January 15th. Celebrated 3rd Monday in January.
3.) Inauguration Day January 20th.
4.) Abraham Lincoln's Birthday February 12th.
5.) George Washington's Birthday February 22nd (Celebrated 3rd Monday in February for Presidents Lincoln and George Washington only.
6.) Easter Sunday (Date varies).
7.) Mother's Day (2nd Sun. in May).
8.) Armed Forces Day (Third Saturday in May).
9.) Memorial Day (Half Staff until Noon) the Last Monday in May.
10.) Flag Day June 14th.
11.) Independence Day July 4th.
12.) Labor Day First Monday in September.
13.) Terrorist Attack on N.Y. and Virginia - September 11th.
14.) Constitution Day Sept. 17th.
15.) Columbus Day (October 12, Celebrated on 2nd Monday.
16.) Navy Day October 27th.
17.) Veterans Day November 11th.
18.) Thanksgiving Day Fourth Thursday in November.
19.) Christmas Day December 25th.
20.) Any additional days as may be proclaimed by the President; the United States; the Birthdays of States. (Date of Admission); and on State Holidays.

Proper Display of the Stars and Stripes.

1.) If the Flag is to be displayed over the middle of the street, the Flag should be suspended vertically with the Union pointing to the north in an east and west street. For proper display if the street runs north and south, the Union should point east.

2.) When displaying the Flag with another flag from crossed staffs, the U.S. Flag should always be on the right (the Flag's own right) and the staff of the U.S. Flag should be in the front of the staff of the other Flag.

3.) When displaying the U.S. Flag at half-staff (half-mast on a vessel), the Flag should be hoisted to the peak and then lowered to the position of half-staff. Before lowering the Flag for the day, it should first be raised again to the peak. The Flag is at the proper position of half-staff when it is positioned at one-half th distance between the top and bottom of the staff (pole). During the Holiday of Memorial Day, the Flag should be flown at half-staff until the hour of 12 noon and at that time it is to be raised to the peak of the staff.

4.) When it becomes necessary to fly the flag of a state, city or a pennant of a society on the same halyard with the Flag of the United States of America, the Flag of the U.S. should always be at the peak. If these other flags are to fly alongside the Stars and Stripes on adjacent staffs, the U.S. Flag should be raised first and lowered last. No flag or pennant shall be flown above or to the right of the Stars and Stripes (U.S. Flag) at the same level, except the church pennant The church pennant may be flown above the Stars and Stripes during religious services at sea.

5.) When displaying the flag from a rope over a sidewalk extending from a house to a pole at the edge of the sidewalk, th Flag should be hoisted out from the building, Union first towards the pole.

6.) When displaying Old Glory from a staff projecting horizontally or at any angle from the window sill, balcony or front of a building, the Union of the Flag should go to the peak of the staff (unless the Flag is to be flown at half-staff).

7. When the U.S. Flag is to be carried in a procession (parade etc.), with another flag or flags, the Stars and Stripes should be on the marching right.

8.) When there is a line of other flags, the Stars and Stripes should be out in front and to the center of that line.

9.) When the U.S. Flag is to be displayed with a number of flags of cities or states or pennants of societies on staffs, the U.S. Flag should be at the center and at the highest point of the group of flags.

10.) When the Stars and Stripes is to be displayed with the flags of other nations, the flags should be flown from separate staffs of equal height and the flags should be of approximately the same size. International usage forbids the display of the flag of one nation above that of another nation in the time of peace.

11.) When the Stars and Stripes is displayed in a manner other than by being flown from a staff, it should be displayed flat, whether indoors or out. When displaying the Stars and Stripes either vertically or horizontally against a wall, the Union should be uppermost and to the Flag's own right (to the observers left). When displaying the Stars and Stripes in a window, it should be displayed in the same way (Union or blue field to the left of the observer in the street.

12.) When the Stars and Stripes is used to cover a casket, the Flag should be placed that the Union (blue field) is at the head and over the left shoulder. The Stars and Stripes should never be lowered into the grave or be allowed to touch the ground. After the ceremony, the Flag is presented to a member of the family of the deceased.

13.) When the Stars and Stripes is to be displayed at the unveiling of a statue or monument, it should be distinctive and prominent, but never used as the covering or veil.

14.) When the Stars and Stripes is to be displayed from a staff in a church chapel

or speaker's platform, the Flag should be placed on the speaker's right. If the Flag is displayed elsewhere than on the speaker's platform, it should be on the right of the audience as they face the platform. When the Stars and Stripes is displayed flat on a speaker's platform, the Flag should be behind and above the speaker with the Union (blue field) to his right. The Union will be above, behind and to the left of the speaker from the view of the audience.

15.) When the Stars and Stripes is passing in parade, being hoisted or lowered, all persons present should stand at attention and salute. Uniformed persons render the military salute; women and uncovered men (no hats) should place their right hands over their hearts. Men should remove their hats and with their right hands, hold them over their hearts until the Flag passes.

16.) If the Stars and Stripes is not present during the playing of the National Anthem (Star Spangled Banner), all present should stand and face the music. Persons in uniform should salute from the first note and hold it until the last note. Others should stand at attention, men removing their hats. Is the Stars and Stripes is present, all should salute; civilians at attention with their hand over their hearts.

17.) No flag or pennant is permitted to be flown above or to the right of the U.S. Flag at the same level, with the exception of the church pennant, which is permitted to be flown above the Stars and Stripes during religious services at sea.

Personal Honors and Salutes:

The Independence of the United States is celebrated by a salute to the Union at 12 noon on the Fourth of July at all military installations where artillery is available. The salute is rendered by the firing of one gun for each state. The United States national salute which is a 21-guns is also the salute rendered a national flag.

A 21-gun salute accompanied by four Ruffles and Flourishes is rendered to the President of the United States upon arrival and departure. The identical salute is rendered to a former President and to a President-elect. Hail to the Chief or the National Anthem (Star Spangled Banner) is played for the President. The National Anthem is played for a former President or a President-elect.

If a sovereign or chief of state of a foreign nation or a member of a reigning royal family is visiting, a 21-gun salute with four Ruffles and Flourishes is rendered upon arrival and departure. Immediately following the Ruffles and Flourishes, without pause, the national anthem of his or her country is played.

John Wayne & Sergeant (later Major) Rick Spooner, USMC. Major Spooner Ret. is always at his restaurant, the Globe & Laurel in Triangle (Quantico), Va.; it's a patriot's delight.

Marines, MCRD, San Diego

111

How To Properly Fold The Flag.

1.) Fold the full length of the flag in half, pulling the striped half up over the blue field.
2.) Fold the full length of the flag again.
3.) Pull the lower striped corner to the right tip to form a triangle. Turn the outer edge inward to meet the upper edge which will form a second triangle.
4.) Continue folding the flag in triangles until the entire length is folded in the form of a triangle. When the flag is completely folded, only the blue field should be visible, in the form of a cocked hat.
The American Flag, folded, resembles a cocked hat.

Long May She Wave!
Lest We Forget

America's yesterday, totally consumed by Valor, Bravery, Sacrifice, and proud determination, has provided Americans of this generation the privilege of enjoying Today, as Free citizens of the greatest nation on earth. Those valiant Americans continue to inspire us to cherish freedom and to protect and defend America from the clutches of tyranny, be it from our obvious adversaries on the outside of our national perimeter or from the inconspicuous elements from within our very precious shores, thus insuring Life, Liberty, and the Pursuit of Happiness.

They too, will share in our great American heritage, with the knowledge that tomorrow will come, even better than Today, and the Legacy left for us from our Forefathers will be handed down until the end of time, a Legacy that has been unmatched since the beginning of mankind.

Our proud American tradition of being the most outstanding example of what Free men can accomplish is, and will forever be inspired by, the actions of all American Patriots, past, present and future, guided by the Grace of God and the magnificent Flag that represents our great nation,
The Stars and Stripes of these United States of America.

God Rest Their Souls.

There's Our Flag

There's our Flag, flying so proud
She's all around in every town
Brings a chill, right through my spine
Our Grand Ole Flag, she's yours and mine

Ole Glory, she's seen it all
Her Stars and Stripes, still standing tall
She's our flag, flying so proud
She's all around, in every town

She's always there for you and me
Our Stars and Stripes will keep us free
What a sight, oh what a sight
The Stars and Stripes all day and night

If you're out at sea or in a plane
You're sure to see the Stars and Stripes
Many brave men have made it be
Our Grand Ole Flag still keeps us free

She's flying proud for the USA
She's standing tall every night and day
There is no way, no way at all
Our Stars and Stripes will ever fall

She's here today, tomorrow too
Ole Glory's here for me and you
So when you see her marching by
Don't feel sad if you want to cry

It's a tear of joy, a happy sigh
Our Grand Ole Flag will never die
There she is, she's standing tall
Protecting us, protecting all

Protecting us, protecting all

Protecting us, protecting all

The Eternal Flag

Flags have come and Flags have gone, but the American Flag is here to stay. As each crisis evolves, Our Flag always waves a little prouder in the wind. Just as a new wave in the ocean appears to take the place of the one that disappeared on the beach, a new American Flag will blow in the breeze more proudly than the one that some tyrant will burn or tear.

Our Flag has always flown as a Beacon of Freedom in the wind for all the World to see, and even as they saw it burning in Tehran, they must have seen the majestic beauty of its disappearance in the wind, only to be reappearing a few feet to the left or right to be burned again. Their barbaric burning of the greatest Flag of them all sent sparks flying that have welded the American people into one, almost as if the smoke from their fires traveled across the ocean and reassembled the Flags to fly higher and prouder than ever before.

During 1983, terrorists struck the U. S. Embassy and the Marine Barracks in Beirut and this dastardly act was followed during 1987 by the deaths of American servicemen aboard the USS Stark when it was hit, supposedly accidentally, by an Iraqi missile. Other atrocities occurred during 1988, including the torture-death of Marine Lt. Colonel Rich Higgins while on UN duty in Lebanon and the downing of the Pan-Am Plane over Lockerbie Scotland.

The Flag again was tested during 1993 when terrorists struck the World Towers in New York, killing civilians. And now during 2001 on a bright September day, terrorists have struck again, savagely hijacking civilian planes and causing massive loss of life. The terrorists intended to destroy the American will, but instead resurrected the American Spirit and unleashed unimaginable determination that the world has never seen.

The New York skyline has fallen, planes with civilians aboard and thousands of unsuspecting workers and rescuers have been lost and the Pentagon has sustained grave losses, but the stamina of America can be seen on the grieving faces of every volunteer. Old Glory rests in a wounded position atop the debris near the harbor and she respectfully drapes the scarred wall in Virginia, but the smoldering smoke and fire is unable to cloak her brilliant illumination that continues to beam signals of hope to all parts of the globe.   Continued:

114

The Eternal Flag continued:

It is time to stop trying to please everyone in the world. Americans have helped at one time or another almost every country in the world, and did so because they wanted to help, not because they needed any glory. Many Americans have literally given their lives to liberate thousands upon thousands of imprisoned people throughout our history. We have not only helped people, but entire nations. And how quickly they forget.

We can be assured of a much greater love of country, freedom, and the foresight to realize that the terrorists and anyone else who have not learned from history what great things America has done unselfishly for the rest of the World, are no longer important, but that it is important that we as Americans be aware of it.

Maybe now, the people in the rest of the world will realize that the American Flag can be wounded, but never fatally. Neither burning or tearing will ever eradicate the Eternal Flag of the United States of America or the unequaled acts of valor and bravery of its countless deeds in defense of Freedom throughout the world.

The American Flag is an indelible mark, for us and our posterity, that possesses the unique ability to shine brighter under stress and the durability to withstand intimidation by adversaries anywhere in the world. She is the symbol of freedom and the invincible spine of the American Spirit. She is the velvet threads of glory, the blood of our ancestors and the oxygen for our posterity. The Stars and Stripes in her majestic beauty shall always sail the seas, blanket the stars and trumpet the advance of her endless line of heroes, the vanguard of Liberty, who will march in noble cadence to safeguard the dignity, character and honor of the United States. Her families have not fallen in vain.

America I salute you and I thank God that the American Flag in the proud American tradition will always be here to help those in need. By God, It Really Does Feel Good To Be An American.

Written during 1979 A.D. during the Iranian Crisis by Bud Hannings Seniram Publishing and revised subsequent to the terrorist attack against the U.S. in New York and Virginia on September 11, 2001.

It's Our Flag

It's our flag, our country
and our land
With our heroes we shall
always stand
As they deploy in faraway
lands
To destroy every terrorist
band

The Stars and Stripes is shining bright
The flag is flying through the night
Our heroes move, but out of sight
Except the planes in constant flight

The Stars and Stripes is underway
Moving against tyranny for the USA
Armed with the memory of that September day
When terrorists struck to take her heroes away

God bless the Army, Navy and Marines
Coastguard and Air Force on the scene
Seek justice, freedom's mobile team
Under God's mighty light beam

It's our flag, our country and our land
With our heroes, we shall always stand
As they deploy in faraway lands
To destroy every terrorist band

United States Trivia

1.) Which U.S. General Officers achieved the rank of Five Stars? **Answer: Generals: 1.)** Henry "Hap" Arnold (USA-USAF); **2.)** Omar Bradley; **3.)** Dwight D. Eisenhower; **4.)** Douglas MacArthur; **5.)** George C. Marshall **Admirals: 6.)** William Halsey; **7.)** Ernest J. King; **8.)** William Leahy **9.)** Chester Nimitz. **Also,** General John Pershing achieved the rank of General of the Armies (September 1919), making Pershing the highest ranking military officer in U.S. history, placing him above the rank of General of the Army, however, Pershing never wore more than four stars. Later, during the administration of President Jimmy Carter, General George Washington would posthumously receive the rank of General of the Armies, placing him above all other Generals of the Army. **2.)** How many Confederate soldiers became recipients of the Medal of Honor? **Answer**: None. Confederates did not serve in the Union Armed Forces. **3.)** How many Indians received the Congressional Medal of Honor during the Indian Campaigns? **Answer**: Eight. During the campaigns against the Apaches, eight Indian Scouts (U.S. Army) became recipients of the Medal of Honor. **4.)** Which General composed the "Bugle Call, Taps?" **Answer**: Union General Daniel Butterfield (Harrison's Landing, Berkeley Plantation VA) during 1862. **5.)** Which U.S. President was nearly killed by a torpedo? **Answer**: President Franklin D. Roosevelt. While en route to a conference overseas, an errant friendly torpedo nearly sinks the USS *Iowa* (November 13-14, 1943). The runaway torpedo is blown up just before it reached the *Iowa*. Admiral King, Generals Marshall and Arnold and fifty other staff officers are also aboard. **6.)** Which world leader's voice was never heard by the citizens of his country from 1926 through 1945? **Answer**: Emperor of Japan, Hirohito. The first time the Japanese heard his voice was when he announced publicly that Japan had surrendered to the United States. **7.)** What was the name of the first aircraft carrier launched by the U.S. ? **Answer**: The USS *Ranger*, launched during 1921. **8.)** How many Confederate Generals graduated from the U.S. Military Academy at West Point? **Answer**: 140. **And** one graduated from Annapolis. **9.)** During 1937, which country did the U.S. promise to protect from Germany, despite having no troops to send to enforce the protection? **Answer**: Greenland. The Greenlanders raise the world's smallest army (fifteen men- Sledge Patrol). **10.)** Which foreign country stationed about 2,000 pilots in Fairbanks, Alaska during World War II? **Answer**: The Soviet Union. Russian pilots, quartered in Alaska accepted U.S. planes and flew them to Siberia escaping the Luftwaffe. **11.)** Who was the first President of the United States to be assassinated? **Answer**: Abraham Lincoln (1865). Three others also are assassinated, James Garfield (1881), William McKinley (1901) and John F. Kennedy (1963). **12.)** Which Presidents survived assassination attempts? Answer: Andrew Jackson, Gerald Ford, Ronald Reagan, Franklin D. Roosevelt and Harry S Truman. Also, former Pres. Teddy Roosevelt survives an assassination attempt. **13.)** Which U.S. President served in the military during World War I and W.W. II? **Answer**: President Dwight D. Eisenhower. Also, Eisenhower and U. S. Grant are the two presidents who graduated from the Military Academy at West Point. President Jimmy Carter graduated from Annapolis (Naval Academy). **14.)** Which President served in both the American War for Independence and the War of 1812? **Answer**: President Andrew Jackson. During the War for Independence, Jackson as a courier and only 13 years old, was captured by the British at Waxhaw, South Carolina.

U.S. Trivia continued

15.) Which code did the Army and Marine Corps use that was never broken by the Japanese (World War II)? Answer: Navajo Indian language codes. **16.)** Which President was elected unanimously? **Answer:** George Washington (both terms) - inaugurated in New York (1st term), Philadelphia (2nd term). **17.)** Which President opposed the Vietnam War? **Answer**: William Jefferson Blythe Clinton. He evaded the draft and attended, but did not get a degree at Oxford as a Rhodes Scholar and he protested the war while in England. **18.)** Who was the first elected President of the U.S. to be impeached? **Answer**: William Jefferson Blythe Clinton for lying under oath. He was later acquitted by the Senate. Andrew Johnson who succeeded Abraham Lincoln was also impeached and later acquitted; however Johnson was not elected. He assumed office upon the death of President Abraham Lincoln. **19.)** Which Presidents surrendered their law licenses? **Answer**: Richard Nixon surrendered his license subsequent to his resignation from the presidency (Watergate Scandal) and William Jefferson Blythe Clinton surrendered his license to practice law for a period of five years in a plea agreement with a special prosecutor over charges of lying under oath. **20.)** How many horses participated in Teddy Roosevelt's cavalry (Rough Riders) charge up San Juan Hill (Spanish American War)? **Answer**: None: The horses were aboard ship.**21.)** Which President was wounded during the Civil War? **Answer**: Rutherford B. Hayes (23rd Ohio), wounded several times during the conflict including serious wounds at South Mountain (September 1862) and at the battle of Cedar Creek (Sheridan's Ride), Virginia (October 1864). **22.)** Which President's plane was shot down in the Pacific during World War II? **Answer**: President George H. Bush. **23.)** Which President was temporarily lost in the Pacific during World War II, when his PT Boat was sunk? **Answer**: President John F. Kennedy (PT 109). **24.)** Under which enemy, did more American captives die during World War II? **Answer**: The Japanese. More than 30% of the U.S. captives died while held by the Japanese. Less than 5% succumbed while held by the Germans. **25.)** During which war did the U.S. sustain the most casualties. **Answer**: The Civil War. Each bullet that killed or wounded, killed or wounded an American. **26.)** Which President surrendered a military force to an enemy? **Answer**: George Washington (French & Indian War), the only time he ever surrendered. **27.)** Which U.S. General became a traitor? Answer: Benedict Arnold. **28.)** Who saved the portrait of George Washington and an original copy of the Declaration of Independence? **Answer**: Dolley Madison (wife of President James Madison, when the British seized the White House (War of 1812). **29.)** How long did it take Paul Revere to finish his ride to warn the Patriots of the approaching British? **Answer**: He didn't finish. The British arrested him. **30.)** How many times since 1776, has a Marine Corps invasion force been thrown back to the sea? **Answer**: Never. **31.)** How many U.S. Presidents were born in the U.S.? Answer: All 43; however, the 7th, Martin Van Buren is the first born after the Declaration of Independence, essentially making the first six, at the time of their birth, under the King of England. **32.)** What is the name of the tune that is played when the flag is raised in the morning? **Answer**: "To The Colors." **33.)** What animal other than horses and mules were temporarily used by the Cavalry during 1855? **Answer**: Camels. They were brought in from Egypt, but the practice ended because they terrified the horses. **34.)** Which Confederate leader was responsible for the establishment of the First U.S. Cavalry Regiment (2nd Cavalry) during 1855? **Answer**: Jefferson Davis.

Trivia Continued: 35.) Which Confederate General was the son of a President of the U.S.? Answer: Richard Taylor, the son of Zachary Taylor. **36.**) Eleven states seceded from the Union, but the Confederate flag had 13 stars. Which 2 states that had not seceded from the Union, were claimed by the Confederacy and represented by stars? **Answer:** Missouri and Kentucky. **37.**) Which U.S. General literally lost his pants during WWII? **Answer:** General Mark Clark. While attempting to get back to a submarine following a clandestine meeting in Algeria (Oct. 22,1942), that was interrupted by French police; he lost his pants to the unruly surf. **38.**) What was the mysterious new weapon introduced by the British that terrified the defenders during the War of 1812 at the Battle of Bladensburg, Maryland? **Answer:** polytechnics (fireworks). **39.**) What caused the British Army to hurriedly leave Washington, D.C. on the day after they occupied it during the War of 1812? **Answer:** A nasty storm. The U.S. defenders had fled to Virginia. **40.**) Which Confederate Generals, subsequent to the Civil War, served in the U.S. Army? **Answer:** Generals Joseph Wheeler, Fitzhugh Lee (nephew of Robert E. Lee), Thomas L. Rosser and Matthew C. Butler (Spanish American War,1898). **41.**) How did the U.S. Marines get the nickname "Leathernecks?" **Answer:** It evolved during the early days of the Corps, the Marines wore leather bands around their necks as protection against swords. **42.**) How did the military tank get its name? **Answer:** When the British introduced the tank during WWI, they were advanced as a ruse and identified as "water tanks." **43.**) Which nation finally declared war on Japan subsequent to the dropping of the atomic bomb on Hiroshima and just prior to the atom bomb being dropped on Nagasaki, Japan? **Answer:** The Soviet Union. **44.**) In which major battle during the Civil War did the Cherokee Indians participate and on which side did they fight? **Answer:** The Battle of Pea Ridge Arkansas. The Cherokees fought as part of the Confederate Army. **45.**) What are the names of two Presidents of the United States that were qualified as bomber or fighter pilots? **Answer:** George H. Bush and George W. Bush in the Navy and National Guard respectively. **46.**) What was printed on a sign on the beach at Iwo Jima that greeted the Marine invasion force on 19 February 1945? Answer: "Welcome to Iwo Jima." It had been placed there by Navy Frogmen who had worked to clear the beach obstacles for the Marines. **47.**) Which country that was liberated by the U.S. during WWI and WWII, compelled the U.S. to remove its military bases? **Answer:** France. It also has often refused its air space to U.S. military planes, despite the urgency of the missions. **48.**) Was there really an "Uncle Sam?" **Answer:** Apparently yes; the legend grew and evolved around Samuel Wilson (supplied meat to government), known as Uncle Sam. He was born in Menotomy (later Arlington), Massachusetts on 13 September, 1766. **49.**) Which President of the U.S. was in office when "In God We Trust" became the National Motto and the words "Under God" were added to the Pledge of Allegiance? **Answer:** President Dwight D. Eisenhower. **50.**) How many women became recipients of the Medal of Honor? Answer: One, Doctor Mary Walker (Civil War); taken away afterwards and later reinstated.

The Star Spangled Banner

Oh, say, can you see, by the dawn's early light,
What so proudly we hailed at the twilight's last gleaming
Whose broad stripes and bright stars, thro' the perilous fight
O'er the ramparts we watched, were so gallantly streaming.

And the rockets' red glare, the bombs bursting in air,
Gave proof through the night that our Flag was still there.
Oh, say, does that star spangled banner yet wave
O'er the land of the free and the home of the brave?

On the shore dimly seen, thro' the mists of the deep,
Where the foes haughty host in dread silence reposes,
What is that which the breeze' o'er the towering steep,
As it fitfully blows, half conceals, half discloses

Now it catches the gleam of the morning's first beam,
In full glory reflected, now shines on the stream;
Tis the star spangled banner, oh long may it wave
O'er the land of the free and the home of the brave.

And where is that band who so vauntingly swore
That the havoc of war and the battle's confusion,
A home and a country should leave us no more!
Their blood has washed out their foul footsteps' pollution.

No refuse could save the hireling and slave
From the terror of flight or the gloom of the grave:
And the star spangled banner in triumph doth wave
O'er the land of the free and the home of the brave.

Oh thus be it ever when freemen shall stand
Between their loved homes arid the war's desolation;
Blest with vict'ry; and peace, may the heav'n-rescued land
Praise the Power that has made an preserved us a nation.

Then conquer we must, when our cause is just,
And this be our motto: **"In God is our trust"**;
And the star spangled banner in triumph shall wave
O'er the land of the free and the home of the brave.

Written by Francis Scott Key during the bombardment of Fort McHenry on September 13 1814. It becomes the national anthem of the U. S. during 1931. Francis Scott Key towards the latter part of the Star Spangled Banner used the words "In God is our trust." Subsequently a similar use of the words becomes the motto of the United States.

Note: On 30 July 1956 (Eisenhower Administration), **"In God We Trust"** became the national motto. It initially appeared on U.S. currency during 1864 and later on all U.S. coins.

FLAGS THAT FLEW OVER AMERICA

Illustrations on pages 111-112

1.) Royal Standard of Spain - Queen Isabella and King Ferdinand subsidized Columbus' voyage. His expedition landed in San Salvador, Oct. 12, 1492.

2.) St. George Cross - The St. George Cross was flown by the English in the year 1497. It was the first English flag flown in this country.

3.) Kings Colors - The British Union Flag and the Union Jack (one and the same, landed in America in 1620 (Mayflower). The crosses of St. George and St. Andrew were combined (by King James I) for this flag.

4.) British Red Ensign - Queen Anne adopted this flag for England and her Colonies in the year 1707. The King's colors placed on a field of red.

5.) Lord Baltimore Flag - This flag was used for 100 years prior to the Revolution and it still remains part of the Maryland state flag.

6.) Continental Flag - The Boston Tea Party in 1773, a prelude to Lexington and Concord, helped bring about the Continental flag.

7.) Rattlesnake Flag (Gadsden Flag) - Several versions of this flag were flown by the Continental Navy throughout the Revolutionary War.

8.) Grand Union Flag - In 1776, the Colonies decided to implant the King's colors on a field of 13 stripes. This would project allegiance to England, yet illuminate their determination to fight for justice and liberty if necessary.

9.) Betsy Ross Flag - The Betsy Ross flag was adopted by an act of Congress on June 14th, 1777. It is generally accepted that George Washington was instrumental in the design, but there is no proof of it.

10.) Bennington Flag - A unique version of our Stars and Stripes. This flag has the number "76" flanked by eleven stars, with two point stars. This flag inspired the Militia to victory at Bennington, Vermont, on August 16th, 1777.

11.) Appeal To Heaven - Washington's Cruisers' Flag - This flag was flown by the vessels ("Webfoot Regiment") outfitted by George Washington.

12.) Cowpens Flag - The flag of the 3rd Maryland Regiment (Continental Line), but named after battle of Cowpens. Original flag in state house, Annapolis, Md.

13.) Bunker Hill Flag - This flag represented New England. Apparently it was supposed to have a red field, but due to an error it became blue.

14.) Fort Moultrie Flag - This flag, named in honor of Col. William Moultrie, flew over Sullivan's Island (Charleston, S.C.) June 1776 against British fleet.

15.) Sons of Liberty Flag - The Sons of Liberty emerged as opponents of the Stamp Act (1765) and included Samuel Adams, John Hancock and Paul Revere.

16.) Guilford Flag - Flew at the battle of Guilford Court House (March 1781).

17.) Fluer De-Lis - First used by either King Louis VI or Louis VII on their coat of arms. The French used this flag (several variations) in America. The Fleur De-Lis (lily) has been in use in France since the beginning of recorded history.

18.) Dutch East India Company Flag - This flag was flown by Henry Hudson when he arrived in America during 1609.

19.) Rhode Island Flag - The Rhode Island Regimental flag that was used

Flag Illustrations continued:

20.) Christopher Columbus Flag - The "F" represents King Ferdinand and the "Y" represents Queen Ysabella (Isabella) on opposite sides of the Cross.

21.) Serapis Flag - Flown on the Serapis, captured by John Paul Jones on the Bonhomme Richard. The flag was used in France to verify his sailors weren't pirates.

22.) Bedford Flag - Flown at the Battle of Concord during April 1775.

23.) Washington's Flag - George Washington's personal flag.

24.) Green Mountain Boys - Used in Vermont under Ethan Allen.

25.) First Navy Jack - This flag is reported to have flown aboard the first naval ship (*Alfred*) during 1776.

26.) Taunton Flag - Used in Taunton Massachusetts during 1774.

27.) Cross of Burgundy - This flag, a symbol of the Duke of Burgundy Philip I, is in addition to the royal banner of Spain and was flown over Spain's colonies.

28.) President's Flag
29.) Vice President's Flag
30.) Alamo
31.) Confederate Flag
32.) Confederate Battle Flag
33.) Second Confederate Flag
34.) Third Confederate Flag
35.) Confederate Navy Jack
36.) U.S. Army
37.) U.S. Navy
38.) U.S. Coast Guard
39.) U.S. Air Force
40.) U.S. Marines
41.) POW Flag
42.) First Stars and Stripes
43.) Star Spangled Banner
44.) Great Star Flag - Thirty-six stars. At about 1818, Captain Samuel Reid and Peter Wendover suggested a star pattern for the stars for use at sea (private vessels and on land). Congress rejects it.

45.) Twenty Star Flag
46.) Thirty-five Star Flag
47.) Forty-eight Flag
48.) Fifty Star Flag

The Flag as it acquired additional stars. Not all examples have illustrations:

1776 - 13 stars and 13 stripes
1795 - 15 stars & 15 stripes (Kentucky & Vermont). Flew over Fort McHenry during 1814. Last flag with 15 stripes.
1818 - 20 stars (Indiana, Louisiana, Mississippi, Ohio and Tennessee).
1819 - 21 stars . . . . (Illinois)
1820 - 23 stars (Alabama and Maine)
1822 - 24 stars . . . . (Missouri)
1836 - 25 stars . . . . . . (Arkansas)
1837 - 26 stars . . . . (Michigan)
1845 - 27 stars . . . . (Florida)
1846 - 28 stars . . . . (Texas)
1847 - 29 stars . . . . (Iowa)
1848 - 30 stars . . . . . . (Wisconsin)
1851 - 31 stars . . . . (California)
1858 - 32 stars . . . . . . (Minnesota)
1859 - 33 stars . . . . (Oregon)
1861 - 34 stars . . . . (Kansas)
1863 - 35 stars . . . . (West Virginia)
1865 - 36 stars . . . . (Nevada)
1867 - 37 stars . . . . (Nebraska)
1877 - 38 stars . . . . (Colorado)
1890 - 43 stars....... (Idaho, Montana, North Dakota, South Dakota and Washington).
1891 - 44 stars . . . . (Wyoming)
1896 - 45 stars . . . . (Utah)
1908 - 46 stars . . . . . . (Oklahoma)
1912 - 48 stars ......(Arizona and New Mexico)
Completes the Continental U.S.
1959 - 49 stars . . . . (Alaska)
1960 - 50 stars . . . . (Hawaii)

Flags that flew over Texas:
Spanish - . . . . 1519 to 1685
French - . . . . 1685 to 1690
Spanish - . . . . 1690 to 1821
Mexican - . . . . 1821 to 1836
Republic of Texas - . 1836 to 1845
United States - . . . . . 1845 to 1861
Confederate States - 1861 to 1865
United States - 1865 to the present.

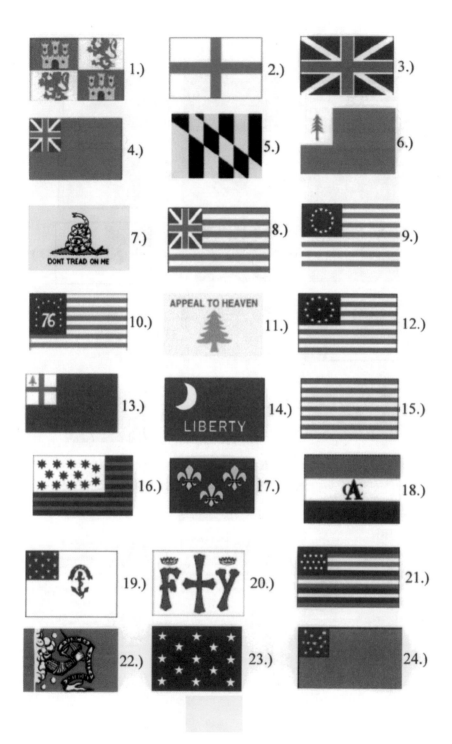

1.)

2.)

3.)

4.)

5.)

6.)

7.) DONT TREAD ON ME

8.)

9.)

10.) 76

11.) APPEAL TO HEAVEN

12.)

13.)

14.) LIBERTY

15.)

16.)

17.)

18.) AC

19.)

20.) F Y

21.)

22.)

23.)

24.)

123

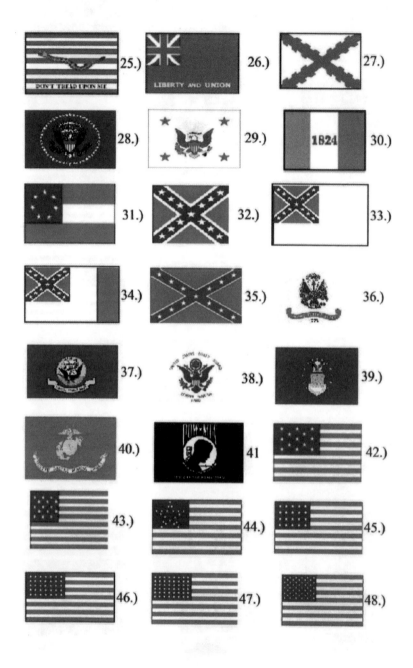

25.)

26.)

27.)

28.)

29.)

30.)

31.)

32.)

33.)

34.)

35.)

36.)

37.)

38.)

39.)

40.)

41

42.)

43.)

44.)

45.)

46.)

47.)

48.)

Listing of the States & Capitals

1.) Alabama (22nd), Dec. 14, 1819- Montgomery.
2.) Alaska (49th) January 3, 1959 - Juneau.
3.) Arizona (48th) Feb. 14, 1912 - Phoenix.
4.) Arkansas (25th) June 15, 1836 - Little Rock.
5.) California (31st) Sept. 9, 1850 -Sacramento.
6.) Colorado (38th) Aug. 1, 1876 - Denver.
7.)Connecticut (5th) Jan. 9, 1788 - Hartford.
8.) Delaware (1st) Dec. 7 1787 - Dover.
9.) Florida (27th) March 3, 1845 - Tallahassee.
10.) Georgia (4th) January 2, 1788 - Atlanta.
11.) Hawaii (50th) August 21, 1959 - Honolulu.
12.) Idaho (43rd) July 3, 1890 - Boise.
13.) Illinois (21st) Dec. 3, 1818 - Springfield.
14.) Indiana (19th) Dec. 11, 1816 - Indianapolis.
15.) Iowa (29th) Dec. 28, 1846 - Des Moines.
16.) Kansas (34th) Jan. 29, 1861 - Topeka.
17.) Kentucky (15th) June 1, 1792 - Frankfort.
18.) Louisiana (18th) Apr. 30, 1812 - Baton Rouge.
19.) Maine (23rd) March 15, 1820 - Augusta.
20.) Maryland (7th) April 28, 1788 - Annapolis.
21.) Massachusetts (6th) Feb. 6th 1788 - Boston.
22.) Michigan (26th) Jan. 26, 1837 - Lansing.
23.) Minnesota (32nd) May 11, 1858 - St. Paul.
24.) Mississippi (20th) Dec. 10, 1817 - Jackson.
25.) Missouri (24th) Aug. 10, 1821 - Jefferson City.

26.) Montana (41st) Nov. 8, 1889 - Helena.
27.) Nebraska (37th) Mar. 1, 1867 - Lincoln.
28.) Nevada (36th) Oct. 31, 1864 - Carson City.
29.) New Hampshire (9th) June 21, 1788 - Concord.
30.) New Jersey (3rd) Dec.18th 1787 - Trenton.
31.) New Mexico (47th) Jan. 6, 1912 - Santa Fe.
32.) New York (11th) July 26, 1788 - Albany.
33.) North Carolina (12th) Nov.21, 1789 - Raleigh.
34.) North Dakota (39th) Nov.2nd 1889 - Bismarck.
35.) Ohio (17th) March 1, 1803 - Columbus.
36.)Oklahoma (46th) Nov. 16, 1907 - Oklahoma City.
37.) Oregon (33rd) Feb. 14, 1859 - Salem.
38.) Pennsylvania (2nd) Dec.12, 1787- Harrisburg.
39.) Rhode Island (13th) May 29, 1790 - Providence.
40.) South Carolina (8th) May 23, 1788 - Columbia.
41.) South Dakota (40th) Nov. 2, 1889 - Pierre.
42.) Tennessee (16th) June 1, 1796 - Nashville.
43.) Texas (28th) Dec. 29, 1845 Austin.
44.) Utah (45th) Jan. 4, 1896 - Salt Lake City.
45.) Vermont (14th) Mar. 4, 1791 - Montpelier.
46.) Virginia (10th) June 25, 1788- Richmond.
47.) Washington (42nd) Nov. 11, 1889 - Olympia.
48.) West Virginia (35th) June 20, 1863- Charleston.
49.) Wisconsin (30th) May 29, 1848 - Madison.

50.)Wyoming (44th) July 10, 1890 - Cheyenne. Arizona's entrance into the Union completes the Continental U.S.

Other Possessions of The U.S. include American Samoa (1900) Guam - claimed by the U.S. June 22nd 1898 and took official control on December 10th 1898 after the signing of the Treaty of Paris at the conclusion of the Spanish American War; **Puerto Rico** - (December 10th 1898 at the signing of the Treaty of Paris; and the **Virgin Islands** - taken over by the United States from Denmark on March 31st 1917. Negotiations for the islands were completed during August of 1916 with the understanding that possession by the United States would become official on January 1st 1917. The U.S. pays Denmark a sum of $25,000,000 (25 million dollars) for these Islands. Also, the **Northern Mariana Islands** (1986), **Wake Atoll** (1898), **Midway Atoll** (1867) and Navassa Island (claimed during 1857) about 40 miles from Haiti and 100 miles from Cuba in the Caribbean. In addition, Washington, D.C. is part of the United States but not a State in itself. Land had been donated by surrounding States (Maryland & Virginia)for use as a Federal Capital and designated as The District of Columbia.

Alabama

Alaska

Arizona

Arkansas

California

Colorado

Connecticut

Delaware

Florida

Georgia

Hawaii

Idaho

Illinois

Indiana

Iowa

Kansas

Kentucky

Louisiana

Maine

Maryland

Massachusetts

Michigan

Minnesota

Mississippi

Missouri

Montana

Nebraska

Nevada

New Hampshire

New Jersey

New Mexico

New York

North Carolina

North Dakota

Ohio

Oklahoma

Oregon

Pennsylvania

Rhode Island

South Carolina

South Dakota

Tennessee

Texas

Utah

Vermont

Virginia

Washington

West Virginia

Wisconsin

Wyoming

Washington, D.C.

Guam

Northern
Marianas

American Samoa

Puerto Rico

U.S. Virgin
Islands

God's Shining Light

I pledge allegiance to our Flag
for Freedom, she's always true
I pray that God's bright shining light
will protect the Red White and Blue

Through unruly seas and stormy days
as Old Glory unfurls and the nation prays
Freedom's heroes move in harm's way
To defend America, our grand USA

Swiftly they move by air and sea
on the advance to ensure Liberty
Through war clouds for Old Glory
That America remains terror free

With Freedom's light and God's might
Our Flag moves fearlessly into the fight
From dawn to dusk and through the night
Old Glory will prevail, with Freedom's light

She'll pave the way, she'll clear the skies
Our Flag will liberate and then fly high
In the vast desert sands and valleys deep
in terrorists' caves and mountain peaks

I pledge allegiance to our Flag
for Freedom, she's always true
I pray that God's bright shining light
will protect the Red White and Blue